*BENJAMIN FRANKLIN*
*IN SCOTLAND AND IRELAND*

GEORGE DRUMMOND
Provost of Edinburgh
From Whom Franklin Received the
Freedom of the City

# BENJAMIN

# FRANKLIN

## *IN SCOTLAND AND IRELAND*

### 1759 and 1771

By J. *ames* BENNETT NOLAN

*A traveller should have a hog's nose,
deer's legs and an ass's back*

**POOR RICHARD**

## *PHILADELPHIA*

### UNIVERSITY OF PENNSYLVANIA PRESS

1956

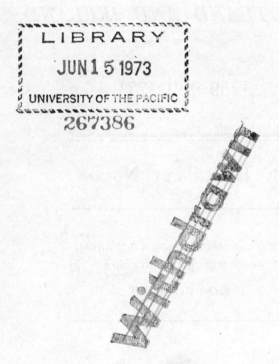
Published in Great Britain, India, and Pakistan
by Geoffrey Cumberlege: Oxford University Press
London, Bombay, and Karachi

*To the Memory of My Friend*

R. TAIT McKENZIE

*Most Eminent of Scottish Americans*

*Most Lovable of Men*

# FOREWORD

In preserving our contact with great men of the past, there is a natural tendency to dwell specially on the permanent value of what they did and on the merit of what they said and wrote. That such should be the case is inevitable, yet a true appreciation of any man can be formed only when we know the circumstances of his time in sufficient detail to visualise the day-by-day conditions of his life—the houses wherein he dwelt, the streets through which he walked, the people with whom he mingled.

This aspect of Benjamin Franklin's life is a task to which Mr. J. Bennett Nolan has given many years of careful research, and he has now reconstructed the incidents of Franklin's visits to Scotland and Ireland in a way which will evoke the gratitude of all who are interested in the great American statesman-philosopher. As one who shares with Mr. Nolan a romantic interest in Benjamin Franklin, it has been to me a peculiar pleasure to see this record grow from small beginnings into the completed form in which it is now presented. I feel certain that many readers will share my pleasure as they study this book, and will recognise the enthusiasm, the meticulous accuracy, and the scholarly charm which the author has devoted to his labour of love.

James C. Irvine

*Office of Sir James Colquhoun Irvine*
*Principal and Vice Chancellor*
*The University*
*St. Andrews*
*July, 1938*

# CONTENTS

# ILLUSTRATIONS

# INTRODUCTION

WHILE Colonial Envoy in Great Britain, Benjamin Franklin made two journeys from London to Scotland, one in 1759 and the other in 1771, the second tour including a six weeks' stay in Ireland. Comparatively little was known of these visits, and until now no attempt has been made to collate the descriptive material or even to approximate the itinerary. The following pages purport to give an account of Franklin's two Caledonian rambles and include the sojourn in Ireland which preceded the second trip.

These journeys have received only a casual and inadequate notice from Franklin's many biographers. Already in 1780 they were half forgotten when Boswell wrote: "Sir Alexander Dick thinks that it was about twenty-two years ago that Lord Kames invited the celebrated Benjamin Franklin and his son to come out and reside with him, which they did, of which inquiry should be made." Inquiry was not made and all succeeding historians adroitly evaded the issue. There is a touch of incongruity in the theme, and perhaps many of the admirers of Poor Richard, accustomed to regard him in sedate Quaker-like garb and in colonial environment, will be as astonished at his portrayal in a Scottish setting as if he were depicted in kilts or stepping a Highland reel. Nevertheless Franklin's Caledonian excursions merit a detailed treatment, first, because of the interesting incidents which featured them, and second, because of the importance of the acquaintanceships he made and the bearing these friendships had upon his subsequent career. For while it may truthfully be stated that few tourists have had the good fortune to meet in one visit such celebrities as David Hume and Adam Smith, Lord Kames and Principal Robertson, it may correlatively be said that only Athens in its golden age and Edinburgh in the last decades of the eighteenth century could vaunt so brilliant a coterie.

Not that the Doctor's propaganda met with the invariable success for which he labored and hoped. The same enthusiastic Irish Parliament which applauded him on the floor of the Commons House on College Green in October 1771 turned a deaf ear, four years later, to the pleas of the American patriots, and passed a resolution deprecating the uprising and sanctioning the recruiting in Ireland of soldiers for the English forces overseas. David Hume, who received the American Philosopher with such gracious cordiality on the same journey, spoke distrustfully of him a few months later and remarked: "I hope you can tell me something in justification, at least in alleviation of Dr. Franklin's conduct. I always knew him to be a factious man and Faction next to Fanaticism is of all passions the most destructive of morality."

But these disappointments were exceptional and, in the main, Franklin's friends in Ireland and Scotland strove manfully to avert a calamitous breach. Even during the period of actual warfare, Sir Alexander Dick, Adam Smith, and Lord Kames in Scotland, Sir Edward Newenham and Dr. Emmett in Ireland, were outspoken in defense of American rights. Bishop Jonathan Shipley, at whose home at Twyford Franklin laid down his unfinished *Autobiography* to undertake the Irish journey, spoke with such rashness in his friend's behalf as to endanger his episcopal office and to provoke the rebuke of the Primate.

Some of the occurrences which featured these tours vie in picturesque appeal with any of the episodes of Benjamin's long and varied career. Among these may be mentioned his elevation as Guild Brother of Edinburgh, the visits to the universities of Edinburgh, Glasgow, St. Andrews, and Trinity, the visits with Sir Alexander Dick, Lord Kames, and Lord Hillsborough, the crossing to Ireland, the presentation in the chamber of the Irish House of Commons, the inspection of the Carron Iron Works, the sojourn with David Hume.

Not the least alluring phase of an interesting research lies in the diverse characters of Franklin's traveling companions. In the post-chaise we may give our distinguished tourist the right-hand seat of precedence. Beside him there first appears his son William, whose urbanity and political dexterity overcame the handicap of a dubious maternity and secured for him the governorship of New Jersey. The seat is successively occupied by the eccentric Professor Anderson of Glasgow, the grotesque pedagogue who taught Boswell and our own Justice James Wilson, then by that curious personality "Omniscient Richard Jackson," old "Two Penny Jackson" of the Inner Temple whose important part in the negotiations between the discontented Colonial Assemblies and the infatuated Ministers of the Crown in those fateful months which preceded the Revolution has escaped the notice of most historians. Next appears young Henry Marchant, the lawyer from Rhode Island, palpably pleased at the honor of making a trip through Scotland with the celebrated Dr. Franklin. Last of all, on the return from the second visit in 1771, Franklin's own son-in-law Richard Bache, whom he is meeting for the first time, mounts timidly to journey down from Liverpool to London and form the acquaintanceship of his wife's father. It is worthy of note that in the twenty-five weeks of travel entailed by the two Scottish and the Irish expeditions, the Doctor was alone only twice, once in the passage from Dublin up to Edinburgh in October 1771 and, a few weeks later, on the return from Edinburgh to Preston.

So much for the fellow tourists, but as usual the Philosopher himself surpasses in interest and appeal. On the first journey of 1759 he was younger and fairly inured to hardship; a man who had campaigned for a winter in the Pennsylvania woods, only three years before, was not likely to be discouraged by bad roads and poor fare. But on the second excursion, in 1771, he was in his sixty-sixth year and softened perhaps by the flesh-pots of Craven Street. How often must he have winced as his springless chaise bumped over the impossible lanes of Lanark and Lothian! Yet he never whimpers, but accepts the privations of the route with a placid fortitude which evokes our admiration after a lapse of two centuries. When he arrives in Edinburgh for his second visit, David Hume becomes voluble upon the inflictions endured by his American guest in the journey across the storm-tossed Irish Sea and over the flooded roads of Ayrshire, but the unperturbed Doctor merely records that he "came through flood and tempest."

No writer should essay a comprehensive treatment of the Caledonian tours without personally retracing Franklin's route, for the various dwellings in which he tarried, one hundred and sixty years ago, are singularly unchanged. His corner bedchamber at Kames House in Berwickshire remains untouched; the trees he planted at Blair Drummond still flourish; his window in the Hume residence in Edinburgh (altered, alas, to the ignoble uses of modern commerce!) still looks down upon the crowding traffic of St. Andrews Square. The gentle Itchen glides beneath the country churchyard at Chilbolton with its historic yew tree and with the mouldering gravestones among which the Philosopher strolled, manuscript of his *Autobiography* in hand.

These are the tangible survivals of two memorable circuits, but the record is best preserved in the unwritten traditions of towns like Hillsborough in Ireland and Preston in England, where the reminiscence of the visits of the great scientist from America is sedulously cherished. One wishes often that the details of the sojourns were more amplified but these local memories, although unsupported by documentary proof, are compelling and omnipresent.

Direct source material dealing with these trips is disappointingly meager. Franklin wrote so sparingly from Scotland and Ireland that there remain not more than half a dozen letters, whose terseness contrasts unsatisfactorily with some of the voluminous and chatty missives which he sent from London. Perhap the discomforts of a racking ramble in lands which were the bane of travelers discouraged lengthy correspondence; perhaps the primitive inns of the period afforded few epistolary facilities.

It is possible, too, that many letters written on the journey have been lost and are not collated in the accepted, published lists of Franklin correspondence. Some unpublished notes have been found during the compilation of this record; more may be found at a future date in the collections of the descendants of those families which Benjamin and his son William visited. Weeks of patient labor in the admirable libraries of Edinburgh, Glasgow, and Dublin, and a faithful following up of every clue have failed to reveal additional proof, but there is always the embarrassing possibility that some letter or diary, neglected through the centuries in a Scottish or Irish attic, may turn up to enlarge or alter this record of the Caledonian tours.

The itinerary of the first journey of 1759 is incomplete. The Envoy's rambles in Derbyshire at the beginning of the trip and his course from the time that he left Glasgow in the last week of September and struck northward into the semi-barbaric Highlands to emerge at St. Andrews, will probably always be conjectural. Nearly a century ago the attention of Henry Stevens, the great bibliophile and collector of Frankliniana, was called to the Caledonian expeditions and he deplored his inability to elucidate all Franklin's movements north of the Tweed. Mr. Stevens, while observing that the Philosopher "was too busy in making history ever to overtake himself and to sit down quietly to record it," expressed the hope that eventually in London, that center of money and mutation, some additional letter written from Scotland or Ireland would turn up. So far this aspiration has been unrealized and it is to be feared that much of Franklin's Scottish data perished with the trunks of papers deposited at the Galloway residence in

Trevose, Pennsylvania, the house which was pillaged by the British soldiery during the Revolution.

It must always be regretted that Benjamin did not give a personal narration of his northern trips in his *Autobiography*, a work which he began while staying at the home of Jonathan Shipley, Bishop of St. Asaph's, at Chilbolton in Hampshire just before his second journey to Edinburgh. It was the understanding of Franklin's grandson, William Temple Franklin, the companion of his later years in Philadelphia, that his grandfather intended to describe his Scottish wanderings at length. Some notes and headings indicative of such a project do indeed survive, but the *Autobiography* remains a momentous and tantalizing fragment with only scattered references to the author's stay in Scotland. "Many a self-asserting artist," writes Stevens again, "has tried to fill out and complete Phidias's matchless but headless figure of Theseus in the British Museum, but no one has yet succeeded."

Why did our Sage ignore the colorful braes of Perthshire in his correspondence? The poet Thomas Gray, who preceded him in the same district, and the great Johnson who rode through it with Boswell a decade later, have left interesting accounts of their tours, but Franklin apparently saw nothing in the Highlands worthy of record. Sir Walter in his novel *Redgauntlet* makes the dilettante Darsie Latimer remark that the Highlanders have degenerated from ruffling bullies to tame cheaters and that the targes of Culloden are used to cover butter tubs. Benjamin's neglect in the setting down of his impressions for posterity savors of the same listless point of view. If the Agent of Pennsylvania had been accompanied by a Boswell to narrate meticulously all his experiences and reactions, the later-day biographer who essays to reconstruct the trip might write with more conviction. But Benjamin's companion in the Highlands was his son William, whose sole concern seems to have been to effect a meeting with Lord Bute, through whose intercession he might hope to secure for himself a governmental job.

This same dearth of fundamental data extends to the Irish visit. Franklin corresponded at length with Sir Edward Newenham of County Wexford, but no memoranda are to be found in the present Newenham residence at Carrigaline. The records of Trinity College in Dublin ignore a visit which he certainly made. The minutes of the Irish Commons are silent as to his reception on the Floor. Only when we come to the second Scottish tour, in 1771, are we miraculously aided by the diary of Henry Marchant of Rhode Island who came over to London early in that year and joined Franklin in Edinburgh. This invaluable record, of which only fragments have been printed, is important not only for the light it throws upon Franklin's movements, but also as a first-hand depiction of the life of American colonials resident in London.

Marchant describes the revels of the over-seas law students from the Temple in the New England Coffee House, the cascades of Vauxhall, the illuminations at Sadler's Wells and Mary-le-bone, the Chief Justices in banc, "a gouty set," the Lord Mayor in his gilded coach. He calls on Lord Chatham and Samuel Johnson, meets Benjamin West and the actor Foote, sups backstage with Garrick, and breakfasts on tea and buckwheat cakes with Dr. Franklin and Mrs. Stevenson. Then on a frosty autumn morning, in the Mall in St. James's Park, he encounters a portly, affable gentleman in a crimson broadcloth waistcoat "squeery-eyed but well-bodied although rather too gross," and knows that he is in the presence of King George the Great, the Good. We have deplored the absence of a Boswell in Franklin's tour of the Highlands; it may as aptly be observed that had he been accompanied by Marchant upon his first Scottish excursion, the posthumous biographer would not need to apologize for so many lapses in the route.

Except for the fortuitous aid of the Marchant diary and

[ 7 ]

for such information as is derived from Franklin's own letters, the Caledonian trips have been reconstructed from local records, observations of contemporaries, a few scattering notices in the newspapers of the period, and from the correspondence of Benjamin's fellow tourists. With the data gleaned from these sources it has been possible to piece together a fairly cohesive recital. The field, to be sure, is infinite, for any man of importance whose career ranged with that of our traveler may afford us a random hint as to his whereabouts. For that reason a list of books and documents consulted is impractical; Franklin's shadow projects itself across the entire eighteenth century and the bibliography would be larger than the narrative itself.

It were equally unavailable to attempt to name all of the courteous scholars and librarians in America, England, Scotland, and Ireland who have labored so indefatigably in this compilation. The author can only hope that the myriad co-workers on both sides of the Atlantic will accept as a partial acknowledgment the achievement of the record of two excursions heretofore little known, an accomplishment made possible only by their unselfish coöperation. If this account of Franklin's Scottish and Irish tours shall throw some additional light upon the movements and character of a subject at once so illustrious and so lovable, the writer will be well content of his task.

# PART ONE

## *THE VISIT TO SCOTLAND*

1759

Benjamin Franklin's Route in 1759

SCOTLAND

PERTH ST. ANDREWS
STIRLING
GLASGOW EDINBURGH
KAMES HOUSE

CARLISLE

IRELAND

YORK
MANCHESTER
LIVERPOOL
SHEFFIELD

WALES DERBY

BIRMINGHAM

ENGLAND

LONDON

Scale-Statute Miles

GEISZEL

# Chapter I

# CRAVEN STREET

IN the summer of 1759 Benjamin Franklin, Agent in London for the Province of Pennsylvania, then in his fifty-fourth year, was lodging in the dwelling of Mrs. Margaret Stevenson at No. 7 Craven Street. The narrow thoroughfare still descends from the Strand to the Thames Embankment, just east of Whitehall, and the house is little changed since Franklin's day. Wealthy American tourists look down upon it from their chambers in the Savoy and seldom realize that it once sheltered the most illustrious emissary whom their Republic has sent upon a mission overseas.

The street took its name from the worshipful Earl of Craven, although until a few years before the Agent's arrival it went by the more modest appellation of Spur Alley. In 1759 there was little of patrician suggestion in the neighborhood except that Northumberland House stood hard by in the Strand and that the luckless Charles the First bestrode his charger and looked majestically down Whitehall just as he does in our own time. The plaza now known as Trafalgar Square was occupied by an assemblage of sordid hovels, the site of the Royal Academy by the King's Mews. Perhaps Dr. Franklin chose the location because of its similarity to that of the dwelling which he had just left in Philadelphia, for Market Street descended to the Delaware in much the same way as Craven Street ran down to the Thames. The circumstance that some barristers from Gray's Inn lived at the upper end of the street gave a contemporary punster an opportunity for descriptive doggerel.

> For the Lawyers are just at the top of the street
> And the Barges are just at the bottom;

Fly, honesty, fly to some safer retreat
For there's craft in the river and craft in the street.

Now the fine world of London has removed to the westward, and only the plaque recording Franklin's residence
remains to testify to the departed glories of Craven Street.
The place is still a boarding house, and the domestics earn
an occasional shilling by pointing out to transatlantic
visitors the second-story front room where the Envoy slept,
the back room where he conducted his electrical experiments, and the garret where lodged the Maryland darkey
whom he brought along as a body servant. Mr. Franklin
with his son William came here shortly after they disembarked at Falmouth in 1757. Benjamin remained until
his departure for Pennsylvania in 1761, returning again in
December 1764 for an additional eleven years of residence.

It is scarcely correct, however, to refer to the establishment as a boarding house. Rather it was a dwelling where
a refined widow took in a select company, and certainly no
man was ever more fortunate in his choice of landladies.
Franklin always held her in high regard, but her culture
—so extolled by indulgent biographers—seems to be evidenced rather in her taste for household embellishment,
Sheffield ware, crockery and napery, than in her letters,
which are the ungrammatical scrawls of a woman of little
education. But landladies are seldom chosen for literary
attainment, and Mrs. Stevenson competently supervised
the domestic routine of her distinguished guest, deferred
to his culinary fancies, and catered to his wishes. Her
daughter Polly, later Polly Hewson, was ever the subject
of Franklin's tender regard. Years afterwards she came to
arrange the Envoy's ménage at Passy and later crossed the
ocean to be with the dying Philosopher in Philadelphia.

The Stevenson house was conveniently located, since
Craven Street was the center of the officialdom of London,
and opportune for all Mr. Franklin's varied interests. The
Crown Ministers whom he must frequently consult in his

capacity of Colonial Agent had their offices in Whitehall, a five minutes' walk. The sulky Proprietors of Pennsylvania, Thomas and Richard Penn, who distrusted the Envoy and had opposed his appointment, lived near by in New Street, Spring Garden, appropriate for the many interviews which were to follow when Franklin was vainly endeavoring to induce the Penns to assume some responsibility of taxation for the upkeep of the Province from which they drew their revenues.

When the Envoy first came to live in Craven Street he was moody and discontented, a state of irritation very evident in his letters to his wife. "I hope if I stay another winter, it will be more agreeable than the last part of the time I have spent in London." [1] He lay sick for many weeks after the grueling voyage on the Atlantic packet, and was disappointed both in his reception and in the unexpected duration of the stay in London. He had counted much upon an interview with Pitt, but the imperious Prime Minister obstinately refused to receive him; and it soon became apparent that the mission which it was confidently expected would be fulfilled in six months might keep him in London for three or four years. In these circumstances the £1,500 grudgingly appropriated by the parsimonious Pennsylvania Assembly was likely to be a most inadequate stipend.[2]

The philosophy of Poor Richard, however, was not to be denied; his indisposition passed and the advantages of London society over that of a remote provincial capital soon atoned for the rebuffs of his official mission. Not that the exclusive clubs of St. James Street ever opened their doors to a colonial ambassador of proletarian antecedents or that Franklin ever crossed the sacred thresholds of Brooks's or Almack's, but plenty of invitations came to receptions and routs in Hanover Square and Albemarle Street, and our Envoy accepted them all, enjoyed himself hugely, and even set up an equipage to comport with the dignity of the Agent of an opulent province.

Your kind advice about getting a Chariot I had taken some time before, for I found that every time I walk'd out I got a fresh cold, and Hackney Coaches at this end of the town, where most people keep their own, are the worst in the whole City, miserable, dirty, broken shabby things unfit to go into when dressed clean and such as one would be ashamed to get out of at any gentleman's door.[3]

All of which afforded a notable contrast to the garret in Little Britain where the youthful Benjamin had lodged, and the ale-drinking apprentices with whom he had consorted when he first came to London as an obscure printer's devil in 1724.

While reveling in this inspiring environment, sometime in this summer of 1759, Dr. Franklin resolved to undertake a journey to Scotland, the Ultima Thule of British travelers of the period, a trip which entailed as much time and far more privation than are involved in a voyage to India in our day. The Doctor, to be sure, was an inveterate tourist with an insatiable interest in strange places, new societies, and unwonted customs, a recurring urge which usually appeared with the advent of fine weather. In America he had made trips to New England and Virginia, to Albany and to Williamsburg, always managing to plead the call of duty and the consideration of health as excuse for his wanderings. In the previous year, when setting out for his excursion to Cambridge and Northampton, he guilelessly explained:

I found the journey advantageous to my health, increasing both my health and spirits and therefore as all the great folks were out of town and public business at an end, I the more easily prevailed on myself to take another journey.[4]

Nowhere in Franklin's correspondence is there a suggestion why he chose Scotland as the scene for his vacation excursion of 1759, but it was not to be supposed that he would remain long in England without visiting the sister kingdom to the north. Moreover in this year his attention had been particularly directed toward Scotland by the circumstance that in February the University of St. Andrews had given him the degree of Doctors of Laws, when eleven professors of that ancient and honorable institution had united with the Rector, David Shaw, in sending to Franklin letters written in English and Latin formally apprising him of the dignity conferred. This diploma is now in the archives of the American Philosophical Society at Philadelphia. The University Minute recites:

Conferred the Degree of Doctor in Laws on Mr. Benjamin Franklin famous for his writings on Electricity and appoint his diploma to be given him gratis, the Clerk and Arch Beadle's dues to be paid by the Library Questar.[5]

This honor seems to have come as a complete surprise to the Agent, who had no intimation prior to the arrival of the diploma in Craven Street. A local historian of St. Andrews intimates that the degree was accorded at the suggestion of Dr. Patrick Baird of St. Andrews who had lived in Philadelphia and been a member of the Junta, Franklin's literary circle, although a later commentator has thrown doubt upon this theory.[6] In any event, the episode gives an additional reason for the Philosopher's northern journey and, anticipating his visit, he had sent a printed volume of his own electrical experiments to the college library.

When, after this gracious gesture from St. Andrews, the Agent of Pennsylvania sought further information upon a tour to Scotland, the opportunities were at hand since many of his closest friends in England were of Scottish antecedents. Next door in Craven Street lived the wine merchant Caleb Whitefoord, a native Caledonian who had kept up his Edinburgh connections. The intimacy between the two neighbors was so well known that in 1782 the British Foreign Office sent Whitefoord as envoy to arrange with Franklin, then in Passy, as to the negotiations of a peace with the revolted colonies, upon which occasion Whitefoord boasted that his friendship with Dr. Franklin had saved a year of warfare. The merchant had graduated at the University of Edinburgh, so that he would be an apt consultant for the proposed trip. If Franklin, as sometimes happened, had a twinge of gravel and must stay within doors, he could discuss Scotland with his physician John Fothergill, also an Edinburgh man. Another Caledonian associate who might well have been a companion upon the journey was his close friend Sir John Pringle, who afterwards went with him to Germany and France. Pringle, who like Franklin held the Copley Medal for scientific attainment from the Royal Society, had been born in Edinburgh and had seen considerable service as an army surgeon in Flanders. He had settled in London, where he became physician, successively, to the Duke of Cumberland and the Queen Consort. The probable reason why he did not accompany Franklin to Scotland lies in the fact that during this summer of 1759 he was engrossed in the American Campaign and his military susceptibilities were enthralled by the exploits of the great Wolfe. Some weeks later, after the death of that hero, there appeared a semi-anonymous biography of Wolfe "by Sir J—n P—n—e, Baronet," the preparation of which pamphlet may have cost Franklin a congenial fellow voyager.

Then there was William Strahan, the printer from Edinburgh, "Scotch Straney" with whom Franklin had corresponded for twenty years, his banker, adviser, publisher, and guide. The two men had formed a warm, enduring friendship and there was even talk of marrying Strahan's son to Franklin's daughter Sally. The advent of the American Revolution brought a rift in this association when the Sage addressed to Strahan his celebrated and oft-quoted reproof: "Look upon your Hands, they are stained with the blood of your Relations. You and I were long friends. You are now my enemy. . . ." All of which sounds very tragic until we note that some months later, when Franklin had crossed from America as Envoy to France, the unperturbed printer sent over to Paris a present of Stilton cheese, which suggests that the misunderstanding, if any really existed, was not of long duration.[7] Besides no one ever quarreled long with "Straney"; he was too good-natured. When Sir Alexander Dick asked Boswell to show Strahan his *British Georgick*, Boswell, charmed with Strahan's affability but never impressed with his talents, wrote: "I evaded his inclination telling him that to show the book to poor Strahan who, as Garrick said, was an obtuse man, would be like showing family furniture to an auctioneer." [8] However, the printer could scarcely have been so inept as Boswell suggests, for he managed to get himself elected to Parliament, and died in 1785 leaving a fortune of £100,000.

As early as June 1750, before Franklin and Strahan had even met, they discussed Scotland and its institutions. On the second of June of that year Benjamin wrote: "The description you give of the company and manner of living in Scotland would almost tempt one to remove thither."

Strahan went up to Scotland in the summer of 1759 a few weeks before Franklin, and it might be supposed that the two friends would have traveled together. But just at this time the canny publisher bought a part interest in the printing rights of Johnson's *Rasselas* for £100, a venture which was far too lucrative in its possibilities to be neglected, and which necessitated an early departure from London and a speedy return.

The Pennsylvania Agent saw many of his Scottish acquaintances at their inn, for just as the American colonials resorted to the New England tavern in Birchin's Lane, so all good Scots resident in London foregathered at the British Coffee House in Cockspur Street.[9] The landlady, a Scotswoman to be sure, was a Mrs. Anderson, who brought popularity to the house by her well-known skill in compounding the national dish of cock-a-leekie, and respectability by the edifying circumstance that her brother was Bishop of Salisbury.[10] So many needy Caledonian adventurers thronged to this hostelry as to lend color to Johnson's gibe that the most entrancing bit of scenery for a Scotchman in his native land was the highway leading to London.

[ 17 ]

Franklin, who neglected few groups where learning and culture obtained, went occasionally to the British Coffee House during the months preceding his departure in August 1759, and met there some illustrious Scotchmen of whom he was afterwards to see much in Edinburgh.[11] Into this courtyard in Cockspur Street rode Principal Robertson of Edinburgh University with the manuscript of his *History of Scotland* in his saddlebags. Thither came "Jupiter" Carlyle of Inveresk, who has given us so sprightly a recital of the times, and David Hume, and the Reverend Mr. Home, pouring a raw egg into his glass of punch, and the printer Strahan, and the oily advocate Wedderburn, later Lord Loughborough, then friendly to Franklin but ferociously to score him before the Privy Council in 1774 during the investigation of the Hutchinson Letters from Massachusetts.

> Sarcastic Sawney, swollen with spite and prate
> On silent Franklin poured his venal hate;
> The calm Philosopher without reply
> Withdrew and gave his Country liberty.

There is a curiously modern touch in Carlyle's account of the dinner which David Garrick gave in his villa at Hampton Court for Robertson, Wedderburn, and others of the inner circle of the tavern. "He had told us to bring golf clubs and balls that we might play at the game on Molesly Hurst." [12] Although Garrick's guests were all from the circle of Franklin's acquaintances,[13] Carlyle does not note Franklin as having been present, otherwise we might record the Envoy's introduction to the Scottish game which has since become so popular in his own land.

The interest engendered in the northern tour by these Caledonian acquaintanceships would be supplemented by Franklin's own contemporary reading. The more important literary works printed in London during the summer of 1759 were the offspring of the Caledonian Muse; for the Attic tradition had shifted to North Britain, and Edinburgh was beginning to be acclaimed as the Athens of the North.

Rivington in Paternoster Row offered a *History of England* by Tobias Smollett, erstwhile student of surgery in Glasgow, the author timidly apologizing for the lack of an index and naïvely promising to prospective purchasers "a promissory note under the Proprietor's hand for the delivery of the plates as soon as the engravings are finished." Millar in the Strand advertised a *History of Scotland* by Principal Robertson of Edinburgh, one guinea in the boards. This northern cult engrossed even the stage, where the tragedy of *Douglas* by the Reverend John Home, a piece banned in Edinburgh by the protests of an outraged Presbytery, led in popular acclaim, and was produced at a theatre much frequented by our Agent of Pennsylvania.[14]

Such in the main were Franklin's Scottish relations in London, but the incentive for the visit had existed long before he set foot in Britain, since in Philadelphia he had had many affiliations with Scotland and with Scotsmen. As the Doctor sat before his comfortable sea-coal grate in Craven Street poring over Kennedy's *Itinerary of Scotland* and planning his tour, he could recall the many Scotsmen whom he had known in America and how they were wont to boast of the charms of their native country. There were: Baird who had been a member of the Junta, and who was back now at St. Andrews,[15] and Andrew Hamilton who designed the Pennsylvania State House, and James Burd the Indian fighter from Tinian near the Susquehanna, and the lanky Professor Alexander Alexander from the faculty of the college on Fourth Street who gave treasonable Jacobite toasts after his third glass, and Barclay of Urie, Comptroller of the Port of Philadelphia, and Thomas Graeme the Aberdonian who had been one of the founders of the American Philosophical Society. Then there was Edinburgh Davey, his own Davey Hall, who had come over to Pennsylvania from Strahan's London printing office in 1744 and had become his partner in 1748. How often had he heard Davey declare that the finest prospect on the entire globe was the view of the Firth of Forth from the Calton Hill! And now honest Davey was making the trip to Calton Hill possible, for without the £1,000 a year which Hall was to pay during eighteen years for the purchase of Franklin's interest in the *Pennsylvania Gazette,* Benjamin could scarcely have lived in luxury, kept a body-servant, and made tours in the summer. So, as the Envoy mused by Mrs. Stevenson's fireside, the fog-bound Thames flowing just beneath his window seemed to vanish, and instead the majestic Delaware rolled past the Assembly Room on Hamilton's Wharf, at the foot of Walnut Street, where on that beautiful summer evening in 1754 he had assisted in the outing of the St. Andrews Society of Philadelphia and the entire company had united in singing "The Bonnie Braes of Balwither."

It is to be hoped, from the standpoint of pleasant anticipation of a well-earned vacation, that Franklin consulted his English friends as little as possible concerning the proposed tour. The average Englishman of the period detested the Scots as a race of impecunious adventurers who had swarmed into London to engross positions and achieve careers at the expense of the native-born. Johnson's sarcastic observations and the oft-repeated taunt from a popular play of the time, that while a Scotsman might die for his country, he would not willingly live in it, are typical of the contemporary feeling. So intense was this hatred that successful Caledonians resident in London often anglicized their names, so that Strachan became Strahan and Menzies became Mengis.

While Scotland was the goal of Mr. Franklin's plans and aspirations, he could not definitely know when he left London whether he would be permitted to extend his journey as far as Edinburgh.[16] His immediate intention, as his correspondence proclaims, was to take a ramble in Derbyshire, make some visits to the estates of the county gentry to whom he had been "recommended," have a sojourn in Manchester and then make the final decision whether to continue his tour northward. In his letter written to Deborah from Liverpool on August 29, hereinafter quoted, he speaks of having "written largely" of his proposed trip, but this previous missive cannot be located.

The Agent's movements would naturally be affected by the state of his health, for a journey such as he was now embarking upon required experience and hardihood. A suggestion of the perils of the Edinburgh Road is afforded by the recital of Mrs. Calderwood of Polton[17] who made the tour a few months before, belted with pistols and accompanied by an armed escort for protection against highwaymen on the lonely moors.[18] Tobias Smollett, who had often traveled between London and Scotland, describes the discomforts of the route in his *Roderick Random,* and "Jupiter" Carlyle, who essayed the northern road a few months before Franklin, paints a deterring picture of narrow clay lanes, impassable after rain, precarious bridges, wretched inns, and uncertain relays of post-horses. Besides the actual dangers of the trip, its tedium was such that Sir Richard Steele took a French teacher along so that he might the more profitably beguile the weary hours.[19]

There were reasons of state, too, which might curtail the absence of a diplomat from London at this critical period when the political atmosphere was so perilously overcharged by the Seven Years' War between Britain and France and by its repercussion, the French and Indian War in America. A few weeks later the situation was materially to improve with a succession of dazzling victories vindicating the sagacious dispositions of Lord Chatham, when the chant of the *Te Deum* at St. Paul's seemed almost continuous and when, as a witty dilettante of the period aptly observed: "It will soon be as shameful to beat a Frenchman as to beat a woman. The park guns never have time to get cool." [20]

But during the weeks when Franklin was preparing for his excursion, the outlook was not so promising. Lally still faced Clive defiantly in India, and Wolfe was patrolling the St. Lawrence declaiming from Gray's *Elegy* and reconnoitering the cliffs of Montmorency through his spyglass; his campaign bulletins were distinctly discouraging: "Today came letters from Wolfe despairing as much as heroes can despair. Quebec is well victualled, Amherst is not arrived and fifteen thousand men encamped defend it," wrote Horace Walpole on July 15. These rumors disturbed Franklin, whose whole soul was bound up in the Canadian Expedition. *"Canada delenda est"* [21] was the slogan which he had personally urged upon the vacillating Ministry, little dreaming that in two decades he would be American plenipotentiary at Paris to conclude a Franco-American alliance against Great Britain. He might have left London in a more cheerful mood had he received the letter predicting the speedy fall of Quebec which Isaac Norris sent from Philadelphia on August 11, but this reassuring missive was to arrive during his absence in Scotland.

Nor was the threat of war restricted to the antipodes; there was a graver menace nearer home. The French Admiral Thurot lay in Dunkirk Harbor with his squadron and fifteen hundred picked infantry assembled for an attack upon the English coast.[22] He slipped out presently, on a foggy morning, evaded the blockade, and bore away into the mists of the North Sea. None could guess his intentions, and a period of panic followed similar to the one which ensued when John Paul Jones appeared off Scarborough in the American Revolution. Horace Walpole might write disdainfully: "Monsieur Thurot is piddling somewhere off the coast of Scotland," but the British public, which had witnessed the ease with which the young Stuart Pretender had marched his army to Derby only fourteen years before, was seriously alarmed. Breastworks were hastily thrown up at Plymouth and Portsmouth, on the Clyde and behind Leith; the trainbands mustered; and the provincial militia drilled on the greens of the county towns [23] as the American traveler rode northward through the long summer evenings.

To disturb further the tranquillity of Franklin's holiday was the imminence of a royal succession. At the time of his departure, George the Second, deaf and almost blind, was still struggling to maintain his formal Court at Kensington.

It does not appear that the Agent of Pennsylvania ever met the King whose coat he once wore as Colonel of the Provincial Militia, but the omission was of little importance, for his Majesty had survived both his influence and his popularity. "He is always going back to Hanover; he thinks of naught but Herrenhausen," wrote gossipy George Selwyn. The youthful exploits of the King at Oudenarde and Dettingen were forgotten. It was obvious that he was dying, and besides, his attitude toward England had always been that of a tolerant exile. The Court looked to Saville House in Leicester Square where dwelt the amiable and promising princeling, the grandson of George the Second, who was shortly to succeed as King George the Third, the same monarch whom the rebel Benjamin Franklin was to vex so sadly in the years that should follow.[24]

In colonial affairs there was a lull, and the Agent for Pennsylvania might leave his post with a clear conscience. The only matter of over-seas concern to come up during the summer in which Franklin left for Scotland was the appointment of a Lieutenant-Governor of Pennsylvania to take the place of the incumbent, Colonel William Denny, who had incurred the displeasure of the Penns; [25] but as this selection was invariably dictated by the proprietorial family, there was little likelihood of the Agent's being consulted.

Doctor Franklin had set the eighth of August as the date for his departure,[26] a notable anniversary, as we shall see. For a traveling companion, the natural and logical choice would be his son William, who had proved so congenial an associate in the trip to Cambridge the preceding year. The notations of the preparations of father and son for the coming holiday are to be read in Franklin's Personal Account Book, now at the American Philosophical Society. In anticipation of the fine folk whom he was to meet in Edinburgh, the Doctor had his wig refurbished by Howard the wig-maker in Jermyn Street. This cost £4 (less half-a-crown discount for cash), and the same amount for Billy's wig. Billy had had a new suit from Regnier [27] some weeks

[ 23 ]

previously, but his father's traveling suit from "Christopher the Taylor" arrived only two days before leaving.

The last days in Craven Street were busy ones. Bowman, the liveryman from whom the Doctor hired his town carriage, called and was paid twenty-one guineas for furnishing a traveling chaise. He got £30 more upon the return, so the trip to Scotland was not a cheap one. Then Mr. Franklin recollected that Isaac Norris had sent him £500 from Philadelphia to invest. He summoned his broker, Chamier, and directed him to put out the sum in a three percent annuity which was bought at seventy-nine and three-fourths percent. For fear that something might happen to him upon the journey, he left a notation explaining that although the annuity stood in his name, it was the property of Mr. Norris. After that, in all the hurry of departure, came an insistent woman from Pennsylvania, Mrs. Henry Flower,[28] who said that she was in great distress and borrowed three guineas. She returned later for a renewed importunity and the soft-hearted Mr. Franklin gave her half a guinea more. Then appeared the landlady, Mrs. Stevenson, who for all her cordiality thought it prudent to balance the account of a guest who was departing upon the perilous excursion to Scotland. She got £11 4s, which paid four weeks' board "including the board of the servants." In view of all these outlays it is a relief to note that one of the late callers, Elias Bland,[29] paid £300 "which was lent," a most opportune reimbursement.

And now with his dispositions all made, the chaise hired, Parliament adjourned, and the members of the Cabinet in their respective country houses, the Agent of Pennsylvania could depart with a clear conscience. The long vacation had set in, William was released from his duties in the Middle Temple; the British countryside with its scenic charm and historic lore was beckoning, so Mr. Franklin closed his office, made his adieus to Mrs. Stevenson, and embarked upon the great adventure.

# Chapter II

# DEPARTURE FOR EDINBURGH

THE two Franklins drove out from Craven Street upon their northern tour on Wednesday, the eighth of August. That morning the poet Thomas Gray left Mr. Jauncey's ordinary, Southampton Row, Bloomsbury, to walk to his desk at the British Museum, hard by. First, as was his daily custom, he took out his weather diary and noted that the wind was west and the day clear and hot.[1] Then as he went down the street, he became aware that some unusual event was toward. The guns of the Tower of London were sounding an insistent *feu de joie;* from Westminster came the triumphant peal of the Abbey bells; at each corner crowds of excited citizens were discussing a bulletin just arrived from Westphalia. Mr. Gray learned that the English and Hanoverian troops under Prince Ferdinand of Brunswick had routed the French under Maréchal de Contades in the glorious victory of Minden.

The sybaritic Horace Walpole, whom only the severe illness of his dear friend Mrs. Leneve could have dragged from the coolness of Strawberry Hill, came into London at the same hour to note: "Every street had one or two bonfires. Every squib in town got drunk and rioted about the streets until morning." [2] The irate mob broke into and pillaged two shops, one in Cornhill and one in Lombard Street, belonging to Quakers who had protested against the campaign. Mr. Franklin, as he drove by, could recollect the momentous summer evening when the news of Braddock's defeat reached Philadelphia and how the rabble had threatened the lives and properties of the non-resisting Friends to whose passivity they attributed the disaster. It appeared that the belligerent tendencies of the British commonalty of the period were not altered by emigration.

[ 25 ]

But this was no time for invidious comparisons. The good news had come most opportunely to cheer the departure, and the two patriotic colonials drove over Finchley Common in high good humor with the jubilant chorus still ringing in their ears:

> Prince Ferdinand has beat 'em;
> Where's now their broad bottoms,
> Bomb-shells or ball?
> Our rights we will maintain
> Proud Gallia's honours drain,
> For Marlboro' lives again,
> God save us all.[3]

So now the Franklins pushed northward through Hertfordshire in the chaise hired from Bowman, glorying in the joys of the English countryside during that "most gorgeous of summers." [4] Benjamin in his new traveling suit from Christopher sat, notebook in hand, taking observations on the postal arrangements, on the flow of the rivers, on the trade regulations of the villages. William was by his side, erect and debonair as became a veteran of the French and Indian War. He took no notes, it is to be feared, but ogled the pretty barmaids at the taverns while the horses were being baited, and ingratiated himself with any great folk whom his father chanced to meet and who might be useful in advancing his own political ambitions.

Nowhere in the correspondence of the travelers is there any direct statement that they were accompanied by a servant. In his letter to Deborah from Liverpool, August 29 (subsequently quoted), Benjamin says that "Peter presents his duty." Peter was the Agent's own body-servant and it may be that he was brought along upon the tour since he is thus referred to when the voyagers were three weeks out from London. William Franklin's negro slave, King, whom he had brought from America, had run away and turned up in the household of a lady in Suffolk, who was negotiating to buy him.

The Envoy could not have chosen a more congenial travel-ing companion than William, and their cordiality is the more marked in view of the later estrangement. In 1759 the political cleavage which was to cloud their sentiments in after years had not yet appeared, and father and son had lately been much in each other's company. Three years be-fore, they had shared the rigors of the campaign of 1755–56 in the ice-bound Pennsylvania woods, and had come over together from Philadelphia. The younger Franklin had been enrolled as a law student at the Middle Temple since the term of 1750–51.[5] He had been diverted, however, to other pursuits in Philadelphia and never crossed to Eng-land until he went with his father in 1757, at which time he resumed his legal studies and was admitted to the English Bar a year later. At the time of his Edinburgh excursion, William was sedulously angling for a political appointment, a vocation which is said to have suggested him to Miss Edge-worth as a model for her character of Cuningham Falconer in the fine novel of *Patronage,* which no one reads now.

Billy was handsome, too handsome perhaps for his own good. When his doting father describes him as "a tall and proper person, very much a beau," one might suspect parental indulgence, but even the unemotional Strahan, little prone to exaggeration, wrote, "I really think him one of the prettiest young gentlemen I ever knew from America." "Straney" liked William, and the insistent whis-pers of scandal attaching to the young lawyer's birth never affected the loving regard. Whether William was really the son of Deborah Franklin, as a painstaking but scarcely con-vincing apologist of our own time has sought to prove,[6] or whether he was "borne of an oyster wench in Phila-delphia" as the ferocious Reverend Bennett Allen pro-claimed in the heat of the American Revolution, we are not likely ever to know.[7] In any event, Strahan stood by William, but his Presbyterian correctness was shortly to be shocked by a graceless episode similar to the circumstances of Wil-liam's own appearance in the world. Perhaps the young

Colonial was not entirely to blame. London in the eighteenth century was a demoralizing place; and, although Billy was twenty-nine years old, he had been brought up rather strictly amid the conventions of a prim Quaker town. Despite, or perhaps because, of this restraint, he became involved in an unseemly connection and, sometime before his departure for Scotland, he learned that he was to become the father of a child.[8] This illegitimate offspring was the boy who afterwards went through life under the name of William Temple Franklin, and who came at an early age to live with Benjamin in Craven Street.

The identity of the mother of Temple Franklin is still undisclosed. Years afterwards, in the summer of 1779, . Thomas Hutchinson, the Loyalist governor of Massachusetts, was dining with Lord Mansfield in London, and his Lordship, in a moment of post-prandial confidence over the port bottle, gave his understanding of the matter.

Dr. Franklin being mentioned, my Lord, said that he (Franklin) carried his grandson (which, by the way, is the natural son of his natural son, both by street women) to Voltaire who said to the boy "Love God and Liberty." I observed to his Lordship that it was difficult to say which of these words had been most used to bad purposes. He seemed pleased with my remark.

Probably the solution of the riddle lies among the agitated letters of female calligraphy and subscription addressed to Benjamin Franklin in Craven Street, letters asking for money, for the payment of doctor's bills, for funds to set up a millinery shop. As one pores over these ill-spelled, ungrammatical ink-stained effusions which appear never to have been immaculate, even when the post-boy left them at the Envoy's door, one wonders: Is this the mother of William's son? Why is this one so insistent? What is this woman's claim? A speculation exhaustive in its ramification and in its futility.

All this to be sure is a far cry from a tale of two Pennsylvanians driving northward to Edinburgh in the half-forgotten days of George the Second, but it is mentioned here as showing the circumstances which attended William's departure. From the meager accounts which we have of his bearing during the tour, the illicit connection does not appear to have in any way dashed his good spirits or affected his zest for the journey.

After leaving London the Franklins set their course northwestwardly to attain Staffordshire, Derbyshire, Liverpool, and the Carlisle Road leading to Edinburgh. By this route they passed near the village of Ecton where three generations of their family reposed under the yew trees of the old churchyard, and Wellingborough where lived their cousin Mary Franklin Fisher, and Birmingham where dwelt their relative Rebecca Flint. They had already called at these three places in their ramble in 1758. As to the first two, there is little likelihood and no proof of a visit in 1759. Birmingham, however, which lay in their direct path, is almost certain to have been included in their itinerary. For while the confident assertions of the local historians that the Franklins stayed in their town in 1759 are not supported by documentary proof, the archives in the Birmingham libraries indicate a sojourn of at least two days.[9] Benjamin's letter to John Baskerville, written in 1760,[10] and referring to a recent visit to Birmingham would be conclusive, but unfortunately it lacks the day and month. It appears, however, to have been written early in 1760.

In Birmingham Franklin saw two men with whom later he was largely to correspond and whose theories and advice were to influence his own scientific essays; these were John Baskerville and Matthew Boulton.

Baskerville, the most celebrated printer and typefounder of his epoch, was then living in his hall, Easy Hill, just outside of the town. Franklin, who admired his work, had in the previous year bought six copies of the Baskerville *Virgil*, one of which he presented to Harvard. "I beg the College to do me the favour to accept a *Virgil* which I sent in the case, thought to be the most curiously printed of any book hitherto done in the world." [11] Poor Richard, who traveled in modest manner with no affectation of state, may well have been dazed at his fellow printer's pomp. Miss Catharine Hutton of Birmingham, writing in advanced age as late as May 1839, gives us a picture of Baskerville at the time of Franklin's visit. "I remember him and his gold-laced waist-coat and his pair of cream coloured horses and his painted chariot, each panel a picture fresh from his own manufactory for he was a japanner as well as a printer." [12]

Just at the period of Franklin's arrival, Baskerville was engaged in removing one of his presses to Cambridge, where he began work upon his Book of Common Prayer. That he found time to talk business with the American and give him some specimens of type is shown by Benjamin's anecdote contained in a letter written shortly afterwards.[13] Some critic came to Craven Street and sought to disparage the art of Birmingham as contrasted with that of Caslon, the typefounder of London. The waggish Agent pulled out a Caslon type and represented it as a Baskerville specimen brought back from his tour. Then he sat smugly by and enjoyed the joke while the detractor pointed out supposed defects in the type produced. However, for all of his praise of Baskerville's work, Mr. Franklin did not give him an order. The sales eloquence of the Birmingham printer was ineffective and the commission for type for the *Philadelphia Gazette* went to Caslon.[14]

Matthew Boulton, the second personage of importance associated with Franklin's visit to Birmingham, was a silver stamper and foundryman who had inherited a large fortune in 1759 and was building a pretentious residence at a suburb called Snow Hill. Even at that early date he was experimenting with a model for a steam engine. Boulton and the Agent of Pennsylvania became friends and correspondents, and in 1766 Boulton sent down to Craven Street his model of a compression engine for Franklin's inspection.[15] One of Boulton's co-workers whom Franklin met in Birmingham was Samuel Garbett, who later went to Scotland and became a developer of the Carron Iron Works near Falkirk. This circumstance was one of the causes which led up to Franklin's visit to the Carron Works in 1771, an episode described later in this narrative.

One Birmingham historian, in speaking of the sojourn of the two Franklins in 1759, asserts that Baskerville introduced Benjamin to Boulton; another maintains that Boulton introduced him to Baskerville. While the question is unimportant, it may be observed that Franklin had certainly made Baskerville's acquaintance in 1758 and does not appear to have met Boulton until 1759.

After our tourists leave Birmingham we know little of their movements until they reappear at Liverpool on the twenty-ninth of August, when Benjamin wrote to Deborah to say:

I wrote to you largely just before we left London. We have been out now almost three weeks having spent sometime in Derbyshire among the gentry there to whom we are recommended, as also at Manchester and this place.[16]

It seems that before entering Derbyshire the travelers visited the pottery district of Staffordshire and acquired some souvenirs. Some weeks after the return to London, Benjamin wrote to his forwarding agents, Hillary and Scott, concerning the insurance upon and the shipment to America of certain earthenware purchased during the Scottish journey. At which of the Staffordshire establishments this material was acquired is not known. The illustrious Wedgwood was just embarking upon his career in the making of pottery at the village of Burlsem, and one would like to believe that his acquaintanceship with Franklin began at this time. However, the first receipt for pottery bought by Franklin from Wedgwood is of a later date and from the Etruria Works.[17]

The tourists passed next into Derbyshire. Their wanderings in this county are uncertain, and there is apparently no possibility of locating the country houses of the gentry to whom they were recommended. These Derbyshire hosts were undoubtedly men of rank whom the Agent had met in London, but their identity is lost except for that of Anthony Tissington of Swanwick. Among the manuscript collections of the British Museum is an anonymous pamphlet subscribed "A Derbyshire Working Miner," printed at the Mews Gate, Derby, in 1766 and deposited at the Museum by Adam Wolley. Upon this pamphlet is the notation by the donor:

W. Ince of Wirksworth, Attorney, told me on November 26, 1794 that this pamphlet was written by Dr. Benjamin Franklin, the celebrated patriot and champion of American Liberty and Independence, during one of his visits to Mr. Anthony Tissington of Swanwick in the county of Derby.[18]

From this reference it would appear that Franklin spent some time at Tissington Hall investigating the operations of the mines in the district. During this sojourn in Derbyshire and perhaps at the Tissington residence, the Agent made the acquaintance of Erasmus Darwin, scientist and poet, grandfather of the great naturalist, as is evidenced by the letter written to Franklin March 19, 1763, wherein Darwin and Tissington convey their compliments to the Franklins.[19]

After leaving Derbyshire the Franklins are next disclosed in Sheffield, and again through the medium of a purchase. Some weeks after his return to London, we find Benjamin writing to Deborah:

By Captain Bolitho I send you two saucepans plated inside with silver instead of tinning. I bought them at Sheffield because I thought they would please you and if you are not much taken with them, I shall be greatly disappointed. I got three but keep the smallest here to make my water gruel. I'll send Sally a case of Sheffield goods instead of the stationary she wrote for to Mr. Hall.[20]

No details are available as to the stay of the travelers in Sheffield or the date of their departure. We only know that sometime in the third week of August they rode into the market place of Manchester, just fourteen years after Prince Charles Edward Stuart and his ragged Highland Army marched into the same square. As reminders of the episode, the heads of the officers of the ill-fated "Manchester Regiment" who had unwisely elected to throw their lot with the luckless expedition were still exposed upon the Manchester Exchange, and devoted Jacobites doffed their hats in passing to testify their respect for a lost cause. The place was full of Stuart reminiscence, and visitors were usually taken to hear the recital of Beppy Byron, an enterprising young lady who had sallied out in a white silk dress to kiss Prince Charlie's hand. Even the choice of an inn had a subtle political significance, for the Tories resorted to the Bull's Head in the Market Place, while good Whigs patronized the Angel Tavern.[21] At which one of these hostelries our travelers descended is not recorded; but it is singular that while Franklin was to proceed almost on the exact route of the Jacobite invasion of the "Forty-Five," he never once mentions it, a circumstance as incredible as for an American in the 1870's to pass over the trail of Sherman's march to the sea and ignore the historic traditions of his route.[22] Perhaps there was too much of practical interest for our serious-minded economist in this great manufacturing center of the Midlands, to permit of his taking the time to study the legends of a romantic past. Manchester already numbered a population of fifty thousand with many looms and, most important of all for a transatlantic observer, a thriving trade in cotton prints with the American Colonies.

An excellent turnpike road led westward from Manchester to Liverpool along which bowled the "Flying Machine," the new stagecoach which made the journey from London to the Angel Inn at Liverpool in the incredibly short time of seventy-two hours. But the Agent of Pennsylvania was not so much pressed for time as driven by the urge of an insatiable scientific curiosity. Someone in Manchester had told him of the marvelous salt mines in Northwich, then as now the great depository of mineral salt for the British Isles. Accordingly, he turned off the direct route and drove in a southwesterly direction to Northwich where he climbed down into the salt caverns, and William secured a glistening stalactite of rock salt to send over to Benjamin's brother, Peter Franklin, in Newport.[23]

These visits and digressions occupied the travelers until the last week in August, and they now turned sharply northward, crossed the Mersey, and drove into the maritime town of Liverpool.

The city of Liverpool, when Franklin visited it in 1759, had a population of thirty thousand and was already a thriving seaport with a harbor so commodious that, as a local newspaper boasted, "A vessel of one thousand tons can enter at low tide." The rich patrician merchants of Liverpool sent out the goods of Sheffield, Manchester, and Birmingham to the coast of Guinea, bartering for slaves, gold dust, or ivory, and to the West Indies in exchange for rum and sugar. The trade with the North American colonies was equally thriving, and more than five hundred vessels passed annually out of the Mersey bound for Boston, New York, and Philadelphia. The district was represented in Parliament by William Pownall of an old Cheshire family, a relative of Governor Thomas Pownall of New York, so that the Agent of Pennsylvania might count upon a courteous reception. There was no lack of distraction in the evening, for the *Liverpool Advertizer* apprises us that a company of comedians from the Theatre Royal in London were performing in *The Refusal, or The Lady's Philosophy*.

Two events of Franklin's visit to Liverpool are reflected in his subsequent writings. A few days before his arrival, the bark *Sarah Ann* laden with sugar came up the Mersey, the first ship to arrive from Guadeloupe since the conquest of that island by the British. The jubilant merchants acclaimed Guadeloupe as a second Jamaica, and proposed that all import duties on its merchandise be forthwith abated. Poor Richard, who could be perverse on occasion, did not share in this enthusiasm. He had profound convictions against the permanent occupation of the island, and launched into print some weeks later to demonstrate that the annexation of Guadeloupe with its alien population and traditions could never be of benefit to Great Britain.[24]

The second circumstance was the state of alarm which obtained in the town over the threatened attack by Thurot and his squadron. As a matter of fact, the French Admiral had not yet sallied forth from Dunkirk, but no one knew where he was, so the Liverpool volunteers were feverishly drilled and batteries of eighteen-pounders installed at the foot of Red Cross Street and in the old churchyard. This apprehension must have impressed Franklin with the vulnerability of the port, for twenty years later, when he was American Envoy at Paris, he wrote to Lafayette to discuss a Franco-American naval descent on the west coast of England, asserting that the rich town of Liverpool, among others, could pay a levy of at least two million pounds sterling to an audacious invader.[25]

Eighty-two years after the Agent's visit, on November 17, 1841, a great Franklin Memorial Service was held in Liverpool. The orator of the day, Reverend Hugh McNeile, delivered a bombastic eulogium which was subsequently printed in pamphlet form, but apparently neither the speaker was aware, nor were any of his auditors, that Franklin had once sojourned in their city.

When our traveler consulted his copy of *Williamson's Liverpool Advertizer and Mercantile Chronicle,* he would observe that two opportunities offered for the sending of letters to America. The merchant ship *Ranger* mounting twelve guns and with space "for freight, Redemptioners, Indented Servants and Passengers" was to depart presently "for the Western Shores of Virginia." Also bound "for Cork, Jamaica and Philadelphia" was the ship *Jason* which carried cotton goods and mail. Perhaps the patriotic Doctor would prefer this latter vessel since she was commanded by Captain George Washington. In any event, on August 29 he wrote and sent the letter (already partially quoted) to his wife to advise her of his progress.

I wrote to you largely just before we left London. We have been out now almost three weeks having spent sometime in Derbyshire among the gentry there to whom we were recommended, as also at Manchester and this place. We shall set out today for Lancaster. The Journey agrees extremely well with me and will probably be many ways of use to me. Billy presents his duty and Peter. I am not certain whether we shall continue our Route to Scotland or return thro Yorkshire and Lincolnshire to London but expect to meet letters at Lancaster that shall determine me. I long much to hear from you and shall endeavor to return early next spring.[26]

Leaving Liverpool on Wednesday, the twenty-ninth of August, the tourists proceeded to Lancaster, where they expected the letters which were to determine their future course. These letters were probably from friends in Edinburgh upon whose coöperation Franklin counted for an interesting stay in the Scottish capital; had the missives been from London or America, they would have overtaken him at Liverpool. In his journey to Edinburgh, Franklin took the western road by Lancaster, Kendal, Carlisle, Hawick, and Selkirk, and not the eastern highway through Berwick-on-Tweed, by which Samuel Johnson entered Scotland in 1773. This is proved by the recital of Dr. Wight, the Presbyterian minister from Dublin, who was crossing from Ireland at the time of Franklin's arrival and speaks of meeting the Agent at an inn along the western route.[27] If Franklin left Liverpool on the twenty-ninth of August, as was his announced intention, and went directly to Edinburgh, he must have taken either three or four days to negotiate the journey, depending upon the condition of the roads.

It is inconceivable that so observing a tourist could traverse the most picturesque parts of the Westmoreland and Cumberland without recording his impressions of the charms of the lake district in September, but if Franklin wrote at all, a painstaking search has failed to reveal his letters. However, as partial compensation the investigation has disclosed a contemporary diary which has been over-looked for nearly two centuries.[28] The American medical student, Jonathan Potts of Potts' Grove and Reading, later an illustrious surgeon in the American Revolution, the friend and correspondent of Washington, landed at Liver-pool in October 1766. He was accompanied by young Ben-jamin Rush of Philadelphia, afterwards Franklin's co-signer of the Declaration of Independence. Both boys intended to take up the profession of medicine and were bound for the college at Edinburgh.

In the absence of a Franklinian account, the Potts rec-ord is valuable as giving us an idea of the details and diffi-culties of Franklin's journey seven years before. At the period there was little transition, and even the inns at which the American lads descended are likely to have been the same which the Franklins patronized. Potts is enthusiastic, even voluble. He tells us about the sights of Liverpool, the castle at Lancaster, the cannon balls imbedded in the walls of Carlisle from the Duke of Cumberland's bombardment in 1745, the hard fare of the northern inns, and the four struggling horses which were required to drag their car-riage through the mud of the Scottish roads.

The Agent of Pennsylvania was now approaching the Highlands, the habitat of seers and divination. If this prox-imity endowed him with any gift of foresight, he would have been aware that his road was taking him close to persons afterwards to be nearly linked to his life and career. When the travelers drove through the old Roman town of Preston in Lancashire, they passed by the home of a family tracing its descent from the Norman Conquest, whose name had formerly been Beche or De la Beche, later corrupted into Bache. A son of this household, Theophylact Bache, had eight years before emigrated to America and become a prosperous merchant in New York. Living at home and impatiently waiting for the time when he could also go out to America was a younger brother, Richard Bache.[29] If Franklin had chanced to meet young Bache that day in the streets of Preston, he would have been looking at his own future son-in-law, for the boy emigrated to Philadelphia and married Sally Franklin in 1768 while the Envoy was still in London. In fact, it was in this very town of Preston, at the end of his second Scottish journey in 1771, that the Philosopher first met the husband of his daughter.

Also resident at Preston when Franklin passed through in 1759 was a dashing dragoon officer with a pair of fine eyes and a talent for writing plays which were seldom produced. His name was John Burgoyne and he had startled the town of Preston by eloping with Charlotte Stanley, eldest daughter of the Earl of Derby. His wife's powerful family had been placated and Burgoyne was being groomed for one of the two seats in Parliament which were the right of Preston and which were largely controlled by the Stanleys. In this summer of 1759 Burgoyne had volunteered for the ill-fated expedition against St. Malo and was awaiting the call to arms.[30] He and Franklin were to have many and weighty communications on both sides of the Atlantic, but the hour of their meeting was not yet.

Near Penryn the road led within a few miles of the port and fishing village of Whitehaven, where lay a small schooner fitting for a trading voyage to Virginia. Among her crew was a lad of twelve enrolled as a seaman's apprentice and about to make his first sea trip. This adventurous boy was the son of a Scots gardener from Kirkcudbright; his name was John Paul; and he was to return as John Paul Jones, under an alien flag, to terrorize this coast of his boyhood. What an opportunity for a historic meeting! But unhappily there is no intimation that our traveler was even aware of passing Whitehaven, much less of a prophetic vision of a sunny morning twenty years later and a graveled walk in Franklin's garden at Passy, with the gray-haired Envoy pacing up and down on the arm of an alert sinewy officer, Commander John Paul Jones of the new American navy.

The great western highway which our tourists were pursuing led them directly through the weaving town of Kendal, and here they tarried long enough to inspect the looms for which the place was famous and to buy a bolt of the well-known "Kendal green." This bale of cloth was forwarded by Hillary and Scott to Cadwallader Colden at New York, who was instructed to send the same on to Peter Franklin at Newport.[31] This transaction, following the purchase of the pottery in Staffordshire, gives a pleasing insight to the benevolence of a traveler who, amid the distractions of a tour in a new and interesting environment, could take time to think of his relatives at home and to acquire remembrances for them.

After leaving Kendal, the only town of any size through which the Franklins passed was Carlisle.[32] We have no record that Benjamin sojourned there, although perhaps he took a meal and formed some acquaintanceships, for after his return to London he received a letter from a Major Senhouse of Carlisle asking for a scientific treatment for his deafness. When the travelers pushed on, they came presently to the river Esk, and as their chaise splashed through the shallow ford, they knew that they were in Scotland at last. The tiny river was the physical barrier, but the two countries were separated by a social cleavage, almost as sharply defined as that between England and France, and born of age-old animosities and prejudices.

The Union of the governments of England and Scotland in 1707 had existed for half a century at the time of Franklin's visit without in any way ameliorating the hereditary distrust between the two countries, an attitude evidenced by the decorous belittlement by Horace Walpole on the one side, and the fulminations of David Hume against the "factious barbarians of London" on the other.[33] Franklin was well aware of this prejudice. He had observed that from Lancaster northward every tavern window was scrawled with scurrility against the Scots; and, once across the border, he was to witness a like intolerance displayed toward visitors from the southland.[34] Our Philosopher was to be received in Edinburgh with generous cordiality, but it should always be remembered that he was welcomed as an American and not as a Southron.

Benjamin has left us no record of his first impression of Scotland, but it may well have been one of disillusionment. The sincere worshipper at the Caledonian shrine must ever regret that he chose the western avenue of approach rather than the more inviting route by Berwick. The Selkirk landscape could not have been exactly repellent, for Franklin passed through while the heather was flaming in early autumnal glory, but it was a poor district, devoid of trees and not apt to impress tourists who were accustomed to the elmlined lanes of New England. A monotonous stretch of lonely, sparsely cultivated moorland bounded by huddles of bare rolling hills mounting aimlessly to the horizon; these were the characteristics of the western counties as the two Philadelphians first saw them on that September day in 1759. Washington Irving, who visited this same border country as the guest of Walter Scott at Abbotsford fifty years later, stared in disappointment at the treeless braes and asked if this were indeed the romantic setting of the Minstrel's Lay.[35] Jonathan Potts describes the county of Selkirk as "A country, the most dismal in all the world, in which the inhabitants are a kind of centaur, as man or beast live all together." Nor is this unflattering impression to be ascribed to transatlantic prejudice. Goldsmith and Gray both traveled to Scotland about the time of Franklin's sojourn. Goldsmith could only say that the Dumfriesshire hills were "black and frightful," while Gray was still more emphatic: "I dread Edinburgh and the itch and expect to find very little in my way worth the perils I am to endure." [36]

And when, after a toilsome journey over impossible roads, the wayfarer came to his resting place for the night, disappointment reached its climax. Benjamin was by no means a fastidious tourist. As Assistant Postmaster General of the American Colonies, he had ridden thousands of miles on horseback and was used to indifferent accommodations. But the American taverns, though often primitive, were seldom unbearable, and some of the better colonial hostelries vied with the comforts of English country inns. When Mr. Franklin journeyed to Boston, he descended at the luxurious Indian Queen in Elizabeth or the Elm Tree in Farmington. When he drove southward, he enjoyed the hospitality of the well-appointed Blue Bell in Annapolis and the Rising Sun in Fredericksburg. In contrast to these cozy quarters, his first night in a Scottish roadhouse was certain to be a nightmare of wretched quarters, filth and vermin, slipshod service and greasy food.[37] Potts's initial experience of a Scottish rural inn was at a tavern near Hawick: "We slept without going regularly to bed but I fear notwithstanding all my precautions, I shall have reason to regret ever entering the house at all. Don't forget the supper!" The poet Gray had such a racking recollection of his Caledonian tour that he collated his impressions in a brochure entitled *Advice to a Friend Travelling in Scotland,* which the Franklins might well have perused with profit and edification.

See your sheets air'd yourself. Eat mutton or hard eggs. Touch no fried things. If they are broiled, boiled or roasted, say that from a child you have eat no butter & beg they would not run any over your meat. There is honey or orange marmalade or currant jelly which may be eaten with toasting bread or the thin oat cakes for breakfast. Dream not of milk. Ask your landlord to sit down and help off with your wine. Never scold anybody especially gentlemen or ladies.[38]

The inn at which the two Pennsylvanians spent their first night in Scotland, and where Dr. Wight met them, was probably at Galashiels. From Galashiels to Edinburgh was twenty miles "and a bittock," that is to say, about five miles more. Allowing for deficiencies of the road, it would have been late on the afternoon of the second of September [39] when the Franklins drove over the hills of Braid on the same route taken by Adam Woodcock and Roland Graeme in that noble Scottish romance, *The Abbot,* and paused for their first view of the ancient and famous metropolis of the north, the couchant lion overlooking the wide estuary.[40] As the Americans gazed, they could note the gaunt, gray castle with the line of slate roofs where the long High Street descended to the Abbey of Holyrood, the heights of Salisbury Crag and Arthur's Seat, and the tossing blue waters of the Firth. From that same eminence Lord Marmion had reined his steed, delighted with the noble prospect of the distant city.

> Such dusky grandeur clothes the heights
> Where the huge Castle holds its state
> And all the steep slope down
> Whose rigid back heaves to the sky
> Piled deep and massy close and high
> Mine own romantic town.

But Sir Walter was not to be born for twelve years; *Marmion* was as yet undreamed of; and besides a practical philosopher from the banks of the Delaware would be more occupied with calculations of the velocity of the wind currents eddying the sable clouds of smoke over the towers of Auld Reekie than concerned with the romantic traditions of an historic town. The Franklins put their chaise in motion, drove along the Bruntsfield Links where King James's army had lain encamped before the Battle of Flodden, passed through the Cowgate Port, and alighted at their tavern within the city walls of Edinburgh.

# Chapter III

# AULD REEKIE

T HE evidence as to the occupation and movements of our tourists during their first days in Edinburgh is happily more detailed and certain than that of their journey from London to Scotland. Franklin's good friend, the printer Strahan, had come up from London to Edinburgh early in August, and the Sage wrote to apprise him of his own arrival in the northern capital.

*Edinburgh, Sept. 6, 1759*

Dear Sir:—

Your agreeable Letter of the 4th August is just come to hand, being sent back to me from London hither. I have been a Month on my Journey; but the first Thing I did after my Arrival here was to enquire at Mr. Kincaid's whether you were yet in Scotland. He told me he believ'd you were out of Town, but not return'd to England, and might be heard of at Mr. Scot's. We went there immediately in hopes at least to have seen Rachie but were disappointed. We left a Note of our Inn; but having now taken lodgings, I write this Line to inform you that we are at Mrs. Cowan's in Miln Square, where I hope soon for the very great Pleasure of seeing you, being,

Dear Friend,

Yours Affectionately,

B. FRANKLIN.[1]

The "Mr. Kincaid" referred to in the letter was Alexander Kincaid, a friend to Strahan who kept a bookshop near the Cross in Edinburgh. He was at one time Printer for His Majesty for Scotland, and in 1776 was elected Lord Provost of Edinburgh, dying in office in 1777.[2] "Rachie" was Strahan's daughter Rachel, an amiable young girl and a great favorite of Franklin. She afterwards married Andrew Johnston, an apothecary of Bread Street, and died in 1765 in her twenty-fourth year. The "Mr. Scot" referred to in the letter was William Scott, one of the best-known Edinburgh bookbinders of the eighteenth century. Some months before Franklin's visit, he had produced a Book of Common Prayer bound in red morocco which had brought him much praise.

Discerning travelers were not likely to bear long with the discomforts of an Edinburgh inn of the period, so that it is not surprising to find our Americans presently installed in the boarding house of Mrs. Cowan in Milne Square, just west of the Canongate, an irregular rookery of dingy flats giving on to a central close. This building stood on the north side of High Street just where the long North Bridge spans the ravine, thus joining the old town with the new fashionable quarter, which Franklin never saw. Many engravings survive of Milne Square. It was once an ancient and dignified edifice planned and partly erected in 1689 by Robert Milne of Balfarg, the Royal Master Mason who built the later portions of the Palace of Holyrood. When the North Bridge was erected in 1772 it cut away part of the eastern end of the structure, and today only a steep, arched passageway remains of the ground plan of the square of Franklin's time. The landlady, Mrs. Cowan, was the sister-in-law of James Cowan, a well-known watchmaker in Parliament Close who died in 1781. Milne Square endured as a lodging house as late as 1823, when a certain Mrs. Reynolds was reputed to keep there "the most respectable boarding house in town." [3]

The building was a typical Edinburgh "land" of the period with a curious suggestion of modernity in that it rose to a prodigious height upon a comparatively contracted area. This multiplicity of stories, a characteristic of the High Street, originated in the circumstance of the city being built along a precipitous ledge with no chance for expansion. The town at the time of Franklin's visit had a population of approximately fifty thousand,[4] but there were only two streets of any length, the High Street stretch-

**MILNE SQUARE**
Edinburgh

ing from the Castle to the Netherbow Port, and the Cowgate which paralleled it.

The upper stories of these "lands" were attained by stone staircases which were really ascending lanes giving on to gloomy low-ceilinged flats where entire families, even of the better classes, were herded. So narrow were these winding stairs that ladies in the voluminous skirts of the period could scarcely pass, and in case of death, the coffin was often lowered from the roof. Conditions were rather worse than the average in the fall of 1759, for there was a scarcity of water following a long drouth, and the *Scots Magazine* for December describes the long lines of servant maids waiting in the cold to secure their supply of water from the few wells still functioning.

Indeed the sanitary state in Edinburgh at the period is almost indescribable. Mr. Franklin, to be sure, was not squeamish. The habits of the Philadelphians were far from ideal, and he had inveighed in his *Gazette* against the good old custom of depositing filth and offal at the curbs in his own High Street. But in Philadelphia there were at least cesspools; in Edinburgh the rocky strata of the foundation precluded many wells. Consequently the stairways and passages were encumbered with "luggies" containing household excrement of every kind. A municipal ordinance directed that at ten o'clock in the evening these receptacles should be emptied into the street below. Accordingly, at the appointed hour, the entire malodorous collection was thrown out from all the windows to the accompaniment of the historic cry "gardy loo" (*gardez l'eau*),[5] and the agonized shrieks of "Haud your hand!" from the unlucky pedestrians who happened to be passing at that moment. The shiftless Edinburgh poet, Robert Fergusson, who reflects so faithfully the usages of his native town, has commemorated "gardy loo" in ringing rhyme.

> On stair wi tub or pat in hand
> The bare-foot housemaid loe to stand
> That antrin folk may ken how snell

Auld Reekie will at morning smell.
Then with an inundation big as
The burn that 'neath the Nor Loch brig is
They kindly shower Edina's roses
To quicken and regale our noses.[6]

Such were the unsavory conditions of residence in the good town of Edinburgh in the reign of his Teutonic Majesty George the Second! Milne Square had the added disadvantage of standing just over the Nor Loch, a body of stagnant water which occupied part of the site of the railroad yards of our own day and which was the approved depository for the dead animals of the city. Small wonder that Gray described Edinburgh as "That most picturesque (at a distance) & nastiest (when near) of all capital cities." And it was in an environment similar to this that Franklin assured Lord Kames that he spent "six weeks of the densest happiness I have ever met with in any part of my life." [7]

In only one way might the Philadelphians have mitigated the discomforts of their stay. We know nothing of the location of their rooms, but it would have been infinitely preferable for their windows to give on to the noble view to the northward rather than to the fetid close within. One recalls the scene in *Guy Mannering* when Colonel Mannering ascends the unpromising stairway of Counsellor Pleydell's lodgings and is so agreeably surprised by the superb panorama from the Counsellor's windows. Had the Americans been forewarned to engage the outside rooms, they might gain a temporary respite from the olfactory horror below, and revel in the prospect of the Calton Hill and Leith Roads and the dancing waters of the Firth extending from Inchkeith to where, in the dusk of the early evening, the primitive pharos glowed on the Isle of May.

It must not be deduced from this unpalatable description that Milne Square was a tenement peopled by the dregs of humanity. On the contrary, it had always been a resort of aristocracy as was proved by the escutcheons and coats of arms which studded the walls and extended from above the doorways. Great men and high-born women lived there, picked their way amid the filth of the contracted staircases, and dwelt in sordid quarters which would not be tolerated by paupers of our own time. At the period of Franklin's sojourn two of the flats were occupied by the family of Charles Erskine of Alva, Lord Justice Clerk. Simon Fraser, Lord Lovat, whose character Stevenson has so unflatteringly drawn in his novel of *David Balfour,* is said frequently to have visited the Lord Justice, and Franklin may have made his acquaintance. Other notable residents were William, Earl of Sutherland, busied at the time in the problems of the defense of Edinburgh against the threatened attack by Thurot; old Lady Glenorchy, and the amiable Earl of Hopetoun—exalted neighbors, these, for an erstwhile printer's apprentice from Boston.

Returning now to the routine of our two visitors from overseas, they are disclosed on the second day of their stay at the printing office of John Balfour, an associate of Strahan, where occurred a transaction which was to cause the elder Franklin both annoyance and embarrassment. Balfour, the son of a bonnet-laird from Pilrig, was a bookseller and paper maker with a shop near the Luckenbooths where he anticipated modern methods by issuing catalogues. Also, excellent man, he inaugurated the custom, while crying his book sales in Writers Court, of always having a punch bowl at his elbow, the contents of which were generously ladeled out to good customers, a practice which is said to have materially enlivened the bidding and one which his successors in the trade might well emulate.

Amid Franklin's varied commercial interests he had had a share in a book and printing establishment at New York with one James Parker, the proprietor of the *New York Gazette.* Also engaged in the publishing business, in Boston and in the island of Antigua in the West Indies, was Franklin's nephew, Bennie Mecom, his sister Jane's son. Both of these American customers owed Balfour for previous purchases, made through the agency of Strahan, and were behind in their payments. Moreover, another consignment, selected by Strahan during his stay in Edinburgh, was in readiness to be sent out to Parker. So when the Agent of Pennsylvania walked into Balfour's shop, the printer naturally inquired about the financial standing of both Mecom and Parker. Just what happened is not quite clear. Parker, who did not want the books, said afterwards that Franklin, without his knowledge, ordered the parcel to be sent. Balfour, anxious perhaps to save Franklin's face, asserted that Strahan, not Franklin, "recommended" that it be sent.[8] In any event, shortly after the American's visit, a large assortment of books in the amount of £57 16s went on the brigantine *Jenny* to New York, where Parker received them without enthusiasm; he had plenty of unsold books on the shelves already, including some previously bought from Balfour.

Parker was honest and plodding, but a wretched administrator. His voluminous correspondence is made up of whines about bad business, ill health, and family troubles. And now, as he had foreseen, the Edinburgh books which his eminent associate had so casually ordered did not move. Five years passed and Balfour, who had received only £20 in response to insistent duns, began to write to Franklin in London asking for the name of a lawyer in Philadelphia who could handle the account. Benjamin, not altogether easy in conscience over his own part in the matter, put pressure to bear upon his partner through Deborah in Philadelphia. Poor Parker, nearly frantic by this time, indited an agitated protest to Balfour (the firm had now become Hamilton & Balfour)[9] in which he stated that he had never wanted the books and did not see why they had been sent ("Why did I ever receeve these Books? Why didn't I sent them Back?") and then, goaded out of his habitual awe for his distinguished partner, he speaks from the heart: "You said you sent them on Dr. Franklin's recommendation and I could not prevail on myself to offer such an affront to his favour as to refuse them."[10]

[ 48 ]

The collection of the Balfour account was not helped by the arrival in New York, in 1769, of two Edinburgh printers, Alexander and James Robertson, who set up a rival newspaper to Parker's *Gazette*, a sheet which they called *The New York Chronicle*. The unhappy publisher of the *Gazette*, forced by this unlooked-for competition to spread the butter thinner, denounced the newcomers to Franklin as "Two Scots paper spoilers—ignorant blockheads," and was less than ever disposed to pay a Scottish account.

Thus the matter stood until July 2, 1770, when it was Parker's humor to die, leaving a substantial amount of the account unpaid. So irregular was the communication of the period that fifteen months afterwards Balfour, unconscious of Parker's passing, was still writing to Franklin about the balance due him.

Oddly enough the Mecom account, which had seemed the less promising of the two in 1759, was paid in full to Balfour through Franklin.[11] Probably the uncle voluntarily assumed his nephew's debt, for in 1764 Bennie Mecom was a hopeless bankrupt, owed Franklin £200, and paid his creditors only four shillings on the pound.[12]

After this ill-starred business venture, the next event in the Franklins' sojourn is their elevation as Guild Brethren of Edinburgh which took place on Wednesday, the fifth of September, the third day of the visit. The promptness with which this signal honor was accorded shows that Benjamin's advent was expected by the municipal dignitaries. Such a ceremony called for some premeditation and could not have been arranged unless the City Fathers had been advised of the approximate time of the arrival of the great scientist from America.

One speculates as to the identity of the influential friend through whose good offices this distinction was so speedily conferred. It is not likely to have been Strahan, for the tourists did not know of his whereabouts in Edinburgh until after the civic pageant.[13] Nor was it David Hume, for he was in London and did not return to Edinburgh until early in November.[14] Perhaps Adam Smith suggested the commemoration, for Smith was gravitating, during that autumn, between Glasgow and Edinburgh and was in the latter city when Franklin arrived. He had just published his *Theory of Moral Sentiments* with Millar of London (one of the few Scottish productions of the time which got away from the enterprising "Straney") and was already making notes for his magnum opus, *The Wealth of Nations*. Many of his associates, such as Sir Alexander Dick of the College of Surgeons, the two professors Munro, *Primus* and *Secundus,* the doctors Cullen and Russell, Henry Home, Lord Kames, and Professor Black, were either known to Franklin or shortly to be presented. These men were of the distinguished group who had gained for Edinburgh its well-deserved title of "The Athens of the North." Franklin describes them some years later in a letter of introduction given to young Jonathan Potts, who proposed to study medicine in Edinburgh:

You have great advantages in going to study at Edinburgh at this time where there happen to be collected a set of as truly great men, Professors of the Several Branches of Knowledge, as have ever appeared in any Age or Country.[15]

Any one of Adam Smith's colleagues, in the list just given, may have proposed Franklin as a Guild Brother of Edinburgh, and somewhere in the diaries or correspondence of these men there must appear a description of the Americans' reception by the Provost. If such a record survives it is buried away amid the accumulations of a Scottish garret to reward the search of some future and more fortunate biographer. For a reconstruction of the social scene in the England of the epoch, there exists a mass of letters and memoirs, but in Scotland, as an acute observer remarks, the writers did not keep copies of their letters for publication and their friends did not keep the originals for love. So that we cannot say who prodded the burgesses, who certainly knew little of Franklin and less of Philadelphia, to their gracious gesture of appreciation.

On the great day of the installation the Town Council of the loyal city of Edinburgh convened with unusual pomp, proclamation by the Crier, display of the mace and solemn parade of the Lord Provost, Bailies, Old Bailies, Deacons, and the various functionaries who made up the formal municipal array of the period. These dignitaries proceeded to the Council Hall, not on the present site, but behind the Law Courts on part of the grounds now occupied by the Signet Library.[16]

The Lord Provost was Sir George Drummond,[17] one of the most enlightened magistrates who ever presided over the destinies of the good town, and a cousin to Franklin's subsequent friend, Lady Drummond Kames. The term of office was two years but Sir George was elected six times, making a total of twelve years of service. Indeed, had it not been for the provision forbidding a tenure in office of more than two consecutive terms, he might well have had the Provostship for life. He was regarded as the father of modern Edinburgh, and was the first to maintain that the city should expand and not be indefinitely constrained inside its feudal walls along a narrow ridge of rock. Unlike many of his fellow Councilors, who were suspected of Stuart leanings, he was a stout Hanoverian, had marched out with a musket on his shoulder to fight against Prince Charlie, and officiated at the historic ceremony when the Jacobite standards, taken at the battle of Culloden, were publicly burned at the Cross of Edinburgh.

The Council assembled. The stately Provost in stupendous wig and flowing robes, ebony staff of office in his hand, was seated on the dais flanked by the Bailies.[18] Before him were the candidates for the Freedom of the historic city arranged in the proper order of reverence due to rank, first the Right Honorable George Lord Lyttleton and his son, Honorable Thomas Lyttleton, then the Franklins (no one

knew William's first name, so he was presented as ——
Franklin), then Ralph Ratcliff and John Tombes, Esquires,
whose identity is long since lost.

The meeting was opened by prayer, as was fitting in a
community which revered the precepts of John Calvin.
Afterwards some routine matters were considered, including repairs to the janitor's house. Then the Bailies began
to construe the Act of July 19, 1583, a subject of some delicacy, it would appear, and the discussion of which may have
prompted a cynical epigram from Poor Richard and ribald
comment from William. The recorded matter of debate
was:

Whether the daughters of Burgesses shall lose their Freedom
if they are not reputed virgins.

If the Bailies, in their collective wisdom, came to any
conclusion in this embarrassing question, their decision
was not announced and the Conclave proceeded to the
formal Presentations of the Freedom of the City, as evidenced by the faded entry still to be read in the Council
Record: [19]

As also to admit and receive Benjamin Franklin of Philadelphia, Esquire, and —— Franklin, his son, to be Burgesses and
Guild Brethren of this city in the most ample form.[20]

It might be supposed that so august an occasion would be
emphasized by the local press, but the *Caledonian Mercury*
ignores the whole affair and the *Scots Magazine* merely
describes a ceremony in the afternoon of the same day when
Sir George Drummond dedicated a poorhouse for the West
Kirk parish, without referring to the Franklins or to the
honor conferred upon them.

From the files of the same *Mercury* it would appear that
other celebrities were visiting in Edinburgh to vie for the
attention of a fickle public. An astounding camel accompanied by a dromedary was on exhibition in Craig's Close
and daily attracted fascinated throngs. Also a certain Doctor

Chevalier Taylor, an impudent charlatan who claimed to have treated the eyes of the Pope and of the crowned heads of Europe, was in residence in Niddry's Close. This mendacious impostor was actually accorded a reception at the University, at which time a member of the faculty wrote a commemorative ode which was published in the *Mercury*:

> A Camel and a Dromedary too
> Now for a sixpence are exposed to view
> But ere you go their properties to spy
> Let Doctor Taylor regulate your eye.
> For though it be afflicted with no ill
> This Chevalier will make you better still.

With such competition there was small likelihood that the newspapers could find space to record the doings of a diffident philosopher from Philadelphia.

Beyond the occupation suggested in Franklin's letter to Strahan, written on the fifth of September and previously quoted, we know little of the activities of the tourists during the two days, Thursday and Friday, which succeeded their elevation as Guild Brethren. From Franklin's subsequent correspondence we may infer that the time was spent in sight-seeing, and it is regrettable that we lack an account of these hours.

No artist has painted Poor Richard strolling up the High Street of Edinburgh, and yet the subject is as appealing as Paul of Tarsus in the Forum of Rome, or Peter the Great gaping at the sights of the Strand. And while no recital survives of the first sortie of Franklin from Milne Square, it is not difficult to reconstruct his morning promenade. The travelers would arise early, since the town was usually astir by five o'clock, but might comfort themselves with the adage "Plow deep while Sluggards Sleep" or some similar appropriate aphorism from their own Pennsylvania almanac. As the bells of St. Giles's were sounding seven, father and son would descend the tortuous staircase, dexterously avoiding the nasty "luggies."

Once in the street, they would pause to marvel at the height of the buildings, so imposing to the colonial imagination, and to admire the carvings on the weather-beaten beams and gargoyles. Then taking their course up the High Street, they would pass the foundations of the Cross of Edinburgh, which an enlightened zeal for improvement had removed some months before their arrival. This had always been a gathering place for gossips, and even now it was a rendezvous for local politicians discussing the latest bulletins brought in by runners from Leith and Glasgow. Dr. Franklin, whose anxious thoughts were continually of the campaign before Quebec, would pause to ascertain whether any news had arrived from General Wolfe.

By now they would be nearing St. Giles's, and all about them the street abounded with life. The caddies or messengers of the town, alert lively youngsters consumed with curiosity as to everybody's business, ran upon their appointed tasks.[21] The antiquated Gaelic city watch who, having begun life with stealing cattle in the Highlands, were now marshaled for the defense of law and order, went by in their red coats, Lochaber axe on shoulder. The ill-paved "causey" was crowded with cavaliers and pedestrians, sedan chairs and great lumbering coaches drawn by six horses. The ladies who tripped along the muddy lane no longer wrapped themselves in the graceful plaid. That picturesque garment had gone out of vogue about ten years before Franklin's visit and had been succeeded by modern bonnets and sacques usually ornamented by a brooch with a miniature of bonnie Prince Charlie, then drinking himself into oblivion in France.

Passing the Drummond Infirmary, the Pennsylvanians noted that the masons were working on a niche for a bust of King George the Second to be dedicated a few days afterwards.[22] Mounting still higher, they reached St. Giles's Church and came presently to the clumsy mass of buildings called the Luckenbooths, which then stood in the middle of the causeway, leaving only narrow passages on either side.

In the Luckenbooths were shops of every description, cutlery stalls and goldsmiths' booths, establishments of mercers, milliners, glovers, and hatters. Here was the bookshop of the celebrated William Creech, where the wits of the town met before taking their gill of brandy when midday sounded from the Tron. The incongruous structure ended in the Tolbooth or town jail, the same Heart of Midlothian which Sir Walter was to immortalize. If Mr. Franklin compared it with the house of detention at Third and Market Streets in Philadelphia, it must have been with a smug conviction that even the prisons were better ordered in America. Beyond the Tolbooth the High Street sloped up to the Castle entrance and here, peering through the arched gateway, our Pennsylvanians might observe the crude stockade behind which some unlucky white-uniformed French prisoners, the predecessors of Stevenson's *St. Ives,* proffered toys for sale and gesticulated for tobacco.[23]

Such was the Royal Mile, as the Pennsylvania tourists saw it for the first time. Their promenade we may suppose to have taken place on Thursday or Friday, the sixth or seventh of September, for on Saturday father and son went out to visit Sir Alexander Dick, President of the College of Physicians, at his seat Prestonfield, on the slopes of Arthur's Seat two miles southeast of Edinburgh.

# Chapter IV

# LATTER-DAY ATHENIANS

S IR ALEXANDER DICK, Franklin's first host in Scotland, was among the very few Scottish gentry who sought to continue in the eighteenth century the lavish hospitality of the feudal era. Nearly every distinguished visitor to Edinburgh sooner or later found his way out to Sir Alexander's estate at Prestonfield, so that it is not surprising that the Franklins should have been invited there for their first week-end. The letter in which the travelers accepted the invitation is still preserved among the Cunnyngham-Dick family archives at Edinburgh.

Dr. Franklin and his son present their respectful compliments to Sir Alex. Dick and shall attend him to Prestonfield tomorrow with great Pleasure. They are extremely obliged to Sir Alex. for his kind invitation to spend some Days at his seat in the country, but doubt the short stay they must make in these Parts will not allow them that advantage.

MILNE SQUARE.                                              *Friday morning.*

Edinburgh was still enclosed by the battlements of its medieval period when the Franklins rode down the High Street on that September day in 1759, on their way to Prestonfield. They passed through the walls at the venerable Netherbow, turned right near Luckey Boyd's tavern, at the head of the Canongate, where Johnson was to stay in 1773, and gained a lane which led over the Dalkeith Road to the Dick mansion.

Sir Alexander Dick was fifty-six years old at the time of Franklin's visit. In his youth he had studied medicine at Leyden, had qualified as a physician, and even found time to introduce the rhubarb plant into Scotland. Later he made the Grand Tour and shot partridges in the swamps of the Romagna with the exiled princeling, Charles Edward Stuart, whom Doctor Dick was next to see marching past Prestonfield at the head of an invading army to hold a brief but brilliant Court in the hall of his royal ancestors at Holyrood. Returning to Scotland after his travels, Sir Alexander began a distinguished medical career which culminated in his election as President of the Edinburgh College of Physicians. In 1773, at the age of seventy, he came to visit Johnson in Edinburgh, upon which occasion Boswell relates: "At dinner this day we had Sir Alexander Dick whose amiable character and ingenious and cultivated mind are so generally known." The great Lexicographer was much impressed with the magnificence of the hospitality of Prestonfield.

> *Johnson:* Were I a country gentleman, I should not be very hospitable. I should not have crowds in my house.
> *Boswell:* Sir Alexander Dick tells me that he remembers having a thousand people in a year to dine at his house, that is reckoning each person as one each time that he dined.
> *Johnson:* That, Sir, is about three a day.

Boswell was a frequent visitor at Prestonfield, and it was here, in the autumn of 1776, that he first heard the news of the British occupation of New York, which tidings he received with such unpatriotic regret.[1]

The Dick family [2] at the time of Franklin's stay consisted of Lady Dick and two daughters, the elder of whom, Janet, aged ten, was Franklin's especial favorite. Janet was a sprightly hoyden well calculated to tease and delight an indulgent, middle-aged Envoy. She grew up a great beauty, was the toast of every hunt ball in Haddington, had the distinction of refusing the suit of Boswell, and died unmarried.[3] The verses which she exchanged with Franklin are still to be read at Prestonfield.

*Lines wrote at Coldstream by Dr. Franklin on his Return to England.*

Joys of Prestonfield adieu,
Late found, soon lost, but still will view
The engaging scene—Oft to those eyes
Shall the pleasing vision rise,
Hearts to warm towards a friend,
Kindness on kindness without end
Easy converse, Sprightly wit
These we found in Dame and Knight
Cheerful meals and balmy rest
Beds that never Bugs mollest
Neatness and sweetness all around
Those at Prestonfield we found
Hear O Heaven the Stranger's Prayer
Bless the hospitable pair
Bless their sweet bairns and very soon
Grant these a Brother those a Son.[4]

These verses were addressed to Lady Dick, and the mischievous Janet collaborated with her friend Robert Alexander in reply.

What Franklin writes appears so fine
I wish his thoughts and words were mine,
Why then so cruel couldst thou be
As send his sprightly lines to me.

Our prayers and sentiments the same,
I love the Knight adore the Dame,
Unlike alone is this our vow
He prays for one Son, I for two.

But see for all he pleased to say
Your beauty could not make him stay
A lover gone you'll understand
Is not so good as one at hand.

Franklin made many warm friendships in Scotland, but his most cherished association, not excepting those with

Lord Kames and David Hume, was the one with Sir Alexander Dick. The two friends exchanged letters and presents, and their cordiality extended to members of the families who had never met. Sally Franklin in Philadelphia received a collection of Scots songs [5] from Lady Dick, Janet Dick got a book of poetry from Deborah Franklin. Sir Alexander's sincerity was to be put to a severe test. He lived to hear his former guest denounced as a proscribed rebel; from the very lawn where he and Franklin had so often paced, deep in their philosophical discussions, he was to hark to the thunder of the American guns as Paul Jones threatened the shipping of the Leith, in 1779. But he never faltered in his devoted loyalty.

There was a butler at Prestonfield for whom Franklin conceived a great liking and to whom he afterwards refers in his letters. Some wag, Sir Alexander himself perhaps, had dubbed him "Pythagoras," and the visitor always calls him by that name and promises to perform a mysterious commission in Philadelphia. Lady Dick, writing to Franklin three years later on the eve of his departure for America, sent greetings from "the honest Pythagorean." [6]

The Dick mansion lay and still lies, for it has not greatly changed, at the base of Arthur's Seat with a fine view of the Duddingston Loch to the eastward. It is a stately mansion with traditions of William Wallace and Mary Queen of Scots. Even now, when its park is oppressed by the rows of suburban villas which modern enterprise has crowded up to its gates, it has an unmistakable air of distinction. Of the three great estates which our traveler visited in Scotland—Prestonfield, Kames House and Blair-Drummond—Prestonfield is the only one which rests in the possession of the family of the original visit. Another Janet, as engaging as the one who charmed Franklin, escorts visitors about the grounds, shows the green where William played at bowls and the bench, under the yew tree brought into Scotland by Mary of Lorraine, where Benjamin conversed with Sir Alexander Dick.

What did they talk about, these two congenial savants, as they sat beneath the historic yew? Of their researches, possibly, and of the electrical experiments which were their common interest; perhaps, too, of the varied vicissitudes of their colorful careers. Sir Alexander might tell of his student days in Holland, his trips on muleback over the Swiss passes, the banished Pretender's gloomy Court at Rome. Franklin would speak of his printing office in the High Street, his quarrels with the Proprietors, his recent campaign amid the Lehigh hills, his hopes and fears, plans and aspirations for the new nation on the western sea-rim.

Despite the Agent's protestations that he could make only a short stay at Prestonfield, he remained five days with the Dick family, returning on the fifteenth of September to Edinburgh, where there ensued the round of lavish entertainment which he afterwards so gratefully acknowledged.

The hospitality of Edinburgh is proverbial, but it is unfortunately impossible to identify all of Franklin's hosts and hostesses. Many of the cards and invitations preserved at the American Philosophical Society bear Scottish names, but as they are seldom dated, it is not easy to say whether they were left at Craven Street or Milne Square. Then, too, the newspapers of the period are exasperatingly lacking in social bulletins. The *Edinburgh Evening Courant* announces "the arrival of the celebrated Dr. Franklin of Philadelphia" and then ignores the remainder of his sojourn. Perhaps the best evidences of Franklin's associates in Edinburgh are his own subsequent letters, since the persons to whom he referred and to whom he wished to be remembered would be those whom he had frequently seen. The names thus mentioned are, first, those of his most intimate friends, David Hume, Lord Kames, and Sir Alexander Dick; and secondly, the Professors Munro (father and son), Adam Ferguson, Joseph Black, Doctors Cullen and Russell,[7] Principal Robertson, and Adam Smith—a notable circle. But then it must be remembered that this was the period when Dr. Aymot boasted that he could stand at the Cross of Edinburgh and every hour shake fifty men of genius by the hand.

Dr. Franklin's social circle in Edinburgh would have furnished a fitting subject of portrayal for the brush of Raeburn or Allen Ramsay; but from the standpoint of picturesque narration only Sir Walter could have done proper justice to the scene. The table might be placed in the Douglass Inn at Anchor Close or in John's Coffee House or in the White Horse in the Canongate. The hospitable board would be strewn with glasses and with long-necked bottles of good French claret; the clouds of tobacco smoke eddying up to the low oaken ceiling. There sat the genial Agent of Pennsylvania, his visage flushed after mighty and unwonted potations, leaning eagerly forward to interpret properly the broad Scotch accent of the attendant babble. William Franklin would be modestly placed at the foot of the table and he, too, would be intent in following the guttural periods of the speaker of the moment. The benevolent gentleman whose lace jabot was invariably stained with snuff would be the celebrated Dr. Cullen, under whom so many American lads had studied and to whom Benjamin West referred as the Blackstone of medicine; Dr. Cullen took a proper pride in his medical attainments but was vainer still of his ability to read *Don Quixote* in the original. The tall, handsome man with pronounced Gaelic features would be Adam Ferguson, philosopher, historian, and man of science, who had fought with the Black Watch at Fontenoy. Next to him we may imagine the erudite Professor Joseph Black, who always spoke with a foreign accent from the circumstance of his having been born in Bordeaux, then Dr. Alexander Munro, teacher of anatomy at the University, who, with his son and grandson, were to form a distinguished academic dynasty, then the amiable Professor Russell and the gaunt, elongated form of eccentric Lord Kames.

Sociability, to be sure, was a characteristic of the intelligentsia of Edinburgh in the period, and all of the circle mentioned, including even the clerical Dr. Robertson, held their meetings at taverns. Our American Envoy was blessed with a strong head and a good stomach, which was fortunate, for nowhere was society so brilliant as in Edinburgh and nowhere so bibulous. Young Henry Marchant [8] of Rhode Island, who was with Franklin in Scotland upon the second visit, speaks of their being escorted home after a late sitting by a servant with a link, which suggests a picture of a portly philosopher following a trifle unsteadily in the wake of an athletic Celt who held aloft a pine torch for guidance through the nameless filth which cluttered the dimly lighted streets.

Sometime in the week following their stay at Preston-field, the Franklins dined with Dr. Robertson at his house in the Cowgate. The Reverend William Robertson was resting from the honors accruing from his successful *History of Scotland,* just published, and enjoying a sinecure in the Kirk as minister of Greyfriar Church. He had met Franklin in London early in 1759, for amongst the Frankliniana at the American Philosophical Society is a card left at the door in Craven Street.

```
Dr. Robertson
at
Mr. Adams
New Bond Street
```

Robertson was a rising man and already being mentioned for the Principalship of the University of Edinburgh, a position to which he was appointed three years later.

When Franklin and his son took dinner with Dr. Robertson there was present that Scottish Pepys, the Reverend Alexander Carlyle of Inveresk, to whose memoirs we are indebted for many intimate glimpses of the social life of the period. Carlyle describes the occasion as follows:

In the middle of September this year I went to Dumfries to meet my friends, as I usually did, and to accompany my friend Dr. Wight, who had come from Dublin to Dumfries, and forward to Musselburgh to visit me. While Wight was here, we supped one night in Edinburgh with the celebrated Dr. Franklin at Dr. Robertson's house, then at the head of the Cowgate, where he had come at Whitsunday after his being translated to Edinburgh. Dr. Franklin had his son with him; and besides Wight and me, there were David Hume, Dr. Cullen, Adam Smith, and two or three more. Wight and Franklin had met and breakfasted together in the inn at (place omitted) without learning one another's names but they were more than half acquainted when they met here. Wight, who could talk at random on all sciences without being very deeply skilled in any, took it into his head to be very eloquent on chemistry, a course of which he had attended in Dublin; and perceiving that he diverted the company, particularly Franklin, who was a silent man, he kept it up with Cullen, then professor of that science, who had imprudently committed himself with him, for the greatest part of the evening, to the infinite diversion of the company, who took great delight in seeing the great professor foiled in his own science by a novice. Franklin's son was open and communicative, and pleased the company better than his father; and some of us observed indications of that decided difference of opinion between father and son which, in the American war, alienated them altogether.

This account has been much quoted as the first record of a meeting in Scotland between Hume and Franklin, but "Jupiter" Carlyle's memory is not always trustworthy, and we have Hume's own testimony to the effect that he was not in Edinburgh before the first week in November, at which time Franklin had already left the city.[9]

Carlyle is not usually malevolent, but there is ever a subtle hint of ill will in his allusions to Franklin. He relates with unctuous glee a conversation he had with the Pennsylvania Chief Justice, William Allen, at Harrogate in England, in which Allen described Franklin as a "turbulent plotter who could embroil three kingdoms," without ex-

plaining that Allen was a fanatical Penn partisan and hardly
an unbiased witness. In another place in Carlyle's *Autobiography* he speaks of meeting Franklin at a dinner at Sir
John Stuart's lodgings in London and finding him "silent
and inconversible." This is an unexpected impression of an
Envoy whose great asset during his diplomatic career at
London and Paris was his affability, but there is perhaps a
reason for this appearance of reticence. The gatherings at
which "Jupiter" Carlyle met Franklin were composed ex-
clusively of Scotsmen, and it must have been very difficult
for an American colonial to understand the dialect. When
the Glasgow justice, Lord Dun, appeared before the House
of Lords, Franklin's friend Lord Kames maliciously remarked, "Deil ae word from beginning to end did the English understand of his speech." This was a formal occasion;
in moments of relaxation, his Lordship would have been
still more unintelligible. Even the most cultured of the
doctors and judges who made up Franklin's circle in Edinburgh were apt to revert to broad Scotch after the claret
decanter had gone its third round. Small wonder that a
transatlantic visitor should give a suggestion of reserve in a
conversation to which his ears were not yet attuned. It may
have been of these argumentative gatherings in the northern capital that Franklin was thinking when he wrote in his
*Autobiography* of the trait of disputation and remarked,
"Persons of good sense, I have observed, rarely fall into it
except lawyers, university men and men of all sorts that
have been bred in Edinburgh."

There was one prominent resident of Edinburgh at the
period, to whom it might be supposed that Franklin would
pay an early visit, for he was the only person in the city who
had known the Philosopher in Philadelphia. This was Peter
Williamson, the Indian captive of Pennsylvania, kidnapped
from Aberdeen and sold into slavery in America, and who
had been back in Edinburgh about a year when Franklin
first came there. His adventures are best to be gleaned from

his own book *French and Indian Cruelty*,[10] which ran into twelve editions, during a period of half a century, and was embellished by a picture of Peter in Indian costume struck from what one of his biographers terms "a very tired plate." Peter's connection with Benjamin Franklin in America is vague. His own unblushing account represents him as running the whole Pennsylvania campaign with the help of some slight assistance accorded him by "General Franklin." The more probable theory is that after his captivity among the Shawanoes in the interior of Pennsylvania, Williamson joined a column which marched from Philadelphia in January 1756 to re-victual Fort Allen on the Lehigh River, which Franklin and his son were then building. Peter certainly served with the relief column and met Benjamin at Fort Allen,[11] although just how much the two men saw of each other during the expedition is not clear. Peter was not likely to minimize the intimacy.

Upon his return to his native Scotland after this American Odyssey, the adventurous Williamson may well have expected something of an ovation, but instead the irate burgesses of Aberdeen accused him of having brought the fair name of their city into disrepute because of his recital of the kidnapping. The unfortunate author was arrested and his book burned by the common hangman. He retorted with a countersuit against the municipality, and the matter was still in abeyance when the Franklins arrived in Edinburgh.

While his cause was pending, "Indian Peter" established a coffee house (where no coffee seems ever to have been drunk) inside the sacred precincts of the Parliament House itself. It was one of the sights of the town which all visitors were taken to see. Boswell relates that he went there to meet the elder Walter Scott, Writer to the Signet, for in the days when lawyers saw their clients in taverns Peter's bar was an approved rendezvous for legal consultation.

This same Parliament House, the stately hall where

Scottish kings were crowned of yore and where the great Montrose had confronted his accusers with serene intrepidity, had fallen upon evil days and lay neglected and forlorn. A row of crudely partitioned booths occupied the north side of the room and upon one of these was displayed the legend:

COFFEE ROOM.
PETER WILLIAMSON
THE INDIAN CAPTIVE
FROM ANOTHER WORLD.
ALL ARE WELCOME

Before the door of this singular place of entertainment stood the wooden figure of a Mohawk in full panoply of war.[12] About the entrance were suspended spears, bows, and quivers of arrows. One article in particular would attract Franklin's attention and if he stepped over to inspect the label, he would read:

Chief Jacob's night cap which Peter Williamson got in a Present from Benjamin Franklin Esq. of Philadelphia.[13]

For customers who had ordered (and paid for) a sufficient amount of claret, Peter was wont to dress himself in Indian costume and do the Mohawk war-dance, ending with a blood-curdling whoop. After a "tappit hen" (a formidable receptacle holding four quarts) he would relapse into maudlin poesy and recite an ode which is printed in the York, 1758, edition of his *Cruelty*.

> See Pennsylvania bleeds in every vein
> Her Houses ravaged and her Children slain
> Rouse, Britons, rouse from Sloth and Delays
> Be what you were in Anne's and Edward's Days.

Poor Fergusson, who took many a tass of brandy at Peter's bar, too many for his own good, deplored the paucity of business when the Courts were not in session.

This vacance is a heavy doom
On Indian Peter's Coffee Room
For a' his china pigs are toom
Nor do we see
In wine the sucker biskits soom
As lights a' flee.[14]

There survives in Kay's *Edinburgh Portraits* a curious woodcut showing Williamson chatting before the Cross of Edinburgh with Bruce, the Abyssinian traveler, but we have no depiction of Peter and Franklin. Apparently the arrival of Benjamin and William, his two former comrades in the Lehigh campaign, stirred the Indian Captive to renewed activity, for in the current *Caledonian Mercury* appeared the following advertisement:

Just arrived from North America and to be seen at John Mitchell's in Sellers Close opposite the upper end of the Luckenbooths from ten to nine at night for a sixpence a person, Statue of King Hendrick the Mohawk Chieftain as big as life, also an Indian Queen in a miniature canoe.

Exhibited by the famous Peter Williamson, author of a book entitled "French and Indian Cruelty," who entertains the publick with the most surprising Indian performance.

Peter was enterprising but scarcely measured up to the technique of a modern showman, or he would have advertised that the performance was to be sponsored by the celebrated Dr. Franklin of America, temporarily in our city.

The career and personality of Peter Williamson have been referred to here because he was the only person in Edinburgh whom Franklin had known in America. To be sure, Benjamin nowhere mentions him, but if we were restricted to the few sentences of original description which survive, the narrative of the Caledonian trips would be compressed into sparse paragraphs. The gift of the Mohawk headdress shows a certain degree of intimacy between the two men. The absence of further detail is regrettable, but Peter's establishment was one of the landmarks of the city

[ 67 ]

which all visitors were taken to see, and he is no more to be excluded from a recital of the Edinburgh of the period than the Castle or the Calton Hill.

And now Franklin's first visit to Scotland drew to a close. Life in the capital was pleasant enough, but perhaps a diet of solan-goose, cock-a-leeky, tup's head, and haggis began to pall upon the American stomach. Besides, Benjamin was far too restless and inquiring a traveler to abide indefinitely amid the fleshpots of the metropolis. He had announced his intention of seeing the interior parts of Scotland, and some time in the third week of September our tourists took the road for Glasgow.

# Chapter V

# THE TOUR IN CALEDONIA

T HE road to Glasgow, a muddy winding trail, led out through the Grassmarket. It was so incredibly bad that the average time for the journey of forty-six miles was twelve hours, and in winter the trip might consume a day and a half. Franklin says nothing about the weather, but it may be that the conditions which had so favored him in England did not hold in Scotland, for a certain disconsolate Francis Gentleman, writing to David Garrick from Edinburgh on the eleventh of September of this same year, complains of the excessive rain, plaintively observing, "I entertain thought of removing into a more favorable climate." [1]

Riding westward through Kirkliston and Linlithgow, the travelers passed by the moor of Falkirk where, thirteen years before, Prince Charlie had turned upon his pursuers in the last gleam of success over the waning fortunes of the luckless race of Stuart. It was the time of the autumn fair, and great droves of highland cattle were being tended by ragged caterans, most of whom had been "out in the Forty-Five." These herds were the symbol of the old romantic agrarian Scotland of the Middle Ages. On the northern horizon the surveyor's rods marked the site of the new Carron Iron Works, emblematic of the industrial Scotland just coming into being. The infant industry was to be linked closely to Franklin's destinies, and one of its very earliest prospectuses advertised ranges "Made on the model of Dr. Franklyn's Philadelphia stove." [2] This commercial connection together with his interest in the embryo Watt Steam engine explains Franklin's protracted visit at Carron in 1771.

Glasgow in 1759 was a sleepy, pedantic, and very decorous

county capital, having a population of twenty thousand. All the gloomy fanaticism of the Covenanters concentrated in this Calvinistic metropolis of the west; no decent burgher went abroad after ten at night, and the silence of the Sunday was preternatural. Some months after Franklin's visit a strolling group of players attempted to give a performance in the town, but the scandalized citizens destroyed the temporary structure which was to house it and so averted the profanation.[3]

The gallant Wolfe, who came to his heroic end on the Plains of Abraham almost at the hour in which Franklin left Prestonfield, had been in garrison at Glasgow a few years before, and wearied out some dull months of service in what he describes as "dismal quarters with suppers of the most execrable food on earth and wines that approached a poison." For all of this indifferent fare there was plenty of prosperity in the place. A thriving ship-building industry had started; and boats laden with rum from Jamaica and tobacco from Virginia were constantly arriving in the Clyde to enrich the merchant princes of the Trongate.

There is no note in the municipal minutes of Glasgow of any official reception similar to the one attended at Edinburgh. The Provost was allowed an annual salary of £200, which was to include "wine for the entertainment of gentlemen who have occasion to wait upon him," but if the Franklins partook of this civic hospitality, the event is unrecorded.

Benjamin's interest in Glasgow would naturally center in the University, where forty students were quartered in a group of mournful gray buildings on the High Street. Franklin's only previous knowledge of the institution was derived from his correspondence with Robert Simson, Professor of Mathematics. In the tedious weeks of April 1757, while he was waiting at New York for the tardy convoy which was to escort his packet-ship to England, he had beguiled the time by writing on a scientific theme to "Mr. Professor Simson" of the Glasgow faculty. Besides his desire to see Simson, and the ordinary curiosity of a traveler, there was a commercial reason for the visit. On the quad was the shop of Alexander Wilson, the father of Scottish type founders.[4] Franklin, always a printer at heart, had a commission from his former partner, David Hall of Philadelphia, to buy a set of type for the *Gazette* press. He knew of Wilson's foundry through Strahan, who bought most of his type there, and had one of Wilson's sons as apprentice in the London establishment. Wilson had furnished type for the College press since 1748, and was a courtier of a sort who enjoyed high patronage. Some years previously he had visited London with Professor David Gregory of St. Andrews and managed to get himself presented to the all-powerful nobleman, later Duke of Argyle, but then Lord Islay. Through Lord Islay's influence, a few weeks after Franklin's sojourn, Wilson was nominated for the chair of Practical Astronomy at Glasgow University. If Franklin talked business at Glasgow, the negotiations came to naught for, after his return to London, he bought a set of Brevier type from Caslon on Chiswell Street and sent it on to Hall in Philadelphia.[5]

Emerging from the Wilson shop, the Envoy called upon the brothers Andrew and Robert Foulis, the celebrated printers, who were installed in this same quadrangle and were considered the peers of any craftsmen of their age. Like Baskerville at Birmingham, they specialized in the classics, and Franklin, who was very proud of his own *Cato Major*, could appreciate the beauty and accuracy of the Foulis *Thucydides*. The brothers conducted an art museum filled with doubtful examples of the great masters injudiciously acquired in Italy and France, but as Franklin's versatility never attained to an adequate conception of painting, it is unlikely that his interest in the Foulis establishment extended beyond the printing shop.

Also on the quad and one door removed from the Foulis workroom labored a frail, sickly young mechanic, son of an obscure ship chandler from Greenock, who eked out a precarious living by mending musical instruments for the members of the faculty and for the townspeople. His name was James Watt, and his thrifty relatives complained that he wasted all his spare time in calculations for a fantastic device which he termed a steam-engine. There is no evidence of a meeting between Franklin and Watt although, considering their mutual scientific interests, it is scarcely conceivable that in so restricted an academic community they did not meet.[6] The agent certainly formed the acquaintanceship of Wilson and the brothers Foulis, for on the second visit in 1771, he had no sooner reached Glasgow than "he went to call upon his old friends, the printers Foulis and Professor Wilson." [7]

Adam Smith, who had just posted back from Edinburgh to give his *Theory of Moral Sentiments* to the press, was Quaestor of the University, met the Franklins and appears to have fallen under the spell of William Franklin's affability. A few months afterwards he wrote to Strahan:

> *Glasgow, April 4th, 1760*
> . . . Remember me to the Franklins. I hope that I shall have the grace to write to the youngest by next post to thank him in the name of the college and myself for his very agreeable present.[8]

The identity of William's gift to the college is not disclosed. Perhaps it was a copy or copies of his *Letter to the Printer* published in the *London General Advertizer* in October 1757, an effusion in which he took great pride and had brought out in pamphlet form. However, a search of the Glasgow University Library has failed to reveal any trace either of William's donation or of the books which Benjamin had previously given.

Franklin, a loyal subject to King George, could certainly not foresee, in 1759, that he would ever subscribe to an American Declaration of Independence. Still less could he divine that with him, in the town of Glasgow during those autumn days of his first visit, was another prospective signer of the same historic document. The Pennsylvanians may have noticed that their tavern was crowded with reverend gentlemen of the cloth, rural preachers of the Kirk of Scotland come up to Glasgow for the Fall Meeting of the Western Synod of Glasgow and Ayr. The Synod opened, a few days after Franklin's arrival, with a sermon entitled "Trial of Religious Truth by Its Moral Influence," [9] delivered by the Moderator, a thick-set, earnest young parson from the Laigh Kirk of Paisley. This was John Witherspoon, later to be President of the College of New Jersey, at Princeton, and member of the Continental Congress. There is no proof for a statement that there was any communication between the Moderator and the two tourists from America, and yet the destinies of the three men were to be singularly entwined. Benjamin Franklin and Witherspoon were to sit together in Philadelphia during the tense debates which preceded the Declaration. Later, when Franklin was at Passy, Professor Witherspoon was to write to him twice, once asking for information as to his son, John, Jr., who was a surgeon on an American privateer and had been taken prisoner by the British, and again inquiring whether France were a proper field of propaganda for the raising of funds for Princeton College.[10]

William Franklin, rather bored, we may surmise, with the entire proceeding, was following his father about the quad. If he observed the Moderator from Paisley at all, he is not likely to have accorded him more than a cursory glance, and yet this landward dominie in hobnail boots and threadbare cassock was to bring him much tribulation. A decade later, while Witherspoon was serving as the sixth president of the college of Princeton, William Franklin became a trustee of the institution by virtue of his official position as Governor of New Jersey. The Presbyterian President suspected the Governor of an insidious plot for bringing the college under the control of the Church of England. Probably his suspicions were warranted, for William was a thoroughgoing Tory and a sincere Anglican. In any event, Witherspoon resented the attempt and, being a member of the Provincial Council of New Jersey at the beginning of the Revolution, he voted to send the Royal Governor into exile and imprisonment in Connecticut.[11]

One of the faculty whom Franklin first met in 1759, and whom he hastened to visit when he arrived at Glasgow in 1771,[12] was the eccentric Professor John Anderson, who guided the Americans through the Perthshire Highlands, a competent but most singular traveling companion. The preceptor was a man of great learning, who knew his Scotland and had written on the Roman ruins of Caledonia, but his vagaries were such as to make him cordially hated by his colleagues in the University faculty. On his side he seems to have regarded his fellow professors with profound contempt and, some years after Franklin's visit, startled the Scottish Commissioners of Education with the proposition:

That an University is rather a hurt than an advantage to a trading town for it has been universally observed of the Merchants of Glasgow that the most ignorant of them have been the most successful.

And at a faculty meeting he gravely suggested:

That the University of Glasgow be dissolved and the Professor of Natural History (Anderson) be despatched to Skye in Hebrides to teach ancient Caledonian music to the inhabitants.[13]

Professor Anderson was of a scientific turn of mind, which may have commended him to Franklin, and was engaged in perfecting a new cannon which he proposed to use against Thurot if the French admiral should threaten the shipping in the Clyde. This gun was conceived upon modern principles in that the recoil was counteracted by the condensation of air. With the advent of the French Revolution, Anderson became an enthusiastic Jacobin and went over to Paris to offer his gun to Robespierre.

A contributor to the *Glasgow Mechanic's Magazine* for 1825, writing in a reminiscent mood, asserts that Franklin assisted the Professor to install a lightning rod on the North

College, regretfully adding that "since Anderson's death, this scientific thunder-rod has been suffered to fall into disrepair." Some lines of unknown authorship preserved in the College archives are supposed to refer to this incident:

> Tell them you can discharge the cloud
> Though fully charged and thundering loud
> And let them know the lightening of the eye
> Has no conductor like a thundering sky.

Now the Franklins, with Anderson as their courier, turn their backs upon the Clyde and vanish into the Highlands, where their movements for the next few days are problematical. Albert H. Smyth, the most responsible and exhaustive of the collators of Franklin correspondence, but too often careless in his documentation, makes the statement that Benjamin and his son joined with Professor John Anderson at Glasgow for a tour of the Perthshire Highlands, proceeding by way of Dunkeld and Perth to St. Andrews.[14] This information is probably authentic, but it is unfortunate that Smyth cites no authority. Franklin wrote once to Deborah from Glasgow and perhaps explained his route, but the letter cannot be found,[15] so that after the Americans' departure from Glasgow, nothing definite can be said about their itinerary until they arrive at St. Andrews.

Benjamin's route led through some of the most picturesque parts of the Highlands, and above Stirling he passed the estate of Blair Drummond, where he was to spend five happy days as the guest of Lord Kames in 1771. The tourist has left us no record of his sensations during this journey, although he must have been impressed by the grandeur of the scenery through which he passed. Even Thomas Gray, that most sybaritic of travelers, takes time from his excoriation of the filth and insects to tell about the prospect of the Grampians, the glories of the thundering Spey, and the plaintive appeal of the Gaelic ballads sung by the gangs of Highland laborers who were constructing the roads.

There is a tradition in Perth that the Franklins and Professor Anderson descended at the old King's Arms Inn. Robertson told Horace Walpole that Benjamin had been to Scone, north of Perth, and had made some sage remark which is supposed to have prompted Macaulay's famous allegory of the New Zealander sitting on the broken arch of London Bridge to sketch the ruins of St. Paul's. The historian Parton, usually very sound in his conclusions, was convinced of the actuality of this incident and quoted it in his biography of Franklin.

Being once at Scone and being told that it was there the old Scottish kings had used to be crowned, Franklin said "Who knows but St. James may some time or other lie in ruins as Scone does now.

These fugitive and semi-apochryphal allusions make up our only information as to Franklin's course in Perthshire, but with the arrival at St. Andrews on the first day of October, we turn from the conjectural narrative to a more solid basis of authority, since here there is contemporary evidence and the movements of the tourists are well substantiated by the records of the college and the town. St. Andrews lay off the direct road from Perthshire to Edinburgh, but the Agent made this digression to express his appreciation of the honor conferred upon him by the faculty in the previous February. He had already given tangible expression of his gratitude by presenting a book to the University, his own *Experiments and Observations,* "Ex dono Auctoris," which is still treasured in the College Library.[16]

Perhaps on the journey down from the Highlands, the Pennsylvanians speculated on what sort of place St. Andrews might be, and pictured a trim college green like their own New Haven or a second Oxford with imposing architecture in appropriate horticultural setting. If this was their expectation, they were doomed to disappointment. The university town was in the depth of decadence, its ecclesiastical prestige had departed; the stately mansions where the Scottish nobility once dwelt lay defaced and ruined. Grass grew on the one principal street, well fertilized by the unsavory manure piles which stood before the doors of the houses. Campbell in his *Scotland Described* gives a lugubrious depiction of the place:

It consists of one street on both sides of which appear the decaying remains of several houses once splendid and stately but now desolate. Its conviviality is enlivened and a maudlin consolation administered to its sorrows by no fewer than two and forty ale houses.[17]

The population of the village had dropped to three thousand. The college, whose glorious traditions dated back to a Bull of the exiled pontiff, Benedict XIII, given at Avignon in 1413, had only twenty students to shiver in its shabby, fireless halls. A few years after Franklin's visit one of the university buildings was actually put up for sale and bought by a professor for a nominal sum.[18]

There is no record of the hostelry at which the Americans and Professor Anderson descended; perhaps it was Glass's Inn, one of the very few Scottish taverns to which Johnson accorded a word of grudging praise, and where he breakfasted so heartily on rissered haddock and mutton chops. The two outstanding events of the stay were the ceremony of the elevation of Benjamin Franklin as a Guild Brother of the town of St. Andrews, and the formal reception by the faculty of the college.[19] The elevation took place on the second of October in the picturesque Tolbooth, long since demolished to make place for the present Town Hall. Benjamin's Certificate or Burgess Ticket, inscribed pedantically in classic Latin and signed by the Burgess, Jacob Lumsdean, is now among the archives of the American Philosophical Society. The honor was accorded only to the elder Franklin. William, who had been made a Guild Brother at Edinburgh, was neglected at St. Andrews.

The academic reception was held in the University Library, the same room which evoked Johnson's caustic comment because it was closed and no one could find the key.

Rector Shaw, who presided at the exercises, was the Dr. David Shaw who guided the great Lexicographer about the quad and wrung from him the reluctant admission, "I took much to Shaw." [20] No official details of the Franklinian ceremony are available beyond the somewhat fulsome minute in the college archives, quoted in our first chapter, but Rector Shaw's successor, the distinguished scholar who now holds the post of Principal of St. Andrews, has given us a fanciful reconstruction of the historic scene. [21]

In imagination we can look on at the ceremony, taking our place on the tier of raised benches flanking the wall: the windows overlook the College Garden where the thorn-tree planted by Mary, Queen of Scots, was even then 200 years old. The center of the floor is empty, the surrounding seats are occupied by senior members of the University while in the background stands a group of scarlet-gowned students. All eyes are turned on the central figure. Clad in the undress gown of a Doctor of Laws (out of the fashion of the University of Paris) Franklin kneels on the graduation stool in front of the President of Senatus who admits him in the customary form:—

"Te ad gradum DOCTORIS LEGUM promoveo, cujus rei in symbolum super te hoc birretum impono."

At the words "hoc birretum" the graduate's head is covered for a moment with the historic "graduation cap." Today little more than a fragile square of black velvet, this cap belonged traditionally to John Knox and its adoption as the symbol of admission to the fellowship of the University began at the Reformation. It is, of course, the fashion of iconoclasts to discredit a story so picturesque but this much is certain. In the University accounts there is a charge for repairing the cap dated nearly a century in advance of Franklin's time; and it is indisputably the same cap which is still in use and is taken out of its safe in the strong room on every graduation day. Whatever its origin, it has rested for a moment on many a distinguished head and only a man utterly devoid of imagination could escape a feeling of exaltation and consecration at its touch.

The hood of scarlet silk lined with white satin having been

draped over the shoulders of the kneeling graduate he rises—no longer Mr. Benjamin Franklin but "Doctor Franklin"—and the simple ceremony, conducted in terms of regulations made in 1428, is over. There is no complete record of those who were present as spectators but an early pen drawing of a graduation shows that students attended on such occasions and the University being in session on 2nd October, 1759, it may be taken as certain that many would avail themselves of the opportunity to see the distinguished visitor.

Among the students who gathered on that October day in 1759 to witness the investiture of the illustrious scientist was a raw-boned, shock-haired country lad named James Wilson whose father was a small landed proprietor in Fife. At Glasgow, a few days before, Franklin had been in proximity to, if he did not actually meet, one prospective signer of the American Declaration of Independence in the person of John Witherspoon; here at St. Andrews was another future signer, a man who was to rank as the keenest legal authority in the American colonies, first associate Justice of the Supreme Court of the United States. Wilson transferred to Glasgow University a few weeks after Franklin's visit but was certainly at St. Andrews for the ceremony.

The local traditions of the St. Andrews visit center about Franklin's intimacy with the Provost, who would naturally extend the hospitality of the institution to an illustrious guest, and about his walks with the Professor of Mathematics, the erudite and pragmatical David Gregory. This is the same Gregory who accompanied Alexander Wilson to London in 1758, where he met Franklin at the house of Strahan. He is best remembered now by the lines of a shiftless student, the Edinburgh poet Robert Fergusson, who took his revenge for many castigations by some mortuary verses which have the flavor of Hudibras.

> Now mourn ye college masters all
> And frae your een a tear let fall,
> Famed Gregory's death has taken awa'
> Without remeid

The skaith ye've met with's nae that small
Since Gregory's dead.

He could by Euclid prove lang syne
A ganging point composed a line,
By numbers too he could divine
When he did read
That three times three just made up nine,
But now he's dead.[22]

At some time during their stay the Franklins met a certain Dr. Patrick Baird, who is mentioned in the *Autobiography* and whom Benjamin refers to (addressing his son William) as "Dr. Baird (whom you and I saw many years after at his native place. St. Andrews in Scotland)." [23] This Patrick Baird was a chirurgeon who left Scotland about 1722 and somehow drifted over to Philadelphia, where he set up an office in a corner of the old Town House on Chestnut Street. Business was not too good, and in spare time he did clerical work, sometimes acting as auctioneer at public sales. When George Thomas was governor of Pennsylvania, he gave Baird the sinecure post of Physician of the Port of Philadelphia, and later made him secretary to the Provincial Council. In 1743 Dr. Baird seems to have become discouraged with his career in Philadelphia, for he resigned his positions and returned to his boyhood home at St. Andrews, where he was living when our travelers came along. It must have been an agreeable encounter for Benjamin, since outside of the half-mythical meeting with Indian Peter in Edinburgh, he had seen no one from America after the departure from London.

The most notable event of Franklin's stay in the old university town was the part he took in curing the sickness of one of the students, David Stuart Erskine, Lord Cardross, who later took the title of Earl of Buchan. It is probable that the Agent had been requested to call upon this boy by Sir Alexander Dick, for the lad, with his younger brother, the illustrious Henry Erskine, spent his vacations at Prestonfield. In any event, Franklin visited the youth, found him dangerously ill and suggested a change of treatment which saved the patient's life. A quarter of a century later the grateful student, then Earl of Buchan, wrote to the Envoy at Paris:

You are entitled to a civic crown on my account a great many years ago when at the University of St. Andrews you gave a turn to the career of a disorder which then threatened his life.[24]

But a great deal of water had flowed over the dam since the Agent of Pennsylvania descended at St. Andrews, and the Envoy to France had completely forgotten the episode. Under date of March 17, 1783 he answered:

I do not recollect the circumstance you are pleased to mention of my having saved a citizen of St. Andrews by giving a turn to his disorder. . . .

This sick boy whose life, in his own opinion at least, Franklin had saved, went on to a long and diversified career. Out of gratitude to Franklin, perhaps, he cultivated an enthusiasm for all things American, invariably speaking of George Washington as his cousin,[25] and offering an abundance of advice on matters of statecraft to the bewildered President. In June 1792, during Washington's first term, Lord Buchan testified his admiration for his distinguished "relative" by presenting him with a box made from the wood of an oak-tree under which Sir William Wallace had reposed after the battle of Falkirk.[26] Just at that time the Scottish portrait painter, Archibald Robertson, was crossing to New York, and the Earl put the box in his charge with instructions to deliver it to Washington, who was to keep it during his life and pass it on in his will to the person whom he deemed most worthy of receiving so valuable a relic. When the President came to write his testament he remembered this injunction and exercised the judgment of Solomon by bequeathing the object to its original donor.

Item. To the Earl of Buchan I re-commit the box made of the oak that sheltered the great Sir William Wallace after the battle of Falkirk, presented to me by his Lordship in terms too flattering to repeat. . . .[27]

Benjamin Rush, who came to the University of Edinburgh in 1766, carried letters to Buchan from Franklin. Half a century afterwards his son, young James Rush, also of Philadelphia, crossed in his turn to Scotland to study medicine. The boy was equipped with an introduction to his Lordship which he duly presented. The old nobleman seems to have come frequently to call on James and to have remained an unconscionable time while he discoursed about America and about Franklin in the old St. Andrews days. Youth is seldom tolerant, and the student confided to his father that Lord Buchan, while very hospitable, was a trifle crazy.

His Lordship is of medium size, his person that of a badly-dressed servant. He wears occasionally a colored neck-cloth and a red waistcoat. He wears spectacles, carries a two-penny stick in his hand and is followed by an ugly cur. He insinuates that from his correspondence with Washington and Jefferson was derived that wise counsel which has made America so prosperous.[28]

As Buchan advanced in years he became a devoted antiquary and purchased the historic Dryburgh Abbey, in whose restoration he was greatly interested. When Sir Walter Scott began to commemorate the Abbey in his early poetry, the Earl was naturally much impressed. In June 1819 Sir Walter lay grievously ill in his house in Castle Street, Edinburgh. Buchan, who had become obsessed with the idea that Scott was going to die, presented himself at Castle Street with the avowed object of extracting from the supposedly expiring author a promise that he would be buried in Dryburgh, and it was only with the greatest of difficulty that the distracted family was able to keep him out of the sick-chamber. Sir Walter recovered, and in April 1829 Buchan himself died at the age of eighty-seven to be buried, as he would have wished, at Dryburgh. On the misty morning of the funeral, Scott rode up the glen from Abbotsford to attend the ceremony. Lockhart records him as saying in emerging from the Abbey, "At least I have not the mortification of thinking what a deal of patronage and fuss Lord Buchan would bestow on my funeral." [29] Such was the passing of the eccentric peer whose life Franklin saved seventy years before in the university town of St. Andrews.

If in the perusal of this recital it should often appear that our Philosopher associated with unusual types during his Caledonian tour, it should be remembered that Scotland of the period was the land of originality. Perhaps in no country at any one time have there been assembled so many characters of such marked individuality. The student who consults the book of portraits etched about the time of Franklin's visit by John Kay, the Edinburgh barber,[30] will be convinced of the aptness of this observation.

No Boswell accompanied the Americans about the decrepit colleges of St. Andrews, so that the gossipy particularity of Johnson's day in the same place twelve years afterwards is unhappily lacking. With two such exceptional and efficient mentors as the professors Anderson and Gregory, the stay of the Franklins in the university town cannot have failed in interest. They remained three days, perhaps four, and always preserved a cordial recollection of their stay. How long Anderson kept company with them or when he went back to Glasgow is not known.

Nor have we any definite knowledge of the road chosen for the journey back to Edinburgh. The shortest route involved the crossing of the Firth of Forth from Inchkeith as contrasted with the more circuitous way by the bridge of Stirling. However, the Inchkeith ferry was not always available for carriages and had other disadvantages. Thomas Gray, who crossed in a four-oared yawl without a sail, writes that he was deadly seasick and was "tossed about rather more than I should wish to hazard again." In any event, it was in the end of the first week of October that Franklin returned to the capital and again took lodgings at Milne Square. He had been on the road for approximately three weeks, his longest journey in Scotland, for never again did he penetrate farther north than Blair Drummond.

# Chapter VI

# THE RETURN TO LONDON

THE days which the Franklins passed in Edinburgh before they departed for London were occupied in a round of sociability. Only on Sunday might the travelers have some moments to themselves, for on that day a portentous Calvinistic pall of sanctity enveloped the good town. Franklin was used to the Puritan austerity of the Boston sabbath, but this was nothing compared with the rigidity of the Edinburgh Sunday. Anyone who idly looked out the window might be reported by the inquisitors of the Kirk and be liable to a fine. Even to walk on the links or enter an alehouse or receive a social visit was an offense to the Presbytery. The Americans could go in the morning to Greyfriars Church as Guy Mannering did, and hear a sermon from the eloquent Dr. Erskine (who corresponded afterwards with Franklin) but the rest of the day must be spent in soul-searching introspection.

From Franklin's letters we may derive the identity of most of his hosts, but it is curious that he makes no mention of entertainment by the two leading celebrities of the day, Lord Kames in his town house at New Street and Lord Monboddo across the way at St. John's Street, Canongate, who vied in the reception of visiting lions. The Agent certainly supped with Lord Kames and probably with Lord Monboddo, but has left us no details of their hospitality.

It cannot be sufficiently deplored that the minutes of the social clubs of Edinburgh for the period of Franklin's visit have been lost. The famous Poker Club, to which all of the Philosopher's friends belonged, was not to be formed until 1762, but the Speculative Society was in full blast and met on Friday evenings in a room at the Advocates Library. The members debated such topics as "Was Brutus right in killing Caesar?" with Lord Kames and Principal Robertson upholding the affirmative and Hume and Dr. Cullen the negative. The debaters always adjourned to the tavern of Luckey Boyd, who served an approved claret at two bob the bottle. It is most unlikely that the American guest was not in attendance at some of these meetings, but a diligent search has failed to uncover any proof of so engaging a surmise.

Equally regrettable is the complete absence of reference to Franklin in the minutes of the University of Edinburgh, although the Sage went there on several occasions and had many intimate friends in the faculty, such as Adam Ferguson, professor of Natural Philosophy, Hugh Blair, professor of Rhetoric, and Alexander Munro, professor of Anatomy. Robertson had not yet succeeded as Principal, and the head of the college was an uninspiring reverend gentleman, Dr. John Gowdie, who had held the Chair of Divinity for twenty-one uneventful and unprogressive years. The college buildings resembled those of St. Andrews in their state of disgraceful disrepair, for which Boswell apologized when he piloted Johnson about the quad fourteen years later.[1] This same university could scarcely have been imposing. It is described as a wretched collection of buildings, two half-formed quadrangles of shabby edifices, which had in the olden days been dwelling houses. The classrooms were dingy and the sordid living chambers, designed for students, had long since been relegated to apprentices and washerwomen. The American visitors were not likely to be impressed by these conditions and perhaps they sought to improve them. The college minutes disclose that the long-neglected books in the library were rearranged during the autumn of 1759, and one would like to believe that this innovation was suggested by Franklin.[2]

It may have been at Edinburgh University that Franklin and James Boswell first met. The diary recently and miraculously resurrected from the débris of the garret at Malahide Castle tells us that Benjamin came to dine with the great biographer in London in the May of 1768, but does not claim that this was their first encounter.[3] Boswell, who was in the college of Edinburgh as a pupil of Professor Stuart, is described as a pompous young fop who toadied to the aristocracy and shocked his Presbyterian colleagues by his leanings toward Roman Catholicism. Just at this time he was very despondent over the loss of his friend William Temple, who had left Edinburgh for Cambridge. Indeed, a few weeks after Franklin's visit, Boswell himself resigned to enter the University of Glasgow.

Passing from the campus our travelers inspected the municipal hospital under the guidance of Sir Alexander Dick and Lord Provost Drummond. Benjamin, always an astute observer, suggested some of the features of the Edinburgh institution for the Pennsylvania Infirmary, and afterwards wrote gratefully to Dr. Dick:

> I enclose you one of our Philadelphia newspapers, supposing that it may give you and my good Lord Provost some pleasure to see that we have imitated the Edinburgh Institution of the Infirmary in that remote Part of the World.[4]

This period of Franklin's second stay in Edinburgh marks the beginning of his friendship with Henry Home, Lord Kames, Judge of the Court of Session, an acquaintanceship which was to endure until Kames's death in 1782. The jurist, in the rare intervals of leisure which he somehow managed to snatch from his arduous legal duties, found time to write works on philosophy, and at the time of introduction to Franklin was busy with his *Elements of Criticism,* published two years later. It was natural that he should prize the comments of the great American philosopher whose fame had spread through the length and breadth of Scotland, and should seek his company.

Lord Kames looks out to us from the canvas of Raeburn on the walls of the National Gallery, but a more intimate depiction is to be found in the pages of Boswell's Malahide diary. The scribe had collected a mass of information about

Kames's personality and career with the announced intention of writing a biography. Had his fickle attentions not been diverted to a still more spectacular figure, Boswell's *Life of Lord Kames* might now be the model of biographies instead of Boswell's *Life of Johnson.*

A thousand anecdotes endure in Edinburgh as to the Lord Justice, tales of his wit and eccentricities, his profundity and talents, his sterling patriotism and brilliant hospitality. He was the son of an impoverished rural laird and owed his education and successful career at the Bar to industry and ability. He was forty-five years old when he compiled the first digest of Scottish law, *Dictionary of Decisions of the Courts of Session,* fifty-eight years old when he took his place on the Bench as a Senator of the College of Justice, and sixty-three when Franklin first walked into the Inner House of the Law Courts. His colleague, Braxfield, is generally considered to have been the prototype of Stevenson's "Hanging Judge" in the novel *Weir of Hermiston,* but Kames with his biting gibes and broad speech, the application with which he began his legal labors at five in the morning, and the sincerity of the potations which invariably ended his working day, seems much more suggestive of the character.

The tradition of Lord Kames's appearance still lingers in that Parliament Hall which he daily traversed,—the long, gaunt, stooping figure with toothless jaws, the keen, piercing eye, the mouth of Voltairian expression betwixt a sneer and a smile.[5] Each day the American tourists could stand before their quarters in Milne Square and see the Justice passing along the High Street from his residence in the Canongate to his labors in the Law Courts; and up this same street, a few days before Christmas in 1782, he walked to greet his judicial brethren for the last time: "Fare ye weel, ye bitches." [6] It was the final flash of that sardonic humor which had amused Franklin twenty-three years before. Four days later he was dead, and the Envoy at Passy received the news with becoming emotion.

The last year carried off my friends Dr. Pringle and Dr. Fothergill, Lord Kames and Lord le Despencer. . . . Thus the ties I had to that Country and indeed to the world in general are loosened one by one and I shall soon have no attachment left to make me unwilling to follow.[7]

October was half advanced, and from their windows in Milne Square the Franklins could observe an occasional fringe of frost to dim the glory of the autumn heather on the distant hills of Fife. At this time disturbing news arrived from London. Joseph Bell, Comptroller of the Foreign Office at the General Post-Office in Lombard Street, with whom Franklin, as Assistant-Postmaster General for the North American colonies, had been associated, died and one John Calcott was appointed in his place.[8] This change required some readjustment of the American postal system and Benjamin began to think of his neglected office in Craven Street. Besides there was William who would want to return to his fashionable friends and who had, perhaps, an uneasy recollection of the parental responsibilities which he had left behind him in London.

So the holiday was brought to an end, the farewell visits paid, the valises packed for the journey home. And just as the departure from Craven Street had been cheered by the announcement of the victory at Minden, so the return was to be gladdened by great news from America. One morning the American tourists were awakened by the booming of canon from the Castle and the shrill acclaim of bagpipes in the High Street. Before the Tron stood an excited messenger reading the proclamation of a glorious triumph for his Majesty's arms in Canada, the fall of the all-important fortress of Quebec and the death of the intrepid Wolfe.[9] Mr. Franklin's most cherished aspiration had been realized at last; French dominion on the North American continent was gone forever. When the Agent first began his anti-Gallic crusade from his seat in the Pennsylvania Assembly, twenty years before, he could scarcely have anticipated that the news of this most auspicious consummation would reach him far overseas from the miry causeway of a northern capital.

At this propitious hour came an invitation from Justice and Lady Kames for a visit at their countryseat in Berwickshire, an overture well timed in that Kames House lay not far removed from the road which the tourists would follow on their return journey. It is to be hoped, for the peace of mind of the Pennsylvanians, that My Lord guided them in person, for even now, with the advantages of an automobile and advanced roads, the journey to Kames House entails some complexity. Soutra Hill, that terror of all eighteenth-century travelers, has been graded; and the slough of despond near Lauder, where so many coaches floundered in the old days, has been filled up, but the devious winding trail over the moors from Greenlaw is just as perplexing as it was in Franklin's time. Boswell in his frequent trips between Edinburgh and Kames House usually broke his journey at the village of Ginglekirk, "where the public-house consisted of two tents, one for a kitchen and one for a dining-room." He descants on the deficiencies of the roads, averring that they were the worst he ever saw (no inconsiderable indictment) and that "you just labor through a deep, stiff clay much more terrible than that in Ayreshire." [10]

Kames House lies in southern Berwickshire a few miles from the Tweed and the English border. It is a fine type of Scottish country house set in a beautiful park, and the gallant officer who is the present chatelain [11] has insisted that the additions harmonize with the dignity of the ancient structure which Franklin saw. The priest's hiding hole has been preserved intact, as well as the formal gardens fringed by historic trees, among them the two sycamores, the elm, and the laburnum which Franklin planted. Boswell, who visited the place in 1761, affords us our best contemporary description:

The house is old and not very good but the most is made of every bit of space in it and the rooms are neatly fitted up.

There is a pretty lawn before the house with trees scattered up and down. There is a group of good enclosures, a handsome garden, a long gravel walk and banks ornamented with flowers and evergreens.[12]

This same narrative gives us the routine of Kames House pretty much as it must have obtained during Franklin's visit. Boswell tells us, in his own inimitable way, how the guests walked and rode in fine weather and enjoyed the well-selected library when kept indoors, how he spent one rainy afternoon playing the flute in his "sweet, handsome bed-room," how he got tipsy one evening and the gentle dignity with which Lady Kames reproved him, how they all went to see the Hunter's Purse run at Kelso and how he lost all his money and was ashamed to ask his host for more, how Lord Kames always read public prayers at bedtime and how sound everyone slept in the cold, sharp air blowing down from the Teviots.

In these yellowed pages we glean our most intimate description of Franklin's hostess:

Her person is tall and genteel and her face is very lovely and expressive of good sense and sweetness of disposition. She has an excellent and a compleat education in every respect. She has a great deal of vivacity and an inimitable vein of drollery.[13]

Oddly enough Franklin, who made so much of Janet Dick during his visit to Prestonfield, never mentions Lord Kames's daughter, who was domiciled in her father's house at the time of his visit. The son of the house was George Drummond, the lad who embarrassed Boswell by his presence when his father and Lord Braxfield engaged in a conversation little suited for juvenile ears: "Lord Kames roared, Lord Braxfield raved, both bawdy." [14]

Like Weir of Hermiston, Lord Kames was an enthusiastic planter. It is related of him that, arriving in the night after the toilsome journey from Edinburgh, he would go out with a lantern to mark the growth of his saplings. The retort of his tenant farmer who was sceptical as to innovation is still a byword on the Tweedside. My Lord had experimented with a new compressed fertilizer and remarked that manure sufficient for an acre of ground could now be carried in the coat pocket. "Aye, and ye'll bring back the crop in your waistcoat pouch," answered his unconvinced factor. The Justice's results were probably those of most gentlemen farmers before and since, and he once summarized his experience in the homely Scottish proverb, "The carles and the cart-avers make it all and the carles and the cart-avers eat it all." In the elucidation of his agricultural theories, Lord Kames found a congenial auditor in Benjamin Franklin. That many-sided man was a farmer of a sort who had a model plantation of his own, and during his military campaign had eagerly imbibed all the information possible as to the farming methods of the Moravians at Bethlehem.

Kames Seat is located in one of the most romantic districts of the Scottish border; no more pleasant place could be conceived for the recuperation of two tired travelers. There was no Abbotsford House as yet, but Melrose and Dryburgh were within easy distance, as were Home Castle and Flodden Field. Franklin's subsequent references to the excursions in the Border country, which he and William made with their host, show his appreciation and delight, his regret, too, that their stay could endure only for a few days.

So that whenever I reflect on the great pleasure and advantage I receive from the free communication of sentiments in the conversations we had at Kames and in the agreeable little rides to the Tweed-side, I shall forever regret our premature parting.[15]

One path in particular, which followed the Tweed to the west of the village of Coldstream, within easy driving distance of Kames House, is still pointed out as Franklin's walk. It winds along the shallow river through a beautiful birch grove with frequent vistas disclosing the romantic hills of Eildon. If the two philosophers extended their ramble and clambered to the summit of the neighboring range of hills, they could look far into England to where the towers of Howick Castle, the seat of the Lords Grey, rise from the shores of the North Sea. In that same castle a portrait of Franklin, painted by the renowned Benjamin Wilson, was to rest for one hundred and twenty-five years. It was acquired by the General Lord Grey—"Paoli Grey" who fought in the war of the American Revolution—and was taken away with him when the British evacuated Philadelphia in 1778. During the Franklin Bicentennial Celebration of 1906, Lord George Grey, Governor General of Canada, a great-grandson of "Paoli Grey," sent the picture back to America in a gracious gesture of international accord. A duplicate now hangs in Howick Hall and the original is in the White House at Washington.

So with walks in the Borderland, drives to the Tweed, congenial discussions and the enjoyment of the tactful hospitality of Lord and Lady Kames, the sojourn formed a fitting ending for a memorable tour. Franklin's letter of acknowledgment reflects his satisfaction.

My son joins with me in the most respectful compliments to you and to Lady Kames. Our conversation till we came to York, was chiefly a recollection of what we had seen and heard, the pleasure we had enjoyed, and the kindnesses we had received in Scotland, and how far that country had exceeded our expectations. On the whole, I must say, I think the time we spent there, was six weeks of the densest happiness I have met with in any part of my life; and the agreeable and instructive society we found there in such plenty, has left so pleasing an impression on my memory, that did not strong connexions draw me elsewhere, I believe Scotland would be the country I should choose to spend the remainder of my days in.[16]

When the Americans set out upon their return, their courteous friends rode with them as far as Coldstream, and in that border village Franklin found time to inscribe the lines, previously quoted, dedicated to Lady Dick in requital of the hospitalities of Prestonfield. In Coldstream were said the final adieus which the guest accepted with so much regret.

How unfortunate I was that I did not press you and Lady Kames more strongly to favor us with your company farther. How much more agreeable would our journey have been if we could have enjoyed you as far as to York. We could have beguiled the way by discoursing of a thousand things that we may never have an opportunity of considering together.[17]

Of Franklin's rambles in the eastern counties of England after leaving Scotland, as little is known as of his visits in Derbyshire at the beginning of the trip. He told Sir Alexander Dick that he "had spent some weeks in Yorkshire and Lincolnshire." [18] This expression "some weeks" cannot be taken too literally. The first entry in the Agent's London Account Book, after his return, is of November second, so that not more than two weeks could have intervened between his departure from Kames House and the arrival in Craven Street.

In passing through Yorkshire Franklin had his first opportunity to study the weaving industry with particular reference to the American trade, a subject to which he afterwards refers with familiarity. In one letter written later to Thomas Cushing [19] he speaks of having

. . . lately been among the Clothing Towns of Yorkshire and by conversing with the manufacturers there, am more and more convinced of the natural impossibility there is that, considering our increase in America, England should be able to much longer supply us with Clothing.

Our traveler speaks of having ridden fifteen hundred miles in England and Scotland, which suggests many digressions from a direct route, since the totality of his journey to Edinburgh and back, including the tour in the Highlands, was not more than nine hundred miles.

The entries in the Craven Street Account Book abruptly close on August seventh, the day preceding the departure. They resume on Sunday, November second. The tourists had left in the torrid heat of an abnormal summer; they returned to the comforts of Mrs. Stevenson's sea-coal grates under the leaden skies of a premature winter. The diary of Horace Walpole, to which we refer for the weather attendant upon their leaving London, is also available for the less agreeable conditions of the return:

Thick fogs and some wet. Go not out of town. Gouts and rheumatisms are abroad. Warm clothes, good fires and a room full of scarlet damask are the best physic.[20]

In the streets the faded decorations of the celebration for Minden were still to be observed, but Minden was forgotten now in more brilliant triumphs in another hemisphere; all the Town was talking of the imposing ceremonies to be conducted a week later when the solemn Te Deum for Wolfe's victory at Quebec was to be sung in St. Paul's.

The pleasant holiday in Scotland was over and the drab routine of official business was beginning. On the Agent's desk was a mass of neglected post, invitations, inquiries, requests, formal suspicious missives from the Proprietors of Pennsylvania, official bulletins from the Clerk of the Assembly in Philadelphia, cordial notes, too, from his new friends in Scotland solicitous for his safe return. Perhaps the travelers thought regretfully of the charms of Berwickshire and of the happy hours they had spent in Edinburgh. No pilgrims from Bœotia returning from a sojourn in the Athens of the golden period of Attic supremacy brought back more vivid recollections of a brilliant intellectual circle.

The tour had been an inspiration and a delight; the voyagers returned refreshed in mind and body. Benjamin wrote enthusiastically to Deborah in Philadelphia gratefully testifying to the pleasure and value of the contacts which he had made; but even his sagacity could not probe the full import of the political mutations which had developed during his absence from London. For with the booming of the salute after the victory at Quebec, a new order began. So long as the white flag of the Bourbons floated over Canada, Englishman and Colonial were united by common apprehension. When the Gallic threat was removed, doubts, dissensions, and ignoble disputes over questions of revenue succeeded; the sinister shadows of an impending fratricidal conflict began to impend. Once again the Envoy from the American colonies was to ride up the Great North Road to Scotland, but this time the cordiality of his reception was to be tempered by the menacing specter of internal discord.

# THE INTERLUDE

## 1759–1771

# THE INTERLUDE
## 1759-1771

TWELVE crowded and eventful years were to intervene before Benjamin Franklin found opportunity to revisit Scotland. Certainly he had not anticipated so long a hiatus when he took his reluctant leave of Lord and Lady Kames by the Tweedside on that October day in 1759. In point of fact, it was the intention of the Franklins to go back to Scotland in the following summer. On September sixth of the next year, 1760, the Agent wrote to Lord Kames from Coventry in Warwickshire to say that it had been his intention to visit Ireland and afterwards cross over from Belfast to Scotland, but that unforeseen litigation with the Proprietor of Pennsylvania was recalling him to London.[1] Again in November of 1761, he wrote to Kames that he had wished to go to Scotland during the preceding summer, accompanied again by his son William, but that their approaching recall to America interfered with the project.[2] There is no doubt of the sincerity of Franklin's intentions. His emphatic and oft-quoted declaration to Lord Kames that "If strong connections did not draw me elsewhere, Scotland would be the country I would choose in which to spend the remainder of my days," is only one sentiment of many which testify to his regard for his Scottish friends and for their land. This feeling is evidenced not only by the correspondence but also by more tangible remembrances which were continually being exchanged between the Philosopher and his acquaintances in Edinburgh—newspapers, pamphlets, and Philadelphia playbills for Lord Kames, scientific essays for David Hume, a design for an improved chimney for Sir Alexander Dick.

[ 99 ]

From Scotland came a purse knitted by Lady Dick, the proceedings of the Edinburgh Philosophical Society and a portrait, supposedly of William Penn, from Lord Kames, and David Hume's affectionate assurance on the eve of Franklin's departure for America in the autumn of 1762.

I am sorry that you intend soon to leave our hemisphere. America has sent us many good things, gold, silver, sugar, tobacco, indigo, etc., but you are the first philosopher and indeed the first great man of letters for whom we are beholden to her.[3]

The first outgrowth of Franklin's Scottish tour was the advent of the brilliant succession of American medical students who went to Edinburgh University, largely at his suggestion. In the spring of 1760, while the Agent was at his desk in Craven Street immersed in new colonial perplexities and fresh bickerings with the truculent brothers Penn, there arrived in London a young probationer from Philadelphia, John Morgan, destined to be the founder of the medical school of the University of Pennsylvania. Morgan seems to have been undecided whether to pursue his studies at the University of Leyden or that of Edinburgh. Leyden, where taught Boerhaave, the Nestor of the surgical profession, had hitherto attracted a great number of English and American pupils. Franklin, however, in the enthusiasm engendered by his recent visit, persuaded Morgan to matriculate at Edinburgh. This was a pregnant decision, since the coterie of Pennsylvania neophytes who came over in the next decade followed Morgan's example, and Edinburgh became the academic Mecca for transatlantic medical students just as the Middle Temple in London already was for practitioners of the law.

While John Morgan was still tarrying in London another medical apprentice, Samuel Bard, son of Franklin's old friend Dr. John Bard of Philadelphia, had embarked at New York upon the Portsmouth packet intent also for Edinburgh and carrying messages to the Agent of Pennsylvania. Less fortunate than Morgan, Samuel's ship was

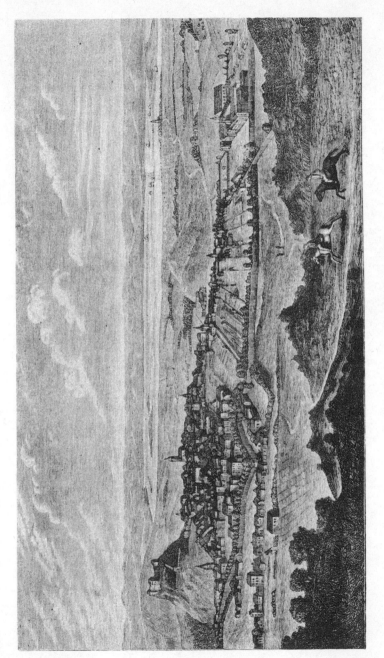

EDINBURGH IN FRANKLIN'S DAY

captured off the coast of Cornwall by a French privateer, and the lad wearied out many weeks of captivity in Bayonne before the Agent could secure a release. Bard finally took his degree at Edinburgh in 1765.

Later in the same year 1760, a storm-tossed bark, whose crew and passengers had subsisted for the last week upon a daily allowance of a quart of water and a meager ration of salt meat, put into Belfast Harbor. Franklin, who must have begun to feel by this time that the cares of the Americas were on his shoulders, presently received a letter from one of the passengers, a lad named William Shippen, also from Pennsylvania, apprising him of his plight and asking for money wherewith to proceed to London, first, and then to the medical school at Edinburgh. The young man's arrival in London and the earnestness of his intention are proved by a somewhat pedantic letter written to his uncle Edward Shippen, the Prothonotary at Lancaster in Pennsylvania:

I do not spend my time trifling about playhouses or operas or reading idle romantic tales or trifling newspapers at coffee-houses as I find many have done before me, but rather in the rich improvement of those advantages which are not to be had in my own country.[4]

Two years later came still another student, Scotland bound, Adam Kuhn of Philadelphia, who had been studying botany in Sweden under the celebrated Linnæus and who was graduated at Edinburgh in 1767. He too was sponsored by Franklin.

Benjamin's solicitude for his charges at Edinburgh extended far beyond the routine of their curriculum. He gave counsel as to boarding houses, advanced money, and was the intermediary for American correspondence. When Billy Shippen married Alice Lee, sister of "Light-Horse Harry" Lee, in London, the Philosopher was present. When John Morgan, in vacation time, made the European tour and visited Voltaire at Ferney, Mr. Franklin outlined his route. Some of the grateful scholars showed their appreciation by dedicating their graduation theses to Benjamin Franklin, and at least three of these are preserved in the archives of Edinburgh University.[5]

The most distinguished of the American students in Scotland, Arthur Lee of Virginia, "Junius Americanus," later co-commissioner with Franklin at the Court of France, matriculated without recommendation or communication from the Agent of Pennsylvania, and entered Edinburgh University upon the suggestion of Dr. Samuel Johnson.[6] The Virginian became intimate with the grotesque Lord Buchan, whose life Franklin had saved at St. Andrews, and sat at the knees of Professors Cullen, Black, and the brothers Munro, yet he never wrote to relate his impressions to Benjamin in London. Had he done so a cordiality might have been engendered at that early day which would have had an important bearing upon the development of American diplomacy and perhaps prevented the later estrangement between the two envoys at Passy. When Lee entered at the Middle Temple in 1770, he became a member of the Royal Society. He and his brother, "Alderman" William Lee, the tobacco factor of Tower Hill, consorted with many of Franklin's friends, including Price, Priestley, and Fothergill. But although Dr. Fothergill got consignments of Virginia wine and tobacco, no Rappahannock claret and no choice rapee were delivered in Craven Street, and the brothers Lee seldom called there.

Returning to the chronological sequence of our narrative, we find that the Agent of Pennsylvania turned his back upon England and Scotland in September 1762 and returned to a colony not entirely appreciative of the labors performed in its behalf. Governor James Hamilton, forgetful of the weeks in which he and Franklin had campaigned together in the snow-clad Pennsylvania woods during the French and Indian War, wrote to Jared Ingersoll, Esq.:

Your friend, Mr. Franklin, and mine, if he pleases, (for it will much depend on himself) is daily expected from England.

I cannot find that his five years' negotiation, at a vast expence to the Province, hath answered any other purpose with respect to the public, than to get every point that was in controversy determined against them. Yet what is this to Mr. Franklin? Hath it not afforded him a life of pleasure, and an opportunity of displaying his talents among the virtuosi of various kingdoms and nations? And lastly, hath it not procured for himself the Degree of Doctor of Laws, and for the modest and beautiful youth his son, that of Master of Arts? And this from one of our most famous universities! Let me tell you those are no small acquisitions to the public, and therefore well worth paying for.[7]

Such were the fulminations of the Governor of the very province for which Franklin had so unselfishly toiled, and such is the ingratitude of commonwealths!

William Franklin did not return to Philadelphia with his father, but tarried some weeks longer in London. It was the gossip of the Town that through his father's influence and his own adroit lobbying he was to be made governor of New Jersey. The official announcement came on the twenty-second day of August, when Lord Egremont affixed his signature to the formal document wherein his gracious Majesty George the Third, King of Great Britain, France, and Ireland, constituted William Franklin of Pennsylvania Royal Governor of the Province of New Jersey in North America. It has been asserted that this honor came to William as a result of an interview with Lord Bute (then Prime Minister *de facto*) in Scotland, but there is no evidence of any such meeting during the Franklins' Caledonian tour. It is significant, however, that Deborah should write from Philadelphia that Lord Bute's picture hung upon the wall of the house in Market Street.

A few days after the publication of William's elevation the *London Chronicle* and *Lloyd's Evening Post* (Strahan's paper) reported the marriage, at the fashionable St. George's Church in Hanover Square, of His Excellency William Franklin, Governor of New Jersey, to Miss Elizabeth Downes, an amiable and aristocratic young lady late a resident of the West Indies. Somewhere in London a wretched, discarded woman was nursing a fatherless child, the illegitimate offspring who was to strut through history under the name of William Temple Franklin. If the abandoned mother read the pompous announcement in the *Chronicle,* it could have afforded her little comfort to learn that the Governor, accompanied by his consort, would shortly sail for New Jersey to assume the duties of his office. Meanwhile the gratified Benjamin, blissfully unaware of the fact that he had acquired a daughter-in-law and a grandson at almost the same time, expressed his satisfaction to his Craven Street neighbor, the wine merchant Caleb Whitefoord.

If he makes a good Governor and a good Husband (as I think he will for I know he has good Principles and a good Disposition), these events will both of them give me continual Pleasure.[8]

Perhaps the only person of whom William made a confidant in this not too creditable matter was Strahan, canny Scotch "Straney," who so successfully handled the ugly details of a scandal which might have cost young Franklin his career. To Strahan the new Governor entrusted the mysterious will, long since destroyed, in which provision was probably made for the child Temple, then two years old. Half a century later, when William Franklin was dying in his house in High Holborn, London, at the age of eighty-two, embittered and forgotten, an exile from his native land, he made another will now in the archives of Somerset House in the Strand. In this second testament William mentions his son Temple coldly and formally as one would refer to a slight acquaintance.

It might be supposed that when Dr. Franklin reached America in December 1762, his interest in Scotland would diminish with the intervention of three thousand miles of gray tossing waters. On the contrary, he wrote to Sir

Alexander Dick from Philadelphia that neither time nor distance had in the least weakened his impression, and that he and William often talked of the pleasant hours they spent in Prestonfield.[9]

The two years at home were too crowded with provincial affairs, colonial politics, quarrels with the Assembly, and perplexities of Indian negotiations to give the Philosopher much time for correspondence with his friends in Scotland. He wrote fairly regularly to Strahan and sometimes inquired for Lord Kames, "the best man in the world," and for Sir Alexander Dick and for Doctors Cullen and Russell of the college at Edinburgh. Amid all his troubles he found time to send Lord Kames a description of the trip across to America and of the call at the romantic island of Madeira with its golden terraces rising from a wine-dark sea, and the clusters of luscious purple grapes which festooned his cabin. Then on a foggy morning in December 1764, the American packet glided up Southampton Water past the Isle of Wight and came to anchor off Portsmouth. Little did Mr. Franklin think, as he debarked upon English soil for the third time, that eleven years were to elapse before his return to America.

Once more installed amid the comforts of Mrs. Stevenson's cheery hostelry in Craven Street, the familiar routine began again. William Franklin was far away in his gubernatorial residence in Burlington, New Jersey, but little Temple Franklin came presently to take his father's place in the Philosopher's household. Just when the grandfather was apprised of the boy's existence is not known, but the Craven Street Account Book soon begins to reflect his tastes and necessities. There are items for Temple's toys, for cutting his hair, for his clothes, and for jaunts to the country. At an early age he was put into the school of Strahan's brother-in-law, James Elphinstone, near Hyde Park Corner,[10] and little Sally Franklin, daughter of Benjamin's cousin Thomas, the dyer of Lutterworth, was brought down to live in the Craven Street house and keep

Temple company. At first the paternity of the boy was not openly acknowledged. Polly Stevenson (now Polly Hewson) writing to Benjamin years afterwards recalled Temple's original ambiguous status.

We are all pleased with our old friend Temple changed into young Franklin. We see a strong resemblance of you and indeed saw it when we did not think ourselves at liberty to say we did, as we pretended to be ignorant as you supposed we were or chose we should be.[11]

But later all pretense was abandoned, and little Temple was openly acknowledged as a Franklin. The grandfather sent glowing accounts of the lad's affability and progress out to New Jersey, and soon the conscience-stricken Governor began to be uneasily aware of his responsibilities and wrote to know whether he could bring the boy back to America without open scandal.

I hope young Temple continues well. I should be glad to know your sentiments about bringing him over with you. He might take his proper name and be introduced as the son of a poor relation for whom I stood god-father and intended to bring up as my own.[12]

Life in Craven Street was pleasant enough at this period, and it is not likely that the Agent of Pennsylvania missed Philadelphia very much, nor are his unctuous protestations about the dolors of a life of banishment from the home circle always convincing. He wrote often and dutifully to Deborah about the prospects of his early return to America, but there were plenty of distractions to beguile his exile in the interval.

Only a step from Craven Street was the diplomatic gallery at Westminster, where a transatlantic visitor might sit enthralled by the sonorous periods of Chatham and of Fox. Equally opportune was the hall of the Royal Society, where on stated days one rubbed shoulders with the great scientists and philosophers of the age and chatted with Collinson or Priestley. In the evening there were the attractions of Drury Lane, at which the entrancing Sylvia Macklin, the toast of the town, played the *Recruiting Officer,* or Covent Garden, where Garrick was winning new laurels in the *Beaux' Stratagem.*

Mr. Franklin was never averse to a social jorum of grog. "For my own part I find I love company, chat, a laugh, a glass, even a song, as well as ever," he wrote to Hugh Roberts. After his diplomatic labors were ended for the day, it was his wont to take his hat and cane and stroll up the Strand under Temple Bar, on the top of which were still impaled the skulls of the gallant Jacobites who had paid the forfeit for their support of the forlorn hope of the unhappy Prince Charlie. Passing along Fleet Street the Doctor would reach the Pennsylvania Coffee House in Birchin's Lane, the approved resort for patriotic colonials where one got the Philadelphia gossip and the latest news from home.[13] Here sat the young American law students from the Temple who were afterwards to write their names so large in the history of their native land, Ben Chew and Tom McKean and Billy Tilghman. The corner table was sometimes graced by the presence of two ex-governors of Pennsylvania, George Thomas and Robert Hunter Morris, who were come to exchange their querulous reminiscences, and rail at the niggardliness of the Penns. Before the diminutive grill were often gathered a bronzed and bearded group in flowing trousers and tarry pigtails, the mariners who plied the Philadelphia packets between Falmouth and the Capes of Delaware. There were Captain Budden of the *Polly Ann,* who had brought over Thomas Mifflin (later first Governor of Pennsylvania), and Captain Kennedy with whom Franklin had sailed, and LeGross of the *Admiral Benbow* and Captain Fowler of the *Neptune.*

Sometimes, too, the Agent went to a club at St. Paul's Coffee House where he met Fothergill and Price and Dr.

Priestley. Boswell, who often attended the sittings, gives a description of the place in his journal, recently found at Malahide.

We have wine and punch on the table. Some of us smoak a pipe. Conversation goes on pretty formally, sometimes sensibly, sometimes furiously. At nine there is a sideboard with welsh rarebits and apple puffs, porter and beer. Our reckoning is about eighteen pence a head.[14]

If, amid all this diversion, the Doctor was beginning to forget about his tour in Scotland and the promises which he had made for a speedy return, his thoughts were recalled to Caledonia in the summer of 1765 by a letter from Sir Alexander Dick. Janet Dick was six years older since Franklin had visited Prestonfield, but apparently as mischievous as ever, for in her feminine calligraphy, on the outside of the missive, appear the cryptic lines:

> Aut Caesar aut nullus,
> Ou bien ou rien,
> Win the horse or lose the saddle.
> Neck or nothing.
> A golden chair or a wooden leg.[15]

Sir Alexander's letter with which Janet had so naughtily tampered concerned a claim of one John Swinton of Edinburgh who conceived that he had rights in an estate in America. The Doctor answered obligingly and promised to interest Governor William in the matter. William went dutifully to Philadelphia and expended four guineas in an investigation which came to naught. Money was never very plentiful in the gubernatorial mansion at Burlington, where the executive's salary appears to have been little more than £1,000 a year, so the Governor writes presently to his father to inquire whether Swinton has repaid the four guineas and when he may expect them.[16]

In the spring of this same year 1765, the Agent secured an importation of Pennsylvania seeds from his friend John

Bartram, the gardener of Philadelphia, and sent some of them to his former hosts in Scotland, including Sir Alexander Dick and Lord Kames. The remaining seeds were divided between His Majesty's superintendent of Kew Gardens and M. de Buffon at the conservatory in Paris.

When the Stamp Act was repealed in 1766 and the excitement in America temporarily subsided, Benjamin breathed a sigh of relief and set off with Sir John Pringle upon a trip to Germany. He had spoken vaguely to Lord Kames about coming to Scotland that year, but the opportunity of visiting the Continent in such congenial company was too tempting and the return to Edinburgh was postponed to another summer. In the following April he was still debating a second Caledonian tour, for he wrote to Kames, "The visit to Scotland and the Art of Virtue we will talk of later." [17] Soon, however, renewed complications ensued and there was no leisure for an extended trip.

Now came more students from America seeking education in Scotland. In October 1766 two seasick, wretched boys, Jonathan Potts, son of John Potts of Potts Grove, and Benjamin Rush of Philadelphia, arrived at Liverpool and began inevitably to bombard Franklin with requests for letters of recommendation in Edinburgh. They were accompanied by a third youth, one James Cummins, a young Scotsman returning from Barbados who was so reduced by the stormy crossing that he died shortly after the arrival. Potts and Rush, who had piously cared for their colleague in his last illness, superintended his burial and then pursued their course northward, as has previously been indicated in this recital. Perhaps Franklin was growing tired of the supervision of the careers of so many of his friends' sons. In any event, Potts wrote two months later from Edinburgh to say that while Sir Alexander Dick, to whom William Franklin had addressed himself in the boys' behalf, had been most courteous, no letters had arrived from Benjamin in London nor had permanent quarters been found. The Agent finally bestirred himself and arranged through Principal Robertson that the lads should be domiciled in the home of the blind poet Blacklock, a thrifty disposition by which, for the payment of £20 a quarter, the students enjoyed bed and board and the company of a son of the governor of St. Christophers and of a nephew of David Hume.

Potts's career in Edinburgh came to a sudden conclusion with the advent of a letter from a sweetheart whom he had left behind him in Philadelphia, imparting some startling and delicate information as to her condition. It was the age of chivalrous impulse, and young Sir Galahad started for London next day. After a journey made in the incredibly short time of nine days, he arrived in Craven Street where he had an embarrassed interview with Dr. Franklin and demanded money enough to pay his bills contracted in Edinburgh and provide for his passage home. It might be supposed that the Doctor, mindful of certain similar episodes in his own career, would have been more gracious, but apparently he was not immediately cordial, for there survives the distressed notation in young Potts's daybook:

> *Pennsylvania Coffee House*
> *February 21st, 1767*

Remember that Doctor Franklin did not use you as you might have expected.[18]

That the Agent eventually relented is shown by his check for £70 drawn on Smith, Wright, and Gray, bankers, of Lombard Street, February 10, 1767, in favor of Jonathan Potts, which amount was repaid to Deborah Franklin by the irate parent after the arrival of the humiliated student in Philadelphia. It is worthy of note that Potts came happily out of his perplexities, placated his father, married the girl, and entered upon a successful medical career in Reading, Pennsylvania, ending with his untimely death in 1781 at the age of thirty-six.

Left behind in Edinburgh, Rush finished his course and came down later to London, where he was domiciled for a time in Franklin's house in Craven Street. From here under the guidance of his famous fellow colonial, the painter Benjamin West, he became engulfed in the brilliant whirl of London Society.

Mr. West introduced me to several of the most celebrated members of the Royal Academy of Artists in London and in particular to Sir Joshua Reynolds by whom I was afterwards invited to dine with Dr. Johnson, Dr. Goldsmith and several other distinguished literary characters.[19]

It is curious that the young student should have been accorded the privilege of a meeting with the great Samuel Johnson, whose acquaintance Franklin himself seems never to have made.

When Rush boarded the American packet at Deal, the sequence of medical students whom Franklin had sponsored for Edinburgh may be said to terminate. Their great hour of service was to arrive six years later, for neither the loyal Agent at London nor the alert pupils who had so well improved their time at Edinburgh could dream that their talents would so soon be used against the land which had afforded them their technical training. At the beginning of the American Revolution, all the Scottish graduates in America, except Dr. Bard of New York who remained true to the Crown, enlisted in the patriot army. A singular destiny attended their military careers. Potts, broken in spirit and body by his unappreciated services with the Northern Army at Ticonderoga, came back to a premature death in Reading. Rush resigned his commission in 1778 owing to dissatisfaction with his heads of the department. Shippen was court-martialed for alleged irregularities in his military hospital. Morgan was displaced through the machinations of an ignoble cabal in the Congress. Perhaps the aggrieved professors at the Edinburgh Medical School saw in these calamities the visitation of a Calvinistic deity outraged at the traitorous misapplication of knowledge obtained in a Scotch college.

In the spring of 1767 Benjamin began to receive agitated

letters from William in New Jersey, informing him that his daughter Sarah in Philadelphia was on the point of marrying a young merchant named Richard Bache, originally from Preston in Lancashire, a man with small expectations and little property, scarcely a suitable or advantageous match for Sarah Franklin. The Agent took the news calmly and wrote to Deborah, "I can only say that if he proves a good Husband to her and a good Son to me, he shall find me as good a Father as I can be." [20] Nevertheless, a few weeks later, when he heard from William that Bache had met with misfortunes in his business, he suggested to Deborah that Sally be sent over to London in an effort to break off an unpromising alliance. Before this proposal could bear fruit, in October of the same year, Sally took matters into her own hands and became Mrs. Richard Bache. Franklin had, of course, never seen his new son-in-law, but was enabled to appraise the character of the family connection on the first day of March 1769, when he received a call from one of the Bache girls from Preston who was temporarily in London. The Agent professed himself much pleased with his visitor and wrote to Deborah that Miss Bache was a comely, sensible young person.[21]

And now Franklin's attention was recalled to Scotland by a procession of young American clergymen who came seeking divinity degrees in Scottish universities and who solicited his influence just as the medical students had done five years before. Already in 1765 the Agent had exerted himself to secure a degree at Edinburgh for Ezra Stiles, later President of Yale College. In the summer of 1767 Principal Robertson at Franklin's request prevailed upon his University to give a degree of D.D. to Samuel Cooper of Boston, afterwards a trustee of Harvard. This was well enough, but when young Andrew Eliot, sometime pastor of the North Church of Boston (who has the doubtful distinction of refusing an election as President of Harvard) came along for a similar honor, Benjamin began to feel that he was imposing upon the Principal's good nature and suggested that the applicant make his plea to the University of Glasgow. Nevertheless Eliot also got his degree, and from Edinburgh. Then a few months later, to Franklin's further embarrassment, there appeared a New York clergyman named Rogers, and he too solicited a Scottish degree. Robertson's complacency was apparently inexhaustible, for he wrote to assure Franklin, "I need not say that every request from you has with me the authority of a command," and that Rogers' degree would be confirmed and a diploma sent. Ever a *canny chiel* in money matters, the thrifty Principal bethought himself of the attendant costs and added as an apparent afterthought, "I have drawn on you for £12 7s 6d."

For one who has been accused of irregularity in religion, Franklin seems to have been much concerned with clerics at this time. In the fall of 1767 and as an indirect result of his first visit to Scotland, he had become involved in the negotiations which led to the election of the Reverend John Witherspoon of Paisley as President of the College of New Jersey at Princeton. Not that the reverend trustees of Nassau Hall, who were convened in November 1766 to choose a successor to President Samuel Finley, recently deceased, had any thought of consulting the Franklins in the matter. They were frankly sceptical of Benjamin's religious convictions and distrustful of Governor William Franklin, whom they suspected of a design for betraying their Presbyterian college to the Episcopacy. Benjamin Franklin was the last man whose aid the trustees would have willingly solicited, and yet there is no doubt that he was conversant with the matter from the beginning.

The young dominie who had presided at the Western Synod when the Franklins visited Glasgow in October 1759 still occupied the pulpit of the Laigh Church of Paisley. But although he remained in an obscure landward parish, he had attained a commanding position in the Kirk and was admired for his eloquence and theological attainments. His pamphlet on *Ecclesiastical Characteristics,* several times reprinted, had been widely circulated in America. So when the dons of Princeton resolved to go abroad for a President, the name of Witherspoon was suggested and he was given a formal call.[22]

Just at this time a resident of Princeton, the lawyer Richard Stockton, who had graduated from Nassau Hall in 1748, during the presidency of the sainted Aaron Burr the elder, was in London upon official business. Like most colonials temporarily resident in England, he had met Mr. Franklin.[23] Upon the arrival of the letter from the college trustees suggesting that he go personally to Scotland and deliver a call to Dr. Witherspoon, it was natural that he should consult with the Agent of Pennsylvania. Much water had run over the dam since 1759 and it is not clear that Franklin remembered the eloquent young preacher from Paisley who had delivered the sermon on "The Trial of Religious Trust by Its Moral Influence" on that autumn morning in Glasgow eight years before, if indeed he had met him at all. He was sure, however, to have a lively recollection of the Scottish roads; and this was midwinter. Stockton, a devoted alumnus, gave one of the earliest examples of the vaunted Princeton spirit by his determination to go at once to Paisley, although he had the warning of Mr. Franklin's experience with Scottish highways and Scottish taverns.

On his journey northward the lawyer carried at his saddle-bow letters from Franklin to Benjamin Rush, who was still pursuing his medical studies at Edinburgh. Rush was himself a graduate of the College of New Jersey in the class of 1759 and was destined, ten years later, to marry Stockton's daughter Julia.[24] He took an active interest in the Witherspoon mission and, as a preliminary step, introduced Stockton to all of Franklin's old friends in Edinburgh. The American was entertained by the Earl of Leven, then Commander of Edinburgh Castle, and received the freedom of the city in the Council Chamber where Franklin and William had stood on that September morning seven years before; but James Laurie was Provost now, and Provost Drummond was gathered to his fathers and slept in the old Canongate churchyard. It must have been with some reluctance that Stockton tore himself away from this pleasant environment to ride over the snowy roads to Paisley, where he arrived in February of 1767.

The terms which Stockton was empowered to offer had seemed generous enough to the trustees of Princeton; a dwelling house on the campus, £250 a year salary, and one hundred guineas for the expenses of the voyage. Witherspoon, however, was not impressed with the munificence of the Board. He had just had a call to Dublin, of all places. Dublin, to use Mrs. Ward's phrase, would seem to have been that part of the world where the Presbyterian beard was least worth the shaving. However, the salary offered was somewhat larger than that suggested by Stockton, and besides, if the Pastor gave up a promising career in the Kirk of Scotland and went into the American wilderness, what assurance had he that his engagement would be permanent? Mrs. Witherspoon, for whom some malicious neighbors had painted an alarming picture of the privations and dangers of pioneer life overseas, was openly rebellious. Stockton despaired, and Rush in Edinburgh, who was emotional at best, took the loss of so likely a candidate the hardest of all. He relieved his feelings in four pages of bombastic lamentation addressed to Witherspoon and ending:

O Nassau Hall, Nassau Hall, in vain rescued and cherished by every Lover of religion, since thou art to fall into the Hands of some—but I cannot express it—my Heart bleeds within me— O Nassau Hall, Nassau Hall.[25]

When this hysterical appeal proved fruitless, Rush went himself to Paisley but was compelled to report to the Trustees that while he might have prevailed upon the Pastor, he was powerless to allay the qualms of Mrs. Witherspoon. So the matter stood when Witherspoon wrote to Stockton on April 18, 1767: "My wife continues in such distress on the subject that for some weeks after you left us she was scarcely ever half a day out of bed at a time."

The trustees of Princeton had given up all hope and had actually elected another candidate in the person of Samuel Blair of Boston (a graduate of Nassau Hall in the class of 1760), when the situation was entirely changed by the arrival in England of the Reverend Charles Beatty of the Presbytery of New Jersey, himself a trustee of Nassau Hall, accompanied by his wife. This was an advocate whose arguments were to prove more effective than the eloquent appeals of Stockton or the hysterical fulminations of Rush.

Beatty and Franklin were old associates. When the Philosopher, most incongruously clad in buff and bandolier, had made his campaign in the Pennsylvania woods in the winter of 1755–56, the chaplain of his little army was the same young preacher, Charles Beatty, a graduate of the Log College at Neshaminy Falls which was the genesis of Princeton University.[26] Franklin in his *Autobiography* pays a tribute to Beatty's services and comments upon the tact with which he mingled his prayers with an adroit distribution of rum, thus securing a full representation of the soldiers at divine service. The two men became great friends during the weeks they spent in constructing Fort Allen in the Lehigh Gap, and when Beatty came over to Ireland and England in 1760 upon a begging mission for Princeton, he brought letters from Deborah Franklin to Benjamin.[27] There is reason to believe that the Pastor and the Agent of Pennsylvania went together to the coronation of King George the Third.

From Beatty's daybook and letters now in the possession of his descendants, it is evident that when he proceeded to Paisley to try his luck with the obstinate Witherspoon, Franklin knew about his errand. Once arrived at Paisley, Beatty registered at the village inn, but Witherspoon, who had learned of his coming, insisted upon his staying at the Parish House. The Pastor was already regretful of his rather curt refusal of the Princeton call, and Mrs. Witherspoon too had become reconciled to the idea of crossing the Atlantic. The visitor from America argued plausibly and with such success that he could presently intimate to Rush that if the offer were renewed, a favorable reply might be expected.

Now the news of Witherspoon's change of heart was relayed to Princeton where it was received with mixed emotions. Young Billy Patterson, a future Associate Justice of the Supreme Court, wrote to his chum, John Macpherson: "Witherspoon is President. Mercy on me! We shall be overrun with Scotchmen, the worst vermin under heaven." [28]

The embarrassed trustees who had considered Witherspoon's refusal as final and had elected Mr. Blair were hastily reconvened. However, Blair behaved very handsomely, mumbled something to the assembled trustees about his youth and inexperience, and discreetly withdrew so that the way was once more clear for Witherspoon's accession. When the President-elect in Paisley heard the news, he posted down to London to buy books and scientific equipment for his new charge in America. The diary recording his movements on this trip existed up to 1868 and was seen by his biographer, Ashbel Green, but has been lost. That Witherspoon consulted with Franklin in these purchases is proved by Beatty's notebook, which has luckily survived.

Witherspoon embarked for Philadelphia and Princeton in May 1768, while Beatty remained behind in Glasgow absorbed in the care of his sick wife. She died in the next autumn and then the bereaved husband journeyed to London to conclude the packing and shipment of the college equipment which Witherspoon and Franklin had ordered. This was the same apparatus which the British troops mishandled so wantonly in their occupation of Nassau Hall in 1776. It is described as "an orrery, a small telescope, an electrical machine with a case of coated jars." [29]

The last inspection of what Beatty calls "philosophical apparatus for the college of New Jersey" took place on March 21, 1769, at the shop of one Lotheby in London. On that morning Beatty hired a coach (the modest sum of two shillings "laid out for the college" is duly recorded by the punctilious diarist) and drove to Craven Street, where he picked up Dr. Franklin, went to the inspection, and then "dined with Dr. Fields."

Beatty sailed for home in June 1769, and perhaps Franklin had expected to go with him. Throughout his correspondence at this period there are repeated suggestions of a termination of his official mission. As early as 1768 Dr. Fothergill wrote, "Dr. Franklin is, I fear, upon the wing to leave us," but still the Agent stayed on. Peter Collinson died in August of 1768 "while on a visit to a Noble Lord in Essex," [30] a great loss to the Agent, who valued his companionship. There had been talk of Franklin and Collinson going together to Edinburgh, but Scotland must have seemed far away from Franklin at this time. Frequently when he called at Strahan's he got word of his old acquaintances in the North, and once, on January 27, 1769, he dined at the printer's with David Hume and Sir John Pringle.[31] At Boswell's lodgings, too, he often met Scotchmen, and on May 14, 1768, Boswell gleefully recorded:

I am really the great man now. I have had David Hume in the forenoon and Mr. Johnson in the afternoon of the same day visiting me. Sir John Pringle, Dr. Franklin and some more company dined with me today, and Mr. Johnson and Lord Oglethorpe one day.

Occasionally the Agent got Scottish news through the missionary Whitefield, who had come down from his last preaching tour in Edinburgh to his home in Tottenham Court Road. Whitefield often came to call at Craven Street to enunciate tiresome homilies. He wrote crazy letters to Franklin depicting the imminent end of the world and his own salvation and announcing that Lord Buchan, whom Benjamin had saved at St. Andrews, had "gotten the call." [32]

Evidently these sporadic reminders of his northern journey were not sufficient to lure the Agent back to Scotland, for both in 1767 and in 1769 he went to France with Sir John Pringle, when he might as easily have gone to Edinburgh. In 1769 his fancy roamed far afield and he bought travel books on China, Norway, Senegal, and Canada. As for Scotland and his friends in Edinburgh, there seemed little likelihood of his ever seeing them again. But in the fall of 1770 his vagrant notion returned to more practical fields of travel and he began to inquire from his friend Robert Alexander of Edinburgh, whom he had met years before at Prestonfield, as to the ships which left the port of London every week for Leith, and as to the feasibility of making the journey to Scotland by sea.[33] Then in the spring of 1771 his humor took a retrospective turn. All through the spring months he worked fitfully upon a recital of his life, the record which afterwards took shape as the *Autobiography*—his greatest literary legacy. The narrative never reached the Scottish episode, but perhaps its composition reminded the writer of old haunts and of friends long unseen. In any event, during the late summer, he set off to pay a belated and much-promised visit to Caledonia, only this time instead of proceeding directly to Edinburgh, he made a preliminary tour in Ireland.

PART TWO

# THE VISIT TO IRELAND AND SCOTLAND

1771

Benjamin Franklin's Route in 1771

N

SCOTLAND

BLAIR DRUMMOND
GLASGOW
CARRON
EDINBURGH
PORT PATRICK
CARLISLE
HILLSBOROUGH
DONAGHADEE
IRELAND
PRESTON
DUBLIN
HOLY HEAD
WALES
BIRMINGHAM
ENGLAND
LONDON

Scale-Statute Miles
0  20  40  60  80  100  120  140  160

GEISZEL

# Chapter VII

# THE DEPARTURE FOR IRELAND

THE winter of 1771 in England was one of unparalleled severity. Storm succeeded storm and Mr. Franklin, going to dine with a friend as late as the twentieth of April, was caught in a heavy fall of snow. He wrote to his son William in the third week of April, to say that not a bud had pushed out nor a blade of grass, and that cattle and sheep were dying by thousands from exposure to the unwonted cold.

Our Agent was now in his sixty-sixth year and far from well, so that the rigors of this untoward season had borne hardly upon him. He was discouraged besides over the uncertainties of the political situation. "I purpose returning to America in the ensuing summer if our dispute should be adjusted," he wrote to DuPont de Nemours. There were insistent rumors that his position as Assistant Postmaster-General was to be taken away from him. The breach between America and Great Britain was widening, and Franklin felt that his eleven years' mission had been a failure. His friends noted his dejection with alarm. Strahan wrote to William Franklin on April 3, 1771:

Your father could not get stir in his business as he is not only on bad terms with Lord Hillsborough but with the Ministry in general. Besides his temper, he has grown so very reserved, which adds greatly to his natural inactivity and there is no getting him to take part in anything.

Benjamin was conscious of his indisposition, and as soon as the roads opened in May he set out upon a tour of recuperation in the Midlands, stopping at Birmingham, Leeds, Sheffield, and Manchester. As the journey was originally planned, his companions were to have been his grandnephew, Jonathan Williams, Jr. (at this time domesticated with him in Craven Street as clerk or secretary) and the Dutch scientist John Ingenhousz, formerly of Breda. Ingenhousz, an old friend and correspondent of Franklin and fellow member of the Royal Society, had been living in England for some years, and in 1771 was just returned from Vienna, where he had inoculated the imperial family for smallpox. Just before the departure Franklin conceived the idea that a quartet would be more agreeable than a trio and wrote to his friend, the pedagogue John Canton, with whom he had been pursuing some studies on the property of electricity, inviting him to go along.

*Craven Street, May 12th, 1771*

Dr. Ingenhousz and myself purpose to set out on Friday next to visit Birmingham and some other Manufacturing Towns, intending to be absent about 10 Days. A young Kinsman of mine accompanies us. Will you make a fourth and so reduce our Triangle to a Square? [1]

Canton, then teaching at the Academy in Spital Square, accepted the invitation and made the tour. The expense accounts of the four travelers, kept by young Jonathan Williams and scrupulously reckoned out to the last farthing, are preserved at the American Philosophical Society.

Franklin's letter to Deborah, written June 5, 1771, gives the general route of the excursion but might be more generous as to details. The party went first to Birmingham. Baskerville was temporarily out of the city, and this circumstance seems to have militated against a long stay, for the travelers proceeded directly to Sheffield where, on the twenty-fifth of May, Franklin drew upon his bankers, Smith, Wright, and Gay, for £42 in favor of Hannah Hazelhurst.[2] Part at least of this rather large sum was expended for cooking utensils. Eleven years before, when Benjamin and William first visited Sheffield, they had bought saucepans for Deborah and Sally Franklin and had sent them on to Philadelphia. Now Franklin made some additional purchases of which he was to be reminded eight years later when he was envoy at Passy and when Ingenhousz wrote to him from London.

> *London, April 9th, 1779*
>
> I will endeavor to bring you the copper pot to roast a chicken in by a bolt of iron which you bought at Sheffield when we were there together.[3]

From Sheffield the party went on to Leeds, where they called upon the great Priestley, who wrote shortly afterwards to continue a scientific discussion about the properties of sound, in which he and Franklin had been engaged during the visit. It is evident that the Doctor was beginning to recover something of his ordinary good spirits.

Franklin's stay with Priestley marks a reversion of his old rôle of mentor for young American hopefuls come over to Europe for their education. Jemmy Bowdoin, son of his friend James Bowdoin of Boston, later Governor of Massachusetts, had left Harvard early in the year 1771 and entered himself at Christ Church, dividing his time very agreeably betwixt Oxford and London.[4] The father, back home in Boston, was uneasily suspicious that Jemmy was not making the best of his opportunity, and suggested that he apply to Dr. Franklin to get an admission to Priestley's Academy at Warrington and that he reside, if possible, in the Priestley home under the Principal's watchful eye. Jemmy, not entirely sympathetic with a plan which would have removed him from the attractions of the metropolis, wrote back that he was very well satisfied, had lately enrolled at the King's Riding School, was studying French and dancing, and would demonstrate his progress by writing a description of the Lord Mayor's fête in French. Also, as living in England was expensive, would the Pater please send over an additional £300 allowance? The discussion was concluded when Franklin wrote to the elder Bowdoin, after his visit to Priestley, that he would gladly have recommended Jemmy as a pupil, but that Dr. Priestley had just left the Academy at Warrington and was now pastor of a congregation in Leeds.[5]

After leaving Leeds the Agent and his companions went to call upon Anthony Tissington at Alfreton, the same rambling Derbyshire hall where he had visited with William in 1759. Tissington was not at home, and wrote shortly afterwards to London to express his regret. His absence was partially compensated for by the presence of old John Whitehurst, the gray-haired, bespectacled clockmaker whose habit it was to bombard Franklin with scientific enquiries. He was in his musty shop in the town of Derby surrounded by horloges and barometers. Franklin, mindful of the trip to Ireland and Scotland which he was shortly to undertake, ordered two traveling clocks, one of which was delivered in Craven Street on August tenth, just before his departure for Dublin. At the same time he gave Whitehurst an order for some engraved silver plates which were sent down to the Stevenson household.[6]

If, on this same Midlands tour, Benjamin had turned to the southward, he might have encountered his old adversary Thomas Penn, who just at that time was taking the waters at Tunbridge Wells. In the period of Franklin's first Scottish visit, a meeting with the Proprietor of Pennsylvania would have been embarrassing and possibly blusterous. But the Thomas Penn of 1771 was a different man from the arrogant, truculent Proprietor of 1759. He was old, sick, and occupied in the making of his will; the former asperity had vanished. His brother Richard, to whom the very name of Franklin was anathema, had died a few months before (February 4, 1771) and Richard, Jr., who was going out as Lieutenant-Governor of Pennsylvania, was in Tunbridge to receive his uncle's last instructions. There is no evidence that the traveler directed his steps or even his thoughts toward Tunbridge, which is to be deplored. A frank interview at this time might have saved much misunderstanding five years later, when the inevitable bickering broke out betwixt the Revolutionary Executive Council of Pennsylvania and the resident Lieutenant-Governor, who still strove to uphold in Philadelphia the waning power of the Crown.

Dr. Franklin returned to London on June fourth to celebrate the King's birthday, thus proving that in spite of his recent differences with the Ministry, he was still a loyal subject of King George. However, he continued to be restless and irritable, and complained of the difficulty with which he breathed the smoke of London. Besides, Mrs. Stevenson, ever a meticulous housekeeper, was in the throes of spring housecleaning. The masons were making repairs to the dwelling on Craven Street and painters were at work on the inside [7]—no repose here for a harassed statesman. Benjamin repacked his bags, gathered up the sheets of rough notes which were to be molded into the famous *Autobiography*, and took himself down to Chilbolton near Twyford in Hampshire, the home of his good friend Jonathan Shipley, Bishop of St. Asaph's.

This Jonathan Shipley, the amiable and talented bishop of St. Asaph's and Llandaff, bound to Franklin by many ties of affection and regard, was the son of a London merchant of means, and a graduate of Oxford. He was a courtly prelate who seems to have well exemplified Shane Leslie's adage that "It is the tradition of the Church of England to place a gentleman in every parish of the British Isles. There have been worse traditions." Bishop Shipley, through his wife's family, had inherited the property of Chilbolton, a stately Tudor mansion approached by an avenue of noble chestnuts, with rolling lawns sloping down to the placid river Itchen. Franklin, writing from overseas years afterwards, dilated upon the agreeableness of his stay at Chilbolton.

How happy I was in the sweet retirement of Twyford, where my only business was a little scribbling in the garden, study, and my pleasure in your conversation and that of your family.[8]

And in 1787, three years before Franklin's own death, when the news came of Bishop Shipley's passing, Benjamin wrote:

That excellent man has then left us. According to the course of years, I should have left this world before him but I shall not be long in following.[9]

The Agent left this pleasant retreat in Hampshire to return to the duties of his office in the middle of July. Already on July twenty-fifth he regretted his leaving and wrote to the Bishop that he proposed to come back to Chilbolton as speedily as possible.

I should have been happy in accompanying your Lordship on that agreeable Party, or in being at Twyford instead of this dusty Town; but Business kept me here longer than I expected. I now purpose to set out on Tuesday next, if nothing at present unforeseen does not happen to prevent me. I hope to find the good family well, which will add greatly to the Pleasure I promise myself in that sweet Retreat.

This second visit lasted three weeks, which the Doctor employed in working hard upon the *Autobiography*. He wrote to Deborah on August 14 to describe the stay and its conclusion.

I spent three weeks in Hampshire at my Friend the Bishop of St. Asaph's. The Bishop's Lady knows what Children and Grandchildren I have, their Ages, &c. So when I was to come away on Monday the 12th in the Morning, she insisted on my staying that one Day longer, that we might together keep my Grandson's Birthday.

The house where Franklin stayed is still standing, although the approach by the chestnut avenue was sadly altered by the cutting of the Portsmouth Road through the premises about the year 1800. This doubtful improvement completely destroyed the privacy of the Shipley residence, and the incumbent of the time, a grandson of the Bishop, was so disgusted that he removed from Chilbolton. The family now resides in another property some miles to the eastward. Past the old hall rushes the teeming traffic of our own day, and thousands of American tourists journeying between London and Southampton Water drive under the high wall without realizing that in the gardens behind it was begun the greatest of American autobiographies. Fortunately the relocation of the highway has spared the rectory and the churchyard with the historic yew tree which Franklin admired.

When the Philosopher left Twyford to journey up to town, he escorted Catharine, aged eleven, the Bishop's youngest daughter, to her school in Marlborough Street.[10] This was the mischievous young lady who had been meted a punishment for drawing a roguish parallel between Franklin and Socrates. The two cronies chatted and quarreled and diverted themselves hugely. They beguiled the way by discussions as to the probable personality of Catharine's future husband and tales of the ghost in the haunted house at Hinton. They lunched at Staines and speculated as to the antics of the squirrel then coming from America as a present to the Shipleys from Deborah, the same Mungo who was killed by a dog in the next year, and for whom Franklin wrote a humorous epitaph. However, our Philosopher's particular favorite in the Shipley family was not little Catharine but her older sister Georgianna, at this time aged fifteen, the girl whose glorious maturity was well to fulfill the promise of a radiant maidenhood. Her biographer (and grandson), Augustus J. C. Hare, whose travel books have delighted three generations, describes her as one who "had studied classics with her father, had been petted by Benjamin Franklin, and learned painting in Reynolds' studio, and was a general favorite for her conversational powers." But neither of the voyagers who traveled up to London on that rainy summer afternoon could guess the tragic destiny which awaited Georgianna through an ill-fated marriage. On March 21, 1785, while Franklin was still at Passy, Richard Price wrote from London:

Your favorite and mine and the favorite of all that conversed with her, I mean Miss Georgianna Shipley, is now Mrs. Hare and resides at Aix la Chapelle. Mr. Hare has been obliged to quit this country for debt. You probably know what inexpressible trouble this has given to the excellent Bishop and his family.

The brilliant woman who charmed all with whom she came in contact was alienated from her kind father, lived most of her life in exile, became blind at the age of forty-eight, and died miserably three years later at Lausanne on Easter day of 1806. Father and daughter, estranged in life, are united beside the chancel of the quaint upland chapel at Twyford. A dignified plaque by the sculptor Nollikins records the virtues of the good Bishop, while a memorial of singular grace and beauty, the work of the great Flaxman himself, testifies to the charm of the lovely and wayward Georgianna.

If Franklin had elected to spend the summer months quietly at London and Twyford and to continue his work upon the *Autobiography,* posterity might have inherited a personal narrative at least of his first trip to Scotland, in which case there would be no occasion for a reconstruction two centuries afterwards. However, Benjamin was too inveterate a tourist to remain long stationary in the fine weather. Already in the spring of 1771 a new note is apparent in the correspondence as his interest focuses upon a trip to Ireland with a possible jump across to Scotland, if opportunity should offer.

It has previously been stated that as early as 1760 the Agent discussed this Hibernian project with Lord Kames. In April of 1769, when the dispute between the mother country and the American Colonies was becoming more and more virulent, the harassed Envoy gratefully acknowl-

edged the sympathy and help proffered him from across
St. George's Channel.

All Ireland is strongly in favour of the American cause. They
have reason to sympathize with us. I send you four pamphlets
written in Ireland or by Irish gentlemen, in which you will find
some excellent well-said things.[11]

Before the Caledonian journey Benjamin had taken care
to inform himself as to the route by conversation and correspondence with his Scottish friends; the same opportunity afforded, on a lesser scale, for the Hibernian
excursion. He had several Irish correspondents, notable
among whom were the scientist, Dean Hamilton of Armagh, of whom more later, and Springett Penn of Dublin,
great-grandson of William Penn, the founder of Pennsylvania. Springett was rather neglected and despised by his
English relatives, but Franklin liked him and termed him
"a sensible discreet young man of excellent disposition." [12]
The young Irishman spent his life in endeavoring to en-
force a claim which he conceived he had to the estate of
Pennsbury on the Delaware, and pestered the Agent of
Pennsylvania with questions as to procedure. He died,
however, in November 1766, and although letters continued to arrive in Craven Street from agitated relations
in Ireland, Gaskells and Fells and Durdins, who had vague
ideas of succeeding to a rich transatlantic patrimony, it
does not appear that Franklin, occupied in the affairs of
his office, ever interested himself much in the matter.

In London there lived an Irish girl whose acquaintance
Franklin had made and who procured for him Irish al-
manacs and gave him travel information.[13] She was Miss
Martin, afterwards married to an Irish Quaker named
Blacker, and she held a position in the General Post Of-
fice. Through her the Agent met two Irishmen of whom
he saw much in Dublin, William Deane and the Reverend
Richard Woodward, later bishop of Cloyne.

Still another Hibernian lure for an erstwhile printer was the arrival in Craven Street in April 1771 of a letter from an Irish typefounder named J. Kettilby, who had a shop in Mitre Alley, Dublin, "opposite the Dean's gardens" where he made types and matrices. Kettilby wrote enthusiastically inviting Franklin to come over and see his work: "I hope by September to alarm ye whole Fraternity with the real Exhibitions of Presses Matrices Moulds types singled in Words." [14]

It was the fashion for visitors of note who chanced to be sojourning in London to pay their respects to the celebrated Dr. Franklin, and among these callers were many Irishmen, particularly of what was known as the patriot faction. The identity of most of these has been lost, but William Samuel Johnson, the Connecticut Agent who dined in Craven Street on May 12, 1769, found there two members of the Irish Parliament, Hercules Langrishe, Esq., the representative for Kilkenny, and Gervase Parker Bushe, Esq., of the borough of Granard, member for Longford.

*London, Friday, 12th May 1769*

Dined at four o'clock with Dr. Franklin. Found Lord Mountmorris, Mr. Bushe (author of the Case of Great Britain and the Colonies), Mr. Langrishe (both of these members of the Irish Parliament and very sensible learned men), Mr. Walker, Agent for Barbados, Mr. Wharton of Philadelphia and Dr. Arthur Lee. Spent the time in much agreeable and useful conversation. [15]

But with all these Hibernian affiliations, Franklin's immediate incentive for the journey came from his old friend Counselor Richard Jackson, who had Irish connections. This was the "Omniscient Jackson" of Charles Lamb's *Old Benchers of the Inner Temple,* long associated with Benjamin in the Agencyship of the Province of Pennsylvania in London, and reputed to be so infallible that when Mrs. Thrale contemplated a tour of Italy, Johnson recommended her to consult Jackson as to her route.

His father, Richard Jackson the elder, a wealthy London merchant, matriculated his son as a Commoner at Queen's College, Cambridge, in 1739.[16] The youth never graduated, although later he was active in the management of the University and served as its counsel. After a term at Lincoln's Inn, young Jackson became a barrister in 1744 and was enrolled at the Inner Temple in 1751. Some of his biographers have confused him with his Irish relative, Richard Jackson, later a member of the Irish Parliament from Coleraine, who was in the Inner Temple at the same time.[17]

About 1752 Jackson begins to be described as "of Weasenham in the county of Norfolk," his father having acquired Weasenham barony. Here the student spent his vacations, here his mother died in 1754, and here in the churchyard of the neighboring All Saints' Church stands the pretentious rococo tomb of the elder Jackson, and the tablet within the church vaunting the talents and ability of his son.

The lawyer very early in his career evinced an interest in American affairs and began to correspond with Franklin. The Doctor, writing to Jared Elliott, speaks of Jackson's agricultural experiments at Weasenham Hall. And, addressing Jackson on May 5, 1753, he comments somewhat harshly upon the character of the German immigrants to Pennsylvania, adverting to the governmental relief measures of the time in a vein strangely prophetic of the conditions in our own day:

To relieve the misfortunes of our fellow creatures is concurring with the Deity; is God-like; but if we provide encouragement for laziness and support for folly may we not be found fighting against the order of God and Nature which perhaps has appointed want and misery as the proper punishment of idleness and extravagance. Whenever we attempt to amend the scheme of Providence and to interfere with the Government of the World, we had need to be very circumspect lest we do more harm than good.[18]

Franklin and Jackson, separated by the broad Atlantic, corresponded in desultory fashion for some years. Benjamin sent maps, pamphlets, and the resolutions of the provincial assemblies. Richard proffered advice for a Bank of Pennsylvania and for new methods of taxation. When Franklin is setting out for Ireland he describes Jackson as "my old friend and fellow-traveler, Barrister Jackson," a mysterious reference, as we have no knowledge of the two men having traveled together before the Dublin excursion.

An interesting glimpse of the youthful Jackson is afforded in the sprightly memoirs of Caroline Powys, who went with the Jacksons, father and son, upon a tour of Norfolk in 1756, visiting at the castle of the aristocratic Coke of Holkham. She draws a picture of young Richard as an ardent boy who rode beside her coach and enlivened the tedium of the journey by his spirited sallies. He was very "wivable" at this period with the prospect of the succession of a lordly manor, and all the ladies of the party set their caps at him. His celibacy was proof against blandishment, for he lived and died an incorrigible bachelor. Sometimes, indeed, he seemed on the point of succumbing, and on these occasions he made confidants of his friends the Franklins. William, who was with Jackson at Tunbridge Wells in 1758, writes to his father that they contemplate a trip to Norfolk but that Richard cannot leave at once "because of the matrimonial affair he mentioned to us." [19] And at Christmas time in 1763 Jackson writes naïvely to Benjamin:

I thank you for your good wishes as to my marriage. I assure you that I have been chiefly prevented from marriage by a resolution I have taken to enjoy a full political independence.

Richard Jackson was appointed as Agent for Pennsylvania in London, a post in which he held equal powers with Franklin. When the Doctor went back to Philadelphia in 1762, the barrister conducted the affairs of the agency until Franklin's return in 1764. He was elected to Parliament in 1763 from the borough of Weymouth, and later represented the Cinque Ports. Jeremy Bentham sneered at his legal abilities and referred to him as "a silk-stocking barrister who never had any briefs," but Jackson took his practice very seriously, and in the good old days when the great Thurlow was Chancellor and Lord Mansfield presided over the Court of King's Bench, Richard Jackson of Norfolk was one of the celebrities of the Inner Temple. Charles Lamb dismisses him all too curtly, but Barrister Blackham in his delightful vision of the old Crown Office Row conjures up an appealing picture:

Here is old Two Penny Jackson, the know-all, shuffling along the brick walk in his slippers while near him Gibbon ponders some point in Roman History and David Garrick struts under the elm trees and Sir Joshua stops a friend to arrange for a sitting.[20]

Somehow we think of Jackson as always old, for omniscience and adolescence are scarcely compatible and there is little affinity between the impetuous youth who showed Billy Franklin about Norfolk in 1758 and the pedantic patriarch whom Temple Franklin met on his visit to London in 1784, and who sent so many messages to his grandfather at Paris. Still less is the resemblance to the embittered recluse who lingered out his later years in Southampton Building on the Strand, and sat down on the evening of May 2, 1787, a few hours before his death, to begin his will "Lest I should die tonight . . ." [21]

A tried man, old Two Penny Jackson of the Inner Temple, member for Weymouth, for Melcombe Regis and for New Romney, attorney for the South Sea Company, counselor for the University of Cambridge, and co-Agent for Pennsylvania. Had his fervid pleas for moderation been heeded, the American Revolution might have been indefinitely postponed.[22]

Franklin and Jackson, as co-agents for Pennsylvania, might in the interest of their clients have gone to Ireland five years before their visit of 1771. In 1766 the Committee of Correspondence of the Pennsylvania Assembly wrote an agitated letter complaining of the falling off of trade between Ireland and the American colonies, and soliciting the immediate attention of their representatives in London.[23] It was not until the spring of 1771 that the Agents definitely decided to go together to Dublin. Then, after Benjamin's return from the first trip to Twyford in July 1771, so many communications, arrangements presumably for the journey to Ireland, passed between Jackson in his chambers in Southampton Building, Chancery Lane, and the house in Craven Street, that a special messenger, one Daniel Evans,[24] was required for the service. In one of these missives is the notation:

Mr. Jackson has the pleasure to send Dr. Franklin a piece of elastic gum with a thousand good wishes and compliments.[25]

Later in the summer Jackson, who had heard of Franklin's trip to Twyford and seemed apprehensive that the Irish visit might not materialize, wrote again:

Does it suit you to go to Ireland with me in a week, a fortnight or three weeks? I am sorry you leave London so soon fearing as I do I may chance to miss seeing you.

This appeal had the effect of curtailing Franklin's pleasant stay in Twyford. On Tuesday evening, the thirteenth of August, he descended in Craven Street, and wrote to Deborah to say that he and Jackson were starting off for Ireland "the next week." By Sunday night, however, far from being busied with preparations for his departure, Franklin was unconcernedly dining at the house of Sir John Pringle, discussing the South Sea Islands and declaring that the journey to Ireland was postponed until the next Saturday—the twenty-fifth of August.[26]

From this procrastination it is apparent that some important affair of state was responsible for the Agent's indecision. The explanation lies in the impending arrival of Henry Marchant, Attorney-General for Rhode Island and special agent for the collection of claims arising from the French and Indian War, claims which demanded the attention and advice of Franklin. Marchant, who was daily expected from America, had actually landed at Dover on the night of Saturday, the seventeenth of August. In his portmanteau were letters to Franklin and to William Samuel Johnson, but while his ship lay in the Downs it was passed by the New York packet *Duchess of Gordon,* Captain Wynne, on board of which was Johnson returning to America, so that Johnson's letter was never delivered.

All unaware that his tardiness was interfering with Mr. Franklin's holiday, Marchant posted leisurely up through Kent, loitering to admire the distant prospect of Calais from the Shakespeare Cliff, inspecting the hop fields and visiting the cathedral of Canterbury. He came to London on the morning of Monday, the nineteenth of August, dined comfortably at the New England Coffee House, and made a belated appearance in Craven Street during the afternoon. He reported his arrival to Ezra Stiles in America:

I saw Dr. Franklin on the day of my arrival which was lucky indeed as he was just setting out for the country and then for Ireland, and from thence to Scotland. He told me he would write me from the country as to when he should be in Scotland so that we might meet there. He told me that William Samuel Johnson was gone, for which I was sorry. Mr. Jackson is going with Dr. Franklin so that I expect much satisfaction in that point.[27]

Marchant's business was important enough to detain Franklin until Sunday, the twenty-fifth of August. The Sabbath was not a good day upon which to begin a journey in the eighteenth century or at any other time, but Jackson's patience was worn threadbare and the Agent indited a hasty note to Jonathan Williams.

*August 25, 1771*

I have not time to add more being this minute setting out on a short trip to Ireland to visit some American Friends or rather Friends of America & take that Portion of Exercise and fresh air which is every year necessary to my health.[28]

The Craven Street expense account for the weeks preceding the departure throws some light on the journey. There is no large entry for coach hire such as the one which attended the 1759 trip, which suggests that Franklin and Jackson used the public stages. It would have been very expensive and scarcely practical to take a private chaise to Ireland, particularly as Mr. Franklin was still uncertain whether he would not continue on alone to Scotland. The Agent called upon his tailor, in anticipation of the state levees in Dublin, and bought a sword belt, at the same time settling young Temple's clothing bill. Temple was to be left at home with Mrs. Stevenson since the responsibility for a lively lad of eleven was not likely to be conducive to repose or convalescence. The boy was still at Elphinstone's School near Kensington, and his grandfather paid the bill for the last quarter's tuition. Jackson had made some outlays for their joint account, comforts perhaps for the voyage, so Franklin sent him £5 5s in payment of his share of the expenditures. Then, as was his invariable habit in setting out upon a tour, he paid Mrs. Stevenson's board bill (£7 3s 7d) and was ready to start. The agency was to be run for the next two months by Jonathan Williams, Jr., and he was given £21 to cover such incidental expenses as might accrue.

Little is known of the course of Franklin and Jackson in the week which followed their departure from Craven Street on Sunday morning. They must have proceeded very leisurely, for in four days they had come only as far as Birmingham. Baskerville was still absent but Matthew Boulton was in town, immersed in his experiments with the steam engine and endeavoring to get James Watt to come down from Scotland and continue his research in

Birmingham. Also resident in Birmingham was an artisan named W. Small, who had written to Franklin in London and asked him to inspect a telescope built upon a new principle which he had discovered.[29]

While staying in Birmingham Franklin found that he needed money. Perhaps in the hurry of a Sunday leaving he had come away without sufficient funds; perhaps he had made some purchases. Baskerville could not have afforded any financial assistance as he was sadly fallen from his former pomp, was offering his plant for sale and writing lugubrious letters to Franklin about the ingratitude of a callous world. Boulton was well off but we have no record of his extending any accommodation. However, our Agent was usually resourceful in money matters and was able to cash a check on his bankers, Smith, Wright, and Gay, for £21 and to go on his way.[30]

Travelers of the period who intended for Dublin had their choice of two routes. They might cross over the Welsh mountains to Holyhead and take the Irish packet, or they could follow a less hilly but more circuitous road to Park Gate, a small seaport west of Chester, which was served by another line of packet ships for Dublin. A new coaching service was established about this time, and young Henry Grattan, on his way from Oxford to Dublin in January of 1772, wrote back to a friend in London:

Tell Tydd that for two guineas, every other day, he may have a place in an excellent post-chaise that will bring him to Holyhead in two days.

Wealthy tourists took their own vehicles, but the body of the carriage must be dismounted from the springs during the transit of the Irish Sea. Tate Wilkinson, who crossed in 1762, records that the traverse was so rough and his horses became so unmanageable that the captain of the packet threatened to cut their throats.

Franklin and Jackson chose the Holyhead route and must have gone on there from Birmingham, for we have the authority of the *Public Register or Freeman's Journal* of Dublin that they sailed from Holyhead for Ireland on Wednesday, the fourth of September.[31] They tarried a day or two at the port of embarkation, no unusual experience, for the Irish packets were small, primitive, and dependent upon the weather. Voyagers were often detained by adverse winds and must rest with as much philosophy as they could muster at a very indifferent inn. The missionary John Wesley, who had been preaching in the Welsh towns before Franklin's arrival at Holyhead and who proposed to cross to Ireland, sat in his wretched tavern, listened to the rain pattering on the roof and wrote in his journal: "I never knew men make such poor lame excuses for not sailing as these Holyhead captains do." And an Irish wit who was similarly delayed beguiled the tedium in rhythmical composition:

> There are unless my memory fails
> Five causes why we should not sail:
> The fog is thick; the wind is high;
> It rains: or may rain by and by;
> Or—any other reason why.

It required a degree of hardihood to embark at all, for while the ordinary passage averaged twelve hours it might take much more, and De Quincey, as late as 1800, consumed thirty hours between Holyhead and Dublin. The sleeping quarters, too, were woefully inadequate and the passengers frequently sought repose upon the hard boards of the deck.[32] However, Mr. Franklin, who had five times crossed the North Atlantic, would have no qualms about the Irish Sea. He had set out to make a tour in Ireland and to Ireland he would go, wind and weather permitting.

# Chapter VIII

# DUBLIN

BENJAMIN FRANKLIN, ESQ., L.L.D., Postmaster General of America and Richard Jackson, Esq., a member of the British Parliament, arrived in the Hillsborough packet from Holyhead on September fifth." [1]

On the afternoon of Thursday, the fifth of September, 1771, the Holyhead packet was to be descried tacking in from St. George's Channel to attain the wharf of the little port of Dunleary on the east coast of Ireland, four miles from Dublin. A few years later travelers from England to Dublin disembarked at Dublin Wall, much nearer the city. In 1771 they often landed at Dunleary, which a contemporary observer described as "a horrible sink of filth inhabited by the dregs of creation." When the portly "First Gentleman of Europe," King George the Fourth, embarked there, after his visit to Ireland in 1821, the name was changed to Kingstown, and it is to be hoped the smells abated. Certainly the aristocratic suburb and bathing resort of our own day gives no suggestion of the unsavory description accorded to it one hundred and fifty years ago.

As the packet beat up to the wharf the usual array of pale, seasick voyagers was to be seen upon the deck, among these two middle-aged gentlemen in traveling costume. The captain of the vessel, duly impressed with the importance of his charges, presently made it known that one of the pair was the barrister Richard Jackson of the Inner Temple, a relative to Richard Jackson, the Irish Member for Coleraine. His companion was none other than the celebrated Dr. Franklin of Philadelphia, whose coming had been rumored for some weeks and whose Poor Richard almanacs were widely read in Dublin.

Franklin and Jackson waded through the slime and ran

the gauntlet of the horde of vociferous porters. They had two alternatives for their transportation to the capital. They might find places in the historic and dilapidated vehicle called the "Long Coach," always overcrowded, which rattled over the incredibly bad causeway to Dublin, or, for an extra outlay, they could hire one of the curious two-wheeled carriages called "Dublin noddies," the predecessors of the jaunting car. An idea of the uncertainties of the route is to be gleaned from the circumstance that highwaymen sometimes stopped the Dunleary coach in broad daylight.

As the tourists drove along they might mark the diverse views of the lordly bay, the soft charm of the distant Wicklow Hills, and the imposing façades of the stately Georgian capital which they were approaching. "Dublin is splendid beyond my expectation," exclaimed Walter Scott half a century later, and Franklin may well have anticipated the sentiment. The "Second City of the Empire," as its inhabitants loved to boast, with a population of one hundred thousand, was being rebuilt in the noble tradition of Inigo Jones. Mr. Jackson could not fail to indicate to his American colleague the spires of St. Patrick's and of Christ Church, the dark mass of the Norman castle and the columns of the new Parliament House where Franklin was so shortly to be honored.

There is no intimation as to where the travelers put up in Dublin. Perhaps they went to the Queen's Head in Bride Street where so many duels were arranged, or to the Phoenix in Werburgh Street, the resort of politicians. More congenial lodgings still would appear to have been Dick's Coffee House in Skinner's Row, which was on the second floor over a bookseller's and much patronized by literary men.[2] Wherever they boarded it is certain that the hospitality of the place savored of the traditional Hibernian bounty so fatal to colonial visitors with weak stomachs. Franklin had marveled at the complexity of the Scottish cuisine, but he was all unprepared for the gastronomic profusion of the Irish metropolis. Mrs. Ann Delaney, who lived in Dublin at the time, relates:

You are not invited to dinner at any private gentleman of £1,000 a year who does not give you seven dishes at one course and burgundy and champagne.[3]

And Arthur Young, another contemporary observer, who has given us a lively portrayal of the social life in the Ireland of the period, says:

Every night in the winter there is a ball or party where the polite circle meet not to enjoy but to sweat each other, a great crowd crammed into twenty feet square gives a zest to the small talk and whist.[4]

Even the digestion of so approved a trencherman as the Agent of Pennsylvania was not equal to these ordeals. Writing afterwards from France he recalled the vexation of his first day in Dublin:

In 1773 [an obvious error; Franklin was in Ireland only in 1771] being in Ireland, I was, after a plentiful dinner of fish the first day of my arrival, seized with a violent vomiting and looseness. The latter continued, no more moderate, as long as I stayed in this kingdom which was four or five weeks.[5]

No precise routine can be assigned for our travelers during the next month, that is to say, for the weeks which intervened between their landing at Dunleary on the fifth of September and their reception by the Irish Parliament in College Green in the second week of October. The task of the subsequent historian would be materially simplified if Deborah Franklin in Philadelphia had preserved her letters for posterity. Franklin speaks of having written to Deborah from Dublin just as he wrote to her on the same tour from Glasgow, but both letters have been lost.

The Doctor gives us no hint of his reactions in his walks about the city, although he afterwards told Thomas Cushing that Dublin was a magnificent town. Indeed, whatever may have been the crudities of the social circle, there was enough of architectural interest to enlist the attention of a discriminating visitor. The Royal Exchange in Cork Street, hard by the Castle, was in course of construction. Trinity College, with its intellectual appeal to a philosopher from overseas, was expanding from the College Green. Across the Green rose the Ionic columns of the new Parliament House, the pride of Ireland. It was true that the winding lanes of the old town were still unpaved and dirty, but the citizens could boast of the fine broad avenues of the new town, of Merrion Square which ranked as the largest square in Europe, and of the stately mansions of the Irish nobility, Moira House on the South Quay, Tyrone House in Marlborough Street, and Leinster House which was to serve the architect L'Enfant as the model for the presidential residence in the new city by the Potomac, the national capital which Franklin did not live to see.

The bookshops existed then just as in the present day, only instead of being situated along the quays of the Liffey they were crowded about the Castle, on Dame Street and Skinner's Row. Sir Walter in his visit to Ireland spent many happy hours browsing there, and one would like to think that Franklin did the same, although we have a record of only one book purchased by him.[6] Our Agent brought along with him to Dublin one of the copies of the proceedings of the American Philosophical Society, just sent out from Philadelphia, which he presented to the editor of the *Hibernian Magazine*. The October number of the magazine, published during Franklin's stay, reviews the proceedings, referring to the achievements of the Society as "No inconsiderable earnest of the great progress the arts and sciences will one day make in the New World." The account is so accurate and authoritative as to suggest the possibility of its having been inspired by Franklin himself. There had been a Dublin Philosophical Society whose constitution had been drawn on lines strikingly similar to Franklin's association in Philadelphia, but it had not survived the bickerings engendered by the Jacobite wars, and was the shadow of a shade in 1771.

Benjamin has left us no description of his visit to Trinity College. He certainly went there once, probably several times, and it would be interesting to have his comparisons between the student body and that of his own College of Pennsylvania.[7] Lockhart, who called at Trinity with Sir Walter some years later, hints at a certain uncouthness, and adverts rather uncharitably to "tattered academic costume and foul linen." On the eve of Franklin's departure for Ulster, the Trinity lads raided the shop of one Michael Mills, a bookseller of Capel Street who had somehow incurred their displeasure, and the police must be called out to quell the riot. These pranks did not militate against the traditional high standard of the institution, for the brilliant Richard Cumberland received his diploma in this same summer of 1771, whilst among the sizars (a position analogous to that of the holder of a scholarship in a modern American university) was John Philpot Curran.

The records of the Trinity Corporation for the period of Franklin's sojourn in Dublin make no mention of the visit of a distinguished philosopher from North America, but are concerned only with the selection of a college brewer and with the finding of a proper custodian for the key to the back park gate, which object, by some inscrutable process of reasoning, was finally entrusted to the Professor of Divinity.

The President of Trinity was the notorious Francis Andrews, a lawyer and a layman; holy orders, the usual attribute of the heads of Trinity, being dispensed with in his case. Andrews was a *bon vivant* and politician who was accused of endeavoring to turn the college into a pocket borough for his own selfish ends. In one respect he would have been very sympathetic with Franklin, for he was devoted to the sciences and at his death bequeathed his telescope to Trinity. There were other members of the faculty with whom the American visitor might have consorted with profit: Dr. Welden, Professor of Mathematics, who had tutored Goldsmith; Dr. Clement of the Department of Botany; and Professor Leland whom Johnson afterwards mentioned with such respect.

Franklin, accompanied by Jackson, went several times to receptions at Dublin Castle and mentions that he there met the Viceroy, George Townshend, and the Lord Chancellor, the Right Honorable James, Baron Liffey, and the Speaker of the Commons, Edmund Sexton Pery, Viscount Pery.[8] He says nothing of two members of the Viceroy's staff who were in constant attendance at the Castle, whom he must have met and with whom he would have been very compatible, the Court physician, Dr. Thomas Addis Emmett, and the viceregal Secretary, Lord George MacCartney. Dr. Emmet had his office in Molesworth Street. His distinguished son, the patriot Robert Emmet, was not born until seven years afterwards; another son, Thomas Addis Emmet, Jr., destined to have so brilliant a career at the New York bar, was a schoolboy at the time of Franklin's visit. The American Agent never saw Dr. Emmet after his departure from Ireland, but he was to meet Lord MacCartney eight years afterwards in Paris under unlooked-for circumstances. MacCartney relinquished his position at Dublin in 1772 and was appointed governor of the island of Grenada in the West Indies. In 1779 Grenada was captured by a French squadron and the Governor was brought to Paris as a prisoner of war. Here he found Benjamin Franklin, whom he had last seen at the Viceroy's levee in Dublin Castle, installed as American Envoy. From the MacCartney papers it would appear that Franklin was asked to use his good offices to secure the illustrious captive's early exchange.

The Viceroy whom Franklin met was George Townshend, Marquis Townshend, then in his forty-seventh year. His Lordship had been a soldier at Dettingen and Fontenoy, had gone out in 1759 as Brigadier General under Wolfe to the siege of Quebec, and been quartered for a time in New Jersey. He had an excellent knowledge of American affairs, so that he and his visitor should have been very congenial. Also (a trait which would appeal to our unassuming Agent) he affected a democratic bearing, walked about the streets of Dublin without escort, and helped a blind beggar at the street corner. However, there were other attributes in the Viceroy which would scarcely commend him to a cultured observer. Franklin could be a two-bottle man upon occasion and was never prudish, but he had the philosopher's detestation for alcoholic excess. When Townshend, through the influence of his distinguished brother Charles, was chosen for the post of Lord Lieutenant of Ireland, a London gossip exclaimed:

Certainly he is the most whimsical character that was ever sent to preside over a great nation but his very conviviality renders him in that jovial and convivial country a not unpleasant chief governor.

This temporary popularity which the Viceroy won by his hospitality soon vanished when he began to quarrel with the Irish Parliament over the inevitable question of revenue.

His temper had grown savage with opposition. He cast every vestige of decorum to the winds. He lived openly with a mistress and her friends, often disappeared from public life to low haunts of dissipation, ridiculed all parties at his own table, scattered abroad satiric ballads on friends and foes and boasted openly of his success in purchasing a majority.[9]

Such was the degenerate Executive who purported to represent the dignity of the Crown while Franklin was in Ireland.

A more worthy representative of the aristocracy of Dublin was the urbane Lord Charlemont, at once a distinguished peer and a devoted patriot. When Charlemont left college to make the Grand Tour he met David Hume in Turin, and it may be that when Franklin came to Ireland

[ 147 ]

he bore letters of introduction from Hume to Charlemont. The Peer's fine town house in Rutland Square was in course of construction at this time and he was living in his villa Marino near Clontarf, the house at which Grattan said he "always met people of wit, humor, gallantry and spirit." Benjamin never refers to Charlemont, but the Charlemont family records state that he called at Marino.

Franklin, always methodical, is at pains to distinguish between the two factions in Dublin: "At Dublin we saw and were entertained by both parties, the Courtiers and the Patriots. The latter treated me with particular Respect." [10] His friends among the "Courtiers" are comprehended in the list just given. Amongst the "Patriots," that is to say, the party which strove for an independent Irish Parliament, the American seems to have seen the most of the venerable Dr. Charles Lucas, the founder of *Freeman's Journal* and member of the Irish Parliament from Dublin city. Franklin, writing to James Bowdoin, described a dinner with Dr. Lucas:

In Ireland among the Patriots I din'd with Dr. Lucas. They are all Friends of America, in which I said everything I could think of to confirm them. Lucas gave Mr. Bowdoin of Boston for his Toast.[11]

Eleven days after Franklin and Jackson arrived in Dublin, Lucas published an open letter to James Bowdoin, James Warren, and Samuel Pemberton of Boston, concerning the Boston massacre, and it seems likely that he consulted with his American guest in its composition. While Franklin never formed a close Hibernian friendship comparable to his association with Sir Alexander Dick or Lord Kames in Scotland, his most intimate connection in Ireland was with this aged physician and patriot. When our Agent first met Lucas, the doctor had become very deaf and had partially lost his powers of locomotion, so that he delivered his speeches while seated. A visitor to the Parliament on College Green who saw Lucas in his prime, dilated upon the majesty of his appearance: "No one entered the Parliament Hall without at once inquiring who was the venerable member with the Olympian form and majestic features." The hand of death was already on Dr. Lucas's shoulder and he expired a few weeks later, while Franklin was still in Edinburgh. All Dublin followed in sorrowing procession when his body was borne to St. Michael's Church where the panegyrist pronounced a fitting eulogy:

No promises or offers could seduce him from untainted patriotism and in this particular he has been more admired than imitated by his countrymen.

Another member of the Patriot faction whose house Benjamin visited was handsome Dennis Daly, the bibliophile, member from Galway and celebrated for his good cellar and fine library. Grattan, who often went there, describes the mansion:

At Mr. Daly's we dined among his books as well as at his table. They were on it, they were lying around it. They were always in his mind which was as well stored with literature as the shelves of his library.[12]

Daly's library would appear to have been a most congenial environment for our Pennsylvania visitor, although there remains only a fleeting reference to his having been there on one occasion. Eight years later, while Franklin was in France, Daly removed to London and Lord Charlemont recorded the end of the noble books which the American had seen in Dublin:

You have, I suppose, been informed of the evil destiny of Daly's books. The ship on which they were embarked foundered off Beachy Head and all the first editions are gone to the bottom.[13]

Franklin's most voluminous Irish correspondent, after his departure from Dublin, was the Collector of Excise, Sir Edward Newenham of County Cork who represented the borough of Enniscorthy in the Irish Parliament. If our Agent met the Collector at all during his stay in Ireland, it must have been immediately after his arrival, for the Dublin newspapers note that Sir Edward sailed for Holyhead on the Bessborough packet on the eleventh of September and did not return until the eighth of October.[14] Newenham afterwards became an ardent advocate of American rights and gave a somewhat rash demonstration of his attachment to the cause by appearing in the Irish Parliament in deep mourning after the arrival of the bulletin announcing the death of the gallant General Montgomery, who fell in the attack on Quebec. Later in the war, when Colonel Ethan Allen of the American Revolutionary army was captured in Canada and brought into Cork, Sir Edward showed the prisoner many courtesies and sent him luxuries and wine.[15] Three years afterwards the situation was reversed and Sir Edward, while making a continental tour with his two sons and a Swiss tutor, was detained at Marseilles as an English enemy when the French entered the American War of Independence. He wrote to Franklin reminding him of his good will to America and particularly of his kindness to Ethan Allen, and requesting that he be allowed to stay in Marseilles without molestation. The Envoy exerted himself in Newenham's behalf and finally secured for him a passport to Ostend and Ireland.

After Franklin had returned to Philadelphia in 1785 his Irish admirer bombarded him with requests for a bust to be installed upon a niche especially built for the purpose in the Newenham library. The bust finally came and the grateful recipient showed his appreciation by ordering the construction of a Connemara jaunting car, which vehicle was actually sent out to Franklin from the port of Galway and arrived in Philadelphia just as the delegates were assembling for the Constitutional Convention of 1787. We have no details as to its reception, but may speculate on the shock to the correct Mr. Washington and the dignified Mr. Jay if they chanced to see their venerable colleague, the former Envoy to France, riding down the High Street perched precariously upon an Irish jaunting car.

The great omission of Franklin's sojourn in Ireland is the lack of evidence of any contact with Henry Flood, then at the head of his powers and influence, the unchallenged leader of the Opposition, before the star of Grattan had risen. It is inconceivable that Franklin and Flood, who moved in the same circles of Dublin society, did not meet, but a careful search has failed to disclose any proof of such an encounter.

These in the main were the representatives of the official-dom of Dublin as Poor Richard saw them in the year of salvation 1771. One could wish, however, for a closer insight of his private companionships. With whom did he stroll over the bridges spanning the Liffey? Who guided him through the maze of lanes which encircled the old castle?

"I hope Billy and Jemmy continue well and will always be as happy as when I knew them," [16] he wrote to William Deane of Dublin two years after his visit. This letter carries a suggestion of cordial intimacy, but we know little of Mr. Deane or his family except that they lived on Dawson Street and that Deane held the position of Clerk of Recognizances. Still more nebulous is the figure of Richard Woodward, Dean of Clogher, to whom Franklin bore messages from his Irish friend in London, Miss Martin. Then there was the Reverend Sammy Pullein from Dromore, sometime chaplain in the establishment of Lord Charlemont. Pullein dabbled in silks and had gained the Madder Prize of the Royal Dublin Society for his translation of the Latin poem "The Silk Worm." Mr. Franklin, whose desk in Craven Street was covered with specimens of American silks, corresponded with Pullein and saw him in Dublin, but we know nothing of their conversation.[17]

It is probable that Franklin and Jackson carried with them to Ireland many letters of introduction, but we have definite knowledge of only two. In writing to Deborah in

August 1771 Benjamin mentions that Bishop Shipley has given him letters to "The Primate and Mr. Jackson." "The Primate" was the magnificent Richard Robinson, Baron Rokeby, Archbishop of Armagh and Metropolitan of Ireland. "Mr. Jackson" was perhaps the Right Reverend Doctor Charles Jackson, Dean of Christ Church, Dublin, and Lord Bishop of Kildare, whose country residence lay seven miles from the city amid the foothills of the Wicklow mountains. After Franklin's return from the Irish journey, he wrote to Bishop Shipley to acknowledge Primate Robinson's affability and to speak of his happy relations with the scholarly Dean.

*London, December 14th, 1771*

I should have thanked you before for your kind letter to the Primate and Mr. Jackson. The Primate was at Armagh and did not come to Dublin until just as I was leaving it. He was exceedingly polite and condescended to honour me with his particular notice in the House of Lords and at the Lord Lieutenant's but I could not accept his hospitable invitations being fully engaged for the little time I had to stay, and my fellow-traveller impatient to be gone on account of pressing Business.

In my life I never saw people more earnestly desirous of obliging a Stranger or more anxiously intent on showing Respect to a Recommendation than the Jacksons and their brother a Mr. Philips.[18] Yet I could not once afford myself the pleasure of dining with that agreeable Family being entangled with numerous engagments in Town and they live in the Country about seven miles from Dublin. It is a handsome Seat, the Gardens and Fields belonging to the house very beautiful, as well as the surrounding prospects. The house is well built, copied, one would think, from yours at Twyford so similar is the disposition of the rooms, stairs, chimneys, etc.[19]

Not the least congenial of Franklin's friends in Dublin, we may suppose, was his fellow craftsman Kettilby, the printer and typefounder of Mitre Alley, who had written over to Craven Street in the preceding year, and whose letter may have partly inspired the journey to Ireland. Kettilby had a shop under the shadows of St. Patrick's Cathedral and hard by the dingy deanery where Swift scribbled page after page of *Gulliver's Travels*. While Franklin was in Dublin, Kettilby advertised in the *Hibernian Journal* inviting subscriptions for *Dr. Bryom's Universal English Short Hand*.[20] An accurate Irish historian [21] claims that the type sold by Kettilby anticipated by six or seven years Henry Johnson's logographic type. When Walter of the *London Times* took over Johnson's invention, he had some correspondence with Franklin, who seems to have made experiments in the same direction. Perhaps the visit to Kettilby first attracted Benjamin's attention to the matter.

The approved gathering place for the Dublin literati of the period was the bookshop of the celebrated, one-legged George Faulkner. O'Keefe described him as "a fat little man with a large well-powdered wig and brown clothes who told good stories about Swift and provided his guests with abundant claret." [22] It was Kettilby's habit to go once a day to Faulkner's shop and it is likely that he took Franklin there, for Franklin afterwards, in semi-sarcastic vein, referred to Faulkner's printing.[23]

In the company of all these agreeable and talented Irishmen the stay of our tourists in Dublin must have been both pleasant and advantageous. It is hardly likely, however, that Franklin and Jackson would have so long protracted their visit except for the circumstance of the approaching opening of the Irish Parliament. Jackson seems to have been a rather restless fellow traveler, since Franklin tells us that he was "impatient to be gone on account of pressing Business." But Benjamin, who had been a member of the Pennsylvania Assembly and had witnessed the functions of the London Parliament, was anxious to see the Commons of Ireland. He vaguely pictured the Hibernian body as a group of patriots whose problems and aspirations were very similar to those of his own colonial assemblies, and looked forward to the opportunity of observing them in session.

# Chapter IX

# THE PARLIAMENT OF IRELAND

TUESDAY, the eighth of October, was officially set for the opening of the Irish Parliament. During the weeks preceding, the inns of the metropolis began to be filled with the members and their families. From Wexford and Cork in the south, from Galway and Ennis in the west, and from Armagh and Londonderry in the north lumbered the ponderous coaches of the gentry of Ireland, drawn often by steeds whose ragged fetlocks betrayed recent usage with the plow. The taprooms were scenes of nightly conviviality; play ran high at Antrey's Club and at Daly's Ordinary. It is true that there was much distress in Dublin this autumn and that the public dinners usually given by the Lord Mayor and the Sheriff were abandoned, the fund being appropriated for charity. Indeed, so acute was the crisis that the Mayor, the Right Honorable George Reynolds, announced from the Mansion House, only three days after Franklin's arrival, that Stephen's Green would be let out for pasturage. However, with Parliament about to convene, an Irish capital could not be dull; there were fireworks at Ranelagh Gardens and performances at the theatre in Smock Alley and at the Royal Theatre in Crow Street. On the Curragh race track Xaverius Blake's bay gelding Trojan beat the Right Honorable Thomas Connolly's bay horse Stroaker. There were public debates at the Music Hall in Fishamble Street, one of which in particular should have interested an erstwhile printer's devil from Philadelphia, since the subject was "Whether a Papist Ought to Be Permitted to Publish Political Tracts in a Protestant Country."

The great day arrived at last, the time of the assemblage of the august Peers and devoted Commons of Ireland with all the power and fashion of the land gathered at the Capitol to hear the opening address of the Viceroy. Dublin was in a ferment; the church bells rang; the guns of the Castle boomed in salute. Crowds lined the streets through which the Viceroy and his glittering escort must pass. Of course, being Irish, the rabble could not remain quiet for long and sometimes united in the strains of a highly disrespectful ballad, then very popular in Dublin, and sung with all the more gusto because few of the ragged rapparees who chanted it could grasp its full import.

> To Albion's Ear ye Breezes bear
> This tale of Ireland's woe,
> That Worth alone exalts a throne
> And Vices bring it low.

However, these evidences of disaffection were soon drowned in loyal acclaim as the state vehicles rolled out of Sackville Street and Merrion Square and Rutland Square to deposit the aristocracy of Dublin at the doors of the new Parliament House on College Green.[1]

Now the fanfare of trumpets and the boom of cannon announced to the waiting thousands that the Viceroy had left the Castle, and presently the imposing procession could be descried descending to the Green, Lord Townshend in his robes of ceremony, the Earl of Hillsborough carrying the Sword of State, the Earl of Tyrone carrying the Cap of Maintenance, and "a nobleman's son" reverently bearing the train of the viceregal robe. Slowly and majestically the cortège moved across the Green and was swallowed up by the great portal of the Parliament House.

When Franklin and Jackson, following in the wake of the array, entered the great hall (now altered to the ignoble purposes of banking) with its sixteen Corinthian columns supporting the rich hemispherical dome, they found the Viceroy already mounted upon his throne of state; Black Rod had been dispatched to summon the Commons, and these came presently crowding into the chamber. The

[ 155 ]

combined assembly was one which might compare in attainments and eloquence with the great parliaments of all time. Swift, the irascible Dean of St. Patrick's, whose biting sarcasm spared none, described the body as

> Scarce a bow-shot from the College,
> Half the world from sense and knowledge,

but in point of fact, few gatherings counted members of such outstanding ability and unique personality. As the visitors gazed about them they might note the spare, graceful form of the imperious Flood, the Olympic features of the venerable Dr. Lucas, Anthony Malone from Westmeath, an early advocate of Catholic emancipation, and the scholarly Dennis Daly from Galway. Massed beside the Speaker's forum were the peers, the noblest names in Ireland, the Duke of Leinster and Lord Charlemont, Lord Tyrone, Lord Drogheda, and Lord Hillsborough. There, too, were the spiritual dignitaries, the lawn-sleeved prelates of the established church, Henry Maxwell, well-beloved Bishop of Meath, Dr. Trail, Bishop of Down, Agar, Bishop of Cloyne, who read Greek as fluently as English, and Robinson, the haughty Primate of Armagh.

Lord Townshend began to read his address, felicitated the members upon the excellent health enjoyed by his Majesty at Windsor (a matter in which they evinced little interest) and then proceeded to the inevitable prodding for revenue. At this there were cat-calls and disturbances in the galleries, and the Viceroy in a temper threatened to have the house cleared. So that Franklin's first experience with a Hibernian public assembly was typical and turbulent.

No honors were accorded to Franklin upon the occasion of the opening ceremony just described; his reception, so often referred to, occurred in the Commons' Chamber two days later. On that morning Jackson and Franklin entered the hall and were on their way to the Visitors' Gallery when they were noticed by the Speaker, Viscount Pery

THE IRISH HOUSE OF COMMONS IN FRANKLIN'S DAY

from Limerick, who had met them at Lord Townshend's reception in the Castle. Then ensued the scene which Benjamin described with such dignity to Thomas Cushing of Boston in his letter of the thirteenth of January in the next year:

Before leaving Ireland I must mention, that, being desirous of seeing the principal Patriots there, I staid till the Opening of their Parliament. I found them dispos'd to be friends of America, in which I endeavoured to confirm them, with the Expectation that our growing Weight might in time be thrown into their Scale, and, by joining our Interest with theirs might be obtained for them as well as for us, a more equitable Treatment from this Nation. There are many brave Spirits among them. The Gentry are a very sensible, polite, friendly and handsome People. Their Parliament makes a most respectable Figure, with a number of good Speakers in both Parties, and able Men of business. And I must not omit acquainting you, that, it being a standing Rule to admit Members of the English Parliament to sit (tho' they do not vote) in the House among the Members, while others are only admitted into the Gallery, my Fellow Traveller, being an English Member, was accordingly admitted as such. But I supposed I must go to the Gallery, when the Speaker stood up, and acquainted the House, that he understood there was in Town an American Gentleman of (as he was pleas'd to say) distinguish'd Character and Merit, a Member or Delegate of some of the Parliaments of that Country, who was desirous of being present at the Debates of his House; that there was a Rule of the House for admitting Members of English Parliaments, and that he did suppose the House would consider the American Assemblies as English Parliaments; but, as this was the first Instance, he had chosen not to give any Order in it without receiving their Directions. On the Question, the whole House gave a loud, unanimous Aye; when two Members came to me without the Bar where I was standing, led me in, and placed me very honourably. This I am the more particular in to you, as I esteemed it a mark of respect for our Country, and a piece of politeness in which I hope our Parliament will not fall behind theirs, whenever an occasion shall offer.

There is an amusing strain of ingenuous vanity in this recital and, reading betwixt the lines, we may infer that few events in Franklin's long and varied career gave him more pleasurable satisfaction. We are restricted to his own account for the details since no minute of the reception is entered upon the records of the Irish Parliament.

This gesture of the Commons, so spontaneous and gracious, was devoid of practical result. Franklin wrote optimistically about the help which might be expected for the American cause from the Dublin legislators. But, four years later, when the news came of the battle at Lexington, this same Parliament put themselves on record as expressing "abhorrence and indignation at the unnatural Rebellion"; Flood himself encouraged recruiting, and four thousand Irish troops went out to fight under the English flag in America.[2]

Nor was the conclave whose members rose to pay their tribute to the distinguished Philosopher from Philadelphia on that October day in 1771 in any sense a representative body. Probably when Deborah and William Franklin received Benjamin's pleased account of his reception on the floor, they pictured a group of ardent patriots similar to the Congress which was shortly to convene at Philadelphia for the assertion of American rights against a headstrong sovereign. Nothing was further from the truth. This Dublin Parliament, so rich in the talents and abilities of its members, was a British-controlled convocation of professional men and large landholders representing but a small proportion of the seven millions of people who then congested the Emerald Isle.

Even the rich and important Presbyterian interest of the North, which symbolized so large a part of the industrial wealth of the land, had little voice in the government. As for the Roman Catholic Celts who comprised three-fourths of the population, they were totally disenfranchised and had little more influence in the deliberations of the Dublin Parliament than had the pigs which they tended. They led a starveling, hand-to-mouth existence, raising the precarious crop of potatoes upon which they lived, shivering over their peat fires and hoping for the best. Not only was the Roman Catholic peasant forbidden to vote, but even possession of property and the public exercise of his religion were prohibited to him under the strict letter of the law. When Franklin, seeking to please his affable Dublin hosts, stated:

It is a fact that the Irish emigrants and their children are now in Possession of the Government of Pennsylvania by their majority in the Assembly as well as of a great part of the Territory, and yet I remember well the first ship that brought any of them over,

he meant emigrants from the Protestant North. Such settlers as came to Pennsylvania from the South of Ireland were indentured servants. The Agent could not foresee the mighty Celtic influx which was to follow the famine of 1845 any more than he could envisage the rollicking, devil-may-care Teague in knee breeches with pick on shoulder and clay pipe in the band of his old caubeen, the character so familiar in antebellum American caricature.

Benjamin, who had prolonged his stay in Ireland that he might witness the ceremonies of the opening of Parliament, now began to think of bringing his visit to a close. He had been away from home for seven weeks and in Ireland five weeks. His stay so far exceeded his original calculation that he seriously debated the giving up of the journey to Scotland and wrote to Henry Marchant that he might come directly back from Dublin to London.[3] However, he had promised Lord Kames a visit and the temptation once more to see his old associates in Edinburgh was too strong to be resisted. So on Thursday, October tenth, when the Irish Parliament adjourned after a short and tempestuous session of three days, Franklin and Jackson made immediate preparations for departure.

# Chapter X

# DUBLIN TO SCOTLAND

THE most direct route from Dublin to Scotland and Edinburgh led northward through Drogheda and Belfast to the little port of Donaghadee in County Down, where there was a packet service to Port Patrick in Scotland, twenty-one miles opposite, the shortest traverse between Great Britain and Ireland. Perhaps Franklin, if left to his own inclination, might have preferred a tour in the South with a visit to Wexford, where his friend Dr. Lucas had a property, and a glimpse of the autumnal glories of Killarney. But he was pressed for time and besides, even before the travelers left England, it seems to have been understood that they were to go to Ulster, for they carried letters from Bishop Shipley to Robinson, Archbishop of Armagh. Robinson was no longer in Armagh, having come down to Dublin for the opening of Parliament, but Franklin adhered to his original intention.

It must always be regretted that the only excursion which our tourist made out of Dublin was to the manufacturing North. Ireland, then as now, was an agrarian country with the real wealth and character of the land typified by the great cattle fair at Ballinasloe. Franklin speaks glibly in his correspondence and in his *Address to the Irish People*,[1] published seven years later, of the economic problems of Ireland, absentee landlords, restriction of exports and misgovernment, but it is not clear that he might not have enunciated these platitudes with as much authority from his desk at Craven Street or from the printing office in Philadelphia. Poor Richard, the greatest commoner of his age, saw little of the commonalty of Ireland. Under the guidance of the fastidious Richard Jackson he

[ 160 ]

moved about in Dublin from the Castle to Leinster House, from the Rotunda to the Assembly in Fishamble Street. But Jackson associated with absentee Irishmen, who spent the most of their time in London or Bath. His circle in Dublin was a brilliant but scarcely representative one of claret-drinking squireens, government functionaries feeding upon an impoverished country, and luxurious clergymen of the Established Church of Ireland who had plenty of leisure for literary discussions, since the contumacious population from whom they wrung their tithes never darkened the doors of their empty churches.

Nor could Franklin learn his Ireland by the medium of romantic narration. Here as in Scotland he came too early to meet those who were first to interpret the real soul of the island. He had been in Edinburgh before the day of Scott and Burns, and now when he was in Dublin the sincere delineators of Irish character, Tom Moore and Maria Edgeworth, Samuel Lover, Charles Lever, and Gerald Banim were unborn or in the cradle. Benjamin's comments on the aboriginal population, after a six weeks' stay in Ireland, are curt and casual: "They live in wretched hovels of mud and straw, are clothed in rags and subsist chiefly on potatoes"; which sounds very like the observations of a traveler in Africa in our own time who gives a passing, curious glance at the native kraals.

Franklin's expense ledgers, now at the American Philosophical Society, throw some light upon his last days in the Irish capital. On September twenty-third he obtained £32 Irish (less a commission) from Oliver Plunkett of Dublin. Plunkett was a merchant on Usher's Quay who did a banking business as a side line. Whether the amount advanced to Franklin was a loan or whether it represented merchandise purchased, is not clear. In any event, our Agent later borrowed £75 Irish from Richard Jackson, probably in contemplation of the large stock of linen which he was to buy in Ulster.

The tourists must have left Dublin on Monday, the fourteenth of October, for on the following day they arrived at Lord Hillsborough's mansion in County Down. From Dublin they had a choice of two lines of Drogheda stages, one setting out from the Boot Tavern in Boston Street and another from Mrs. Robinson's ordinary in Bolton Lane. The turnpike was acclaimed as better than similar roads in England, but the expedition was not without its perils. The marauding bands known as the Heart of Oak Boys and the Heart of Steel Boys (said to be the progenitors of our own unsavory Mollie Maguires of a later date) still raided the countryside and occasionally held up mail coaches.

Before the departure, however, there occurred the memorable meeting between Franklin and Lord Hillsborough at the Lord Lieutenant's reception in the Viceregal Lodge at Dublin, an encounter which was to alter the original plan of travel and must be described at length. Wills Hill, Viscount Hillsborough of Hillsborough in the County Down, was an Irish nobleman of wealth and station, who had been Secretary of State for the American Colonies since 1767. In this position he had many negotiations with Franklin, and some of their interviews had been unsatisfactory, even turbulent. Ten years later, in the disastrous November of 1781 when the news of Cornwallis' surrender at Yorktown had convinced all England of the hopelessness of attempting further coercion against America, the old Peer staggered to his feet in the House of Lords to express the hope that Great Britain would never acknowledge the independence of the revolting colonies, ending his philippic with the dramatic warning: "America lost, everything which we possess as a great trading and maritime nation must shortly follow." [2]

Franklin, who had little cause to love the uncompromising old nobleman, scored him unmercifully in a letter to Samuel Cooper:

His character is conceit, Wrongheadedness, Obstinacy, and Passion. Those who speak most favourable of him allow all this; they only urge that he is an honest man and means well. If this be true, as perhaps it may, I wish him a better place where only Honesty and Well-meaning are required.[3]

From which prelude it would seem that when Benjamin crossed the Irish Sea, the last person whom he might expect to meet on friendly terms would be Lord Hillsborough; and yet at the levee in Dublin Castle the two men did meet, with a resultant bearing upon the visitors' itinerary. Franklin's own account of the occurrence is contained in his letter of January 30, 1772, to his son William:

We met first at the Lord Lieutenant's. Mr. Jackson and I were invited to dine there, and when we came, were shown into a Room, where Lord H. was alone. He was extreamly civil, wonderfully so to me whome he had not long before abus'd to Mr. Strahan, as a factious turbulent Fellow, always in Mischief, a Republican, Enemy to the King's Service, and what not. He entered very frankly into Conversation with us both, and invited us both to stop at his House in Hillsboro', as we should travel Northward, and urged it in so polite a Manner, that we could not avoid saying we would wait on him if we went that way. In my own Mind I was determin'd not to go that way, but Mr. Jackson thought himself oblig'd to call on his Lordship, considering the connection his Office forms between them. His Lordship dined with us at the Lord Lieut's. There were at Table, the Lord Chancellor, the Speaker, & all the great Officers of State. He drank my Health & was otherwise particularly civil.

Despite these overtures, Franklin was not convinced of his Lordship's sincerity and decided not to visit the village of Hillsborough. The town lay on the direct road to Belfast but could be avoided by digressing to the westward and passing through Armagh. Benjamin had good reasons for wishing to call at Armagh. He would be interested to meet his correspondent and fellow member of the Royal Society, the learned Dean Hugh Hamilton whose recent pamphlet, *Remarks and Hints on the Improvement of Barometers,* had attracted much attention. Jackson must have been in somewhat of a dilemma, for being a politician and anxious to retain a seat in Parliament he could not afford to jeopardize the good will of the influential Hillsborough. Franklin's recital as to why he gave up the trip to Armagh and went instead to Hillsborough is as follows:

He [Lord Hillsborough] went from Dublin some Days before us, And when we were on the Road, it was my purpose to have turn'd off for Armagh on a visit to Dean Hamilton, let Mr. Jackson go to Hillsborough alone, and meet him at Belfast; But it so happened that where we were to have parted, no Post Chaise was to be had for me, nor any other to proceed with but that we came in, so I was oblig'd to go forward with Mr. Jackson to Hillsborough, and as soon as his Lordship knew we were arriv'd at the Inn he sent a Message over for us to come to the House. There we were detained by a 1000 civilities from Tuesday to Sunday.[4]

The mansion where Lord Hillsborough entertained his guest from Pennsylvania was demolished some years afterwards to make room for the palatial structure now occupied as a residence by the Duke of Abercorn, Governor of Northern Ireland. The Hillsborough family no longer dwell there, and the present Lord, who takes the title of Marquis of Downshire, lives in England and seldom visits the land of his ancestry.[5] Of the village which Franklin saw, little survives except the beautiful stone church with its graceful spire, the pride of the countryside, which was in course of erection in 1771.[6] Hillsborough was very vain of his church (under which he lies buried) and must have taken great pleasure in explaining his plans to the American visitor.

My Lord affected great state, and had a castle guard with cocked hats and Dutch breeches modeled after the escort of William of Orange "of glorious memory." For all of his foibles he was a good landlord, beloved by his tenants, and his pertinacity only made itself apparent in affairs of state. He posed, too, as a sponsor of the muses, and it was under his patronage that Goldsmith brought out *The Deserted Village*.

This quiet Ulster hamlet offered a grateful interlude for the relaxation of two travelers jaded with the gaieties of a Dublin season in parliamentary year. The estate ranked as the model of all Ireland, and Arthur Young, who went there in 1776, was impressed by its order and cleanliness which afforded such a contrast to the slatternly villages of the South.

Lord Hillsborough has marked the approach to his town by many small plantations on the tops of the hills. Hillsborough is a well-built and flourishing town and the inn is a noble one for Ireland.[7]

Almost the only details of the stay of Benjamin at Hillsborough are those contained in his letter to Thomas Cushing:

He [Lord Hillsborough] seemed attentive to every thing that might make my Stay in his House agreeable to me, and put his eldest Son Lord Kilwarling into his Phaeton with me to drive me a Round of Forty Miles, that I might see the Country, the Seats, Manufactures, etc. covering me with his own Great Coat, lest I should take Cold. And in short, seem'd in every-Thing extreamly solicitous to impress me, and the Colonies thro' me, with a good Opinion of him.[8]

This "Lord Kilwarling" (more properly termed Arthur Hill, Lord Kilwardin, later Earl of Hillsborough and second Marquess of Downshire) who so graciously guided Franklin during his stay in Ulster, was then in his eighteenth year and was an undergraduate at Magdalen College, Oxford. When he succeeded his father in the peerage of Downshire, he reversed the political traditions of his family by espousing the patriot side in Irish politics, and even refused a dukedom rather than vote for the iniquitous Union of 1800.[9]

Kilwardin was in France on his honeymoon in 1786, but

as Franklin had just terminated his embassy at Passy and gone home to Philadelphia, it is not likely that the two men ever saw each other again after the meeting in Hillsborough. There is, however, a curious circumstance connected with this same French tour of the young Irish peer. While visiting in the city of Lyons he made the acquaintance of a Frenchman named Charpentier and some courtesies were exchanged. Three years later, at the advent of the Reign of Terror, Charpentier, feeling himself about to die, sent his two children, a girl and a boy, over to the charge of Lord Kilwardin in England. His Lordship, although somewhat embarrassed by the responsibilities thus thrust upon him, accepted the trust and sent the boy out to a position in the East Indian service. The girl, Charlotte Charpentier, was put into the household of the Dean of Exeter, who conscientiously rebaptized her into the Church of England and brought her up as his daughter. Years passed and in the fall of 1797 the Bishop and his family, including Charlotte, went for a holiday among the English lakes where the party remained for some weeks in a hotel at Gilsland. Down from Edinburgh came a young lawyer, slightly lame, with few briefs and small prospects, much given to the reading of Border ballads and old Scots romances. His name was Walter Scott; he promptly fell in love with the engaging French exile; and the two were married on Christmas Eve at St. Mary's Church, Carlisle. But the nuptials could not be solemnized without first obtaining the consent of Charlotte's guardian, the Marquess of Downshire, the same amiable Lord Kilwardin who had driven Franklin through the winding lanes of Ulster on those chilly autumn mornings forty-six years before.[10]

While we have Franklin's statement that he remained at Hillsborough House until Sunday, the twentieth of October,[11] there is no certainty as to where he went in his excursions about the county. Those familiar with the terrain and with the state of the roads at the period estimate that if he drove with Lord Kilwardin over a circuit of forty miles, he may have called at Armagh. If Benjamin really went to Armagh and paid his respects to Archbishop Robinson, he must have been received with great pomp, for Richard Cumberland writes that the prelate maintained the state of a Prince Palatine and rode out from his palace in a coach drawn by six horses with three running footmen behind.[12] However, the Agent, in writing to Bishop Shipley after his return to England, speaks only of the courtesies shown to him by the Archbishop in Dublin and makes no mention of a visit to Armagh.

A suggestion of how the Ulster countryside may have looked to our American tourist in 1771 is afforded by the recital of James Boswell, who visited Hillsborough two years before.[13] Boswell pronounced the scenery between Hillsborough and Belfast as the finest he had ever seen and was particularly interested in the linen industry.

It was very agreeable to see the number of bleach-fields, the cloths looking so white on the green grass and the people looking so clean.

The Scotch gardener Atkinson, from Dunse, who showed Boswell about the house and grounds, is likely to have performed the same service for Franklin and Jackson since he remained in Lord Hillsborough's employ for twenty-three years.

At some point in his Ulster excursion, probably at Lisburn, where the Huguenot emigrants had established their looms, our Agent acquired the formidable amount of linen which is noted in his Account Book.[14] For Mrs. Stevenson his purchases aggregated £75 Irish currency, or £69 English currency. To Deborah he sent a more modest consignment for which he dispensed £6 5s Irish currency, or £5 15s English currency. Deborah's parcel, to which Franklin alludes as "a fine piece of Holland," was sent via the island of Antigua and through the agency of the Philadelphia sea captain All who happened to be in Ireland. Captain All's presence is rather surprising and is perhaps explained by the announcement in the *Dublin Gazette* of the approaching departure of the snow *Ambrose* from Londonderry for Philadelphia laden with "servants." The trade in Irish indentured emigrants was as brisk and scarcely less inhuman than the slave traffic between Guinea and Charleston at a later period.

Franklin's visit at Hillsborough could well have had an important bearing upon the destinies of the North American colonies. The stage seemed all set for a fortuitous agreement; but the issue was disappointing. The two men were fairly representative of their respective countries. Franklin, Agent for four of the colonies, was the acknowledged spokesman at London for all. Lord Hillsborough was Colonial Secretary for North America, had the ear of the King, and was high in the councils of his party. It might have been expected that two such experienced politicians would have reached some compromise whereby the rising discontent in America would be allayed and the ensuing hostilities averted. More than once in English history, meetings at country houses have prevented political crises no less formidable than the one which impended in 1771. But at the Hillsborough conference no accord could be attained; perhaps because neither of the parties trusted the other sufficiently. Franklin asserted that the noble Secretary "threw me away as an orange that would yield no more juice and therefor not worth more squeezing," and that he was not even received when he called upon Lord Hillsborough in London to thank him for the civilities shown him in Ireland. As for his Lordship, it does not appear that after the obligations of hospitality were concluded, he was ever again on terms of cordiality with his distinguished guest. In fact, a few months later he uttered the classic observation, recorded by Fitzmaurice, that "Ben Franklin instead of walking the streets of London ought to be in Tyburn or Newgate."

A personal and detailed search in the archives at Hillsborough and Belfast yields no hint of Franklin's movements

from Saturday, the twentieth of October, when he terminated his stay at Hillsborough, until the following Saturday
when he arrived at Edinburgh. His probable crossing, and
indeed the only one which he could have made in the
limited time allowed to him, was from Donaghadee to Port
Patrick. His host, Lord Hillsborough, went over to England
by this same ferry a few weeks later. Franklin and Jackson
may have gone directly to their point of embarkation,
Donaghadee, by way of Newtown, and so have avoided Belfast, but it is scarcely likely that such alert travelers would
pass so near that important and thriving town without a
visit, unless indeed they had already driven to Belfast with
Lord Kilwardin.

Once arrived at Donaghadee, the tourists could put up
at the Hillsborough Arms (a wretched hostelry, it seems,
since Boswell describes it in emphatic phrase as "a bad
house") [15] and observe the misty mountains of Galloway
looming up over the waters of the strait, with the thatched
roofs of Port Patrick and the rocky, winding lane leading
eastward to Stranrear and Ayr. The passage, though short,
had an evil name. Boswell engaged his own private boat
and went immediately below, but got very sick nevertheless.
Franklin afterwards told his Edinburgh friends that he got
across between two storms, so perhaps he escaped the tempest which had raged for weeks in the Irish Sea.[16] How he
got over and when he took leave of Richard Jackson we do
not know, but on Saturday evening, the twenty-sixth of
October, he descended at his inn in Edinburgh, and David
Hume wrote Strahan that Mr. Franklin was arrived at last
after as many adventures as had been endured by St. Paul.

# Chapter XI

# EDINBURGH AGAIN

BEN FRANKLIN rode through the Cowgate Port of Edinburgh and alighted at his tavern twelve years, almost to the day, since he and William had left that city for Berwickshire to visit Lord Kames. The Agent was alone now and William was in the great Government House at Burlington in New Jersey, sick and despondent after endless bickering with a recalcitrant Assembly.[1] The bells of St. Giles's were tolling a merry peal, and the innkeeper explained that it was the anniversary of the King's accession. Benjamin could well remember the corresponding day in 1760 when he was returning to London from his trip through Wales and was informed of the death at Kensington Palace of poor, blind George the Second, the hero of Dettingen, and how all the court was hurrying to Saville House in Leicester Square to pay their respects to the new sovereign, King George the Third.

Twelve years had made a difference in Dr. Franklin. He was no longer as active or alert as when he and Billy had walked the High Street from the Castle to Holyroodhouse. His eyesight, too, was beginning to fail, although it was to serve him for nineteen additional and eventful years. If our visitor, on the morning after his arrival, took his stick for a walk amid the once familiar scenes, he would observe that the good town was also changed in the interval. The same smells assailed his nostrils, the same tireless caddies ran upon their endless rounds, the same stalls lined the Canongate, but there were mutations and improvements. His old lodgings at Milne Square had been altered and the eastern end of the great "land" partly demolished to make room for a splendid bridge which spanned the ravine to the northward. Provost Drummond's dream had come true!

The unsavory Nor Loch extending beneath the windows of Franklin's chambers of other days was drained, the hollow bridged, and the new town was groping out over the braes where sheep had grazed in 1759. As he passed the Council Chamber in High Street he could look up to the windows behind which he and William had stood to receive the Freedom of the City. John Dalrymple, a younger brother of Lord Hailes and a Director of the Royal Bank, had succeeded as Lord Provost. He was not likely to make any gesture of official recognition, for he was unfriendly to America, and had he foreseen all the developments of Dr. Franklin's mission in Great Britain he might have been even less cordial. For during his second term of office, in 1778, the worthy Provost was to be much vexed by the raids of American privateers upon the shipping in the Firth.

Time had dealt lightly with the old literary circle, except that Provost Drummond and Lady Dick were dead.[2] Lord Kames had inherited the estate of Blair Drummond, and lived for part of the year in the Perthshire Highlands. But despite these omissions the former associations remained almost intact. Robertson was Principal of the college and had just published his *History of Charles the Fifth*. Across the Firth of Forth in Kirkcaldy, Adam Smith was writing the last pages of his *Wealth of Nations*. Even old Peter Williamson was still living in the Luckenbooths. The former Indian captive had closed his tavern in Parliament Hall and was preparing material for the first Edinburgh directory, eking out a precarious subsistence meanwhile by selling cards for fortune tellers.[3] His garrulity had not decreased with the passing years, and it was remarked that the gruesomeness of the details of his stories of Indian cruelty had amplified with much telling.[4] The foppish student, James Boswell, who had stared at Franklin when he visited the University in 1759, was now a popular figure and posed as a champion of the rights of man. Only a few weeks before he had conducted the Corsican patriot, Pascal Paoli, on a triumphant tour through the streets of Edinburgh.

If on that first morning Mr. Franklin leaned on the parapet of the new North Bridge and looked curiously across at the expansion of the town, west of the Calton Hill, he might have observed a recently finished house in St. David Street south of St. Andrew Square, a structure which bore a singular resemblance to his own dwelling in Philadelphia.⁵ This was the mansion to which his friend David Hume had just removed from his former lodgings in James's Court. The Agent, who must presently return to the discomforts of an Edinburgh inn, would have been relieved to know that he was that very day to exchange his primitive quarters for the luxuries of the Hume residence. Once installed in his pleasant domicile, he hastened to inform Strahan of the good fortune.

Edinburgh, Oct. 27, 1771

Dear Friend,

Thro' Storms and Floods I arrived here on Saturday night, late, and was lodg'd miserably at an Inn; But that excellent Christian David Hume, agreeable to the Precepts of the Gospel, has received the Stranger and I now live with him at his House in the new Town most happily. I purpose staying about a Fortnight, and shall be glad to hear from you. I congratulate you on certain Political Events that I know give you Pleasure. Let me know how it is with you and yours, how my Wife does and Sir John Pringle, and our other Friends.

With sincerest Esteem, I am, my dear friend<br>Yours most affectionately,<br>B. FRANKLIN

The thrifty Mr. Hume, cannily embracing the opportunity to get a free letter through to London on the frank of his distinguished guest, wrote to Strahan two days later.

Edinburgh, Oct. 29, 1771

You will see by the franking of my letter whom we have with us. I was so happy as to prevail on the Doctor to be my guest during his stay here, which we hope will be for ten days or a fortnight. He got over from Ireland in a short interval between two hurricanes by a particular Providence. At least I hope that he considers it in that light.

> I am, dear Strahan,
> Yours, etc.
> DAVID HUME [6]

When Franklin appeared in Edinburgh, Hume had just returned from a visit to the Duke of Argyle at Inveraray, and it may be that the American was the first guest in the dwelling in St. David Street. Peggy Irvine, the cook who had ruled the Hume establishment at James's Court in the old town with a rod of iron, now presided over the new house. She had possession of the front door key and probably regulated Dr. Franklin's movements just as she did those of the rest of the household. David was very proud of his house and of the culinary proficiency of his Peggy, protesting that her sheep's head soup was the best in the world, and that "the Duc de Nivernois would bind himself apprentice to my lass to learn to make sheep's head soup." Hume aimed to make his new residence not only the intellectual but the gastronomic center of Edinburgh, and loved to go into the kitchen and concoct a *soupe à la reine* after the recipe given him in France by Madame de Boufflers. Henry McKenzie, "the man of feeling," praised a *bouilli* which David cooked for him, and Boswell marveled at three kinds of ice cream.

What a wealth of interest must have lain in the talks of these two great philosophers during the fortnight of Franklin's sojourn! They had not seen each other since Benjamin's last Scottish trip except for an occasional casual meeting in London. In the interval both had traveled much, and they could chat of their friends in many lands, of Pringle and Strahan in London, of Newenham and Charlemont in Dublin, of Dalibard and Dubourg, the Marquise de Deffand and Madame de Boufflers in Paris. Unfortunately no details of their conversation survive, and the accounts of Henry Marchant, who was present at many of their sittings, are all too concise and uninspired.

There is little of moment to record concerning Franklin's movements for the next four days or until his meeting with Marchant on the Thursday after his arrival. From what Dr. Robertson told Marchant we learn that the Agent called at Edinburgh University, and while there saw his old friends Doctors Cullen, Black, and Munro. As he passed down the narrow College Wynd he could have noticed at the window of the second story a short, swarthy woman holding an infant boy then eight weeks old. The house was that of Walter Scott, Writer to the Signet, the woman was his wife, Ann Rutherford, and the baby was another Walter Scott whose fame was to ring down the ages with as much insistence as that of Poor Richard himself.

Principal Robertson had been sick before Franklin's visit to the University, and in the faculty minutes his absence at the meeting on the fourteenth of October "because of indisposition" is noted. He left his sick bed, however, to greet his American caller, and by the following Wednesday was sufficiently recovered to write and arrange an interview.

Henry Marchant had left London some weeks after Franklin's departure for Dublin, and journeyed northward by easy stages to arrive in Edinburgh two days after the Agent's coming. Marchant was accompanied during this excursion by a fellow colonial whom he terms "Mr. Church of Boston" to whom a degree of interest attaches because this "Mr. Church" was Edward Church, Harvard 1759, son of Benjamin Church the Indian fighter, and younger brother to the notorious traitor Dr. Benjamin Church, Jr.[7] Marchant and Edward Church had been boyhood playmates in the old days at Newport. Afterwards Church went on to Harvard and Marchant to the College of Philadelphia, each graduating in his respective institution with the class of 1759. When Marchant was sent to England in 1771 as the official agent of Rhode Island for the adjustment of some claims arising from the French and Indian War, he induced Church, then an auctioneer and merchant in Boston, to accompany him. The two men lived together in London, and when Marchant went to Scotland, Church recollected that his sister Elizabeth had Scottish connections living at Kirkliston, nine miles west of Edinburgh, and decided to go along.

Elizabeth Church had married a Scotch printer named John Fleming, who came to Boston and published a loyalist newspaper called *The Boston Chronicle*. He was an avowed Tory and had much to do with the subsequent downfall of his brother-in-law, Dr. Benjamin Church, who once ranked high in the patriot councils as a stout Whig and a colleague of Warren, Hancock, and Samuel Adams.[8] In 1775, during the siege of Boston, when Dr. Church was tried for espionage and treason by a tribunal presided over by Washington himself, his conviction was based upon the evidence of an agent,[9] who carried letters through the lines from the accused physician to Fleming in Boston, presumably for delivery to General Gage. Edward Church, who had no share in the disloyalty, saw his brother thrown into Norwich jail whence he was released after some months of imprisonment, a broken and disgraced man. On a night in June 1776, Edward rowed the culprit down the Charles River and put him on the sloop which was to bear him into ignominious exile in Jamaica. The two brothers never saw each other again for the vessel foundered and all on board were lost.

In 1771 no shadow impended as yet over the honored name of Church, and Edward spent much of his time while in Scotland with his sister's relatives at Kirkliston and in particular with Alexander Fleming, John's older brother. He saw little of Marchant and Franklin until the expedition to Glasgow in November.

Marchant had recommendations from Dr. William Hunter of Rhode Island to Mr. David Bennet, a functionary of the Edinburgh post-office, who received the American courteously and secured him lodgings at an inn. Neither Marchant nor Franklin knew of the other's presence; the Rhode Islander supposed that Benjamin was still in Ireland until informed by Robertson that he was actually in Edinburgh. The description in his diary of the first meeting with Franklin is as follows:

Mr. Bennet wrote a line to Dr. Robertson last Evening informing Him that I would wait upon Him this Morning if he was at Leisure. Dr. Robertson returned him for Answer that He should be proud to wait upon me but as he was this Day engaged upon Publick Affairs if it would suit as well he should be glad to wait upon me at his House to breakfast with Him Tomorrow Morning—When he should have the Pleasure of having Dr. Franklin also at his House to introduce me to. But nevertheless if it was not convenient he would put Affairs in such a Situation as to wait upon me to-day. Mr. Bennet had returned him for an Answer that he was sensible Tomorrow would Answer as Well. The Intelligence of Dr. Franklin's being around in the City gave me inexpressible Pleasure, as I had given over all Hopes of the Dr's. coming at all to Edinburgh. He having wrote from Ireland that he believed he should return from thence directly to London.

This was on Wednesday; the occurrences of the following day, the thirty-first of October, are again set forth in Marchant's diary:

Went with Mr. David Bennet to Breakfast with Dr. Robertson Who rec'd me with much Politeness. At Breakfast His Lady & Daughter with two other young Ladies set at Table— His Daughter about 18 is very handsome & conducted the Tea Table with much Ease—His Lady was also very agreeable, the Conversation was much on America's Affairs. The Geography of ye Country &c &c with somewhat respecting Scotland—& England and her Policy with the Colonies. Dr. Robertson from his Conversation I take to be a Friend to Civil & Religious Liberty & fully imagines America must in some future Period be the Seat of a Mighty Empire. After Breakfast he waited upon me to see Dr. Franklin, who lodged with the Celebrated Mr. David Hume in an Elegant House in the New Part of the City.

Mr. Hume is a Gentleman I should think of about sixty very large & heavy built. His Face is by no Means an Index of the

Ingenuity of his Mind, especially of his delicacy & vivacity. But in Truth he is a very pleasant Gentleman in Conversation. One Mr. Allexander one of the first Merchants in Edinburgh was also in Company—and displayed great Knowledge in ye trade of Europe & America. The Meeting Dr. Franklin with all this good company was vastly agreeable. It was one o'clock before we parted.

The "Mr. Allexander" mentioned by Marchant was Robert Alexander, an Edinburgh merchant of the firm of William Alexander and Company, whom Franklin first met while visiting the Dick mansion at Prestonfield. The two men corresponded, and in 1770 Robert endeavored to persuade the Agent to come by sea from London to Leith and Edinburgh, thanking him at the same time for his interest in the purchase of a pianoforte. So devoted was the merchant to Franklin that he commissioned Benjamin of London to paint the Philosopher, a portrait which hung as late as 1876 in Airdrie House, Airdrie, Scotland.

Now Dr. Robertson's diploma mill begins to grind once more, and there is injected into our narrative still another of the many applications from American scholars seeking Scottish degrees through Franklin's influence. This particular solicitation came as usual from a Harvard man, for the relations between Harvard and Edinburgh at this period seemed to have been as close as those between Harvard and the University of Göttingen half a century later. John Winthrop of Boston had graduated at Harvard in the class of 1732 and was almost as old as Benjamin himself. He was an astronomer of note, held the chair of mathematics and natural philosophy at his college, and is said to have been Franklin's main support in his theories on electricity. Already in 1766 Ezra Stiles had written to Craven Street to intimate that it would be very appropriate if Winthrop were made a Fellow of the Royal Society. Again in 1768 the Reverend Samuel Fayerweather of Cambridge, Massachusetts, wrote Franklin a rambling letter about his baptisms and his beagle dogs, deftly interposing the suggestion that if Franklin intends going back to Edinburgh, it will be highly advantageous for his friend Professor Winthrop to have a degree.[10] Winthrop himself must have had some reason to hope that an academic honor would be accorded him, for he sent some money by Marchant to Benjamin, presumably for the diploma.[11] The good Dr. Robertson was perfectly willing to oblige any deserving friend whom Dr. Franklin recommended, but no one got a degree at Edinburgh without paying the costs. The degree of LL.D. was duly granted, and Marchant's comments upon the transaction are illuminating:

Dr. Robertson informed me that upon the application of Dr. Franklin, London, to Him he had procured a Degree of Dr. Law for Dr. Winthrop Professor of Natural Phylosophy in Cambridge, New England. That he Dr. Robertson was told that application had been made first at Oxford College but upon discovering Mr. Winthrop was a Dissenter, they for that circumstance alone refused to give him a Degree. How has Bigotry beset the World that it should so insinuate itself into the learned Class of Mankind.

On Friday the two Americans went their separate ways. Marchant spent the day rambling about the palace of Holyroodhouse with Henry McKenzie, whom he describes as "a most pleasant agreeable man, the author of *The Man of Feeling* which speaks his mind, heart and ability." Mr. Franklin's occupations on this day are not disclosed. The *Edinburgh Advertiser* for that date gives a belated announcement of his coming and relates that at noon a salvo of guns was fired from the Castle, not in honor of a visiting scientist from America, but because the day happened to be the anniversary of the Gun Powder Plot. On Saturday the Agent was again with Marchant.

Saturday, Novr. 2d. This morning Dr. Franklin waited upon and breakfasted with me. And we had a good Dish of tete-a-tete. The conversation upon American Affairs &c &c lasted till one o'clock. The Doctor was pleased to open very freely & to enter minutely into Many Matters, interesting as well as entertaining. Mr. Church & his Friend, Mr. Allex'd Fleming, dined with me at our Inn & we spent the Afternoon together—And in the Evening we all went together to Mr. Flemmings 8 miles out of ye City at a Village called Kirkleston.

Marchant stayed at Kirkliston over Sunday and was taken to the church next door to the Fleming residence for a doleful Calvinistic exercise with an interminable sermon. Franklin remained in Edinburgh for the sabbath, but whether he attended divine service from the house of the godless David Hume is not disclosed.

On Monday the weather turned inclement, with a light fall of snow. Marchant rode back to town and was pleasantly surprised by a call from Dr. Franklin. The reasons which brought the Philosopher plodding through the slush of the long North Bridge soon made themselves apparent. The visitor first announced that he was empowered to offer Marchant a degree from the inexhaustible supply of the complaisant Edinburgh University.[12] He then invited the younger man to go with him upon a western tour which should include a visit to Glasgow and a stay with Lord Kames at his new estate, Blair Drummond. Marchant, much flattered at being asked to make so agreeable an excursion in distinguished company, accepted promptly. The details must have been gone over at this meeting in the tavern, for on the next day the journey is spoken of as completely arranged. Afterwards the Rhode Islander escorted his caller back to St. Andrew's Square where they both dined with David Hume.

I had not been arrived at my Inn many Minutes before Dr. Franklin come in to see me & by a most open disengaged Frankness in his Conversation afforded me much Pleasure and made me a genteel Tender by honorably commending me to the Edinburgh University. He brought me also the Compts. of the Celebrated Mr. David Hume, inviting me to Dine with Him in Comp'y with the Dr. which I accepted.

Being only with ourselves we set with much free Sociability

till after Tea in the Evening when his Servt. lighted me Home. I mention this last Circumstance as his Servt. refused to take Money saying it was not customary nor allowed of. This is much to the Honor ye Edinburgh Gent'm. if it is indeed general.

On the next morning, Tuesday, the fifth of November, Benjamin's pleasant vacation routine was rudely broken by the arrival of a dunning letter from his old associate, John Balfour the printer.[18] The vexatious specter of the unpaid account for the books sent twelve years before to James Parker reared its head again. Balfour had somehow found out that Franklin was in Edinburgh, and wrote politely but insistently to inquire what the Doctor could do about his bill. There is no suggestion that Franklin paid up, but it is characteristic of his meticulous preservation of letters that he should have brought Balfour's missive back with him to London and Philadelphia. That the annoying episode did not prevent him from buying more books in Edinburgh is evidenced by his sending four shillings to Nourse, the London bookseller, after his return, for "transportation of books bought in Edinburgh."

Marchant's diary apprises us that the day so inauspiciously begun had a more agreeable ending. He had gone on that same Tuesday morning to hear some medical lectures at the College and there received an invitation from Franklin to dine with the faculty, again at the house of that indefatigable entertainer, David Hume.

*Dr. Franklin* sent me a Billet desiring to see me at *Mr. David Humes.* I waited upon Him and it was to sup with them and with the Faculty. Accordingly I supped with Them. We were introduced to the President & so to all the Members; And here I found all the Doctors whose Lectures I had heard in the Morning. At the Hour of Eleven o'clock we excused Ourselves as Dr. Franklin and I had agreed to set by six in the Morning for Lord Kames at Blair Drummond 6 miles beyond Stirling.

Franklin had now been upon his travels for ten weeks. One would suppose that after his perilous crossing from

Ireland and the toilsome journey northward, he would be inclined to relax quietly in the congenial atmosphere of the Hume mansion. However, there were several motives which prompted him to make a western trip. Lord Kames had invited him to Blair Drummond, and our tourist was naturally curious to see the marvelous estate of which he had heard so much; Professor Wilson had written from Glasgow to describe a new type of his own manufacture which he wished his American colleague to inspect; old John Anderson was still at Glasgow University and waiting to exchange reminiscences about the Highland journey which he had made with Franklin in 1759. Marchant, whose imagination fired at the idea of a glimpse of the west of Scotland, was eager to set out, so Wednesday, the sixth of November, the morning after the dinner with the faculty, was fixed for the departure.

# Chapter XII

# JOURNEY TO GLASGOW

I T required some hardihood on the part of a portly philosopher to rise an hour before dawn on a snowy morning, but the wintry days were all too short and Poor
Richard had opined, "Let not the sun look down and say
'Sluggard here he lies.' " When Wednesday morning broke,
the American's post-chaise was well on its way to Linlithgow. That bower of the ancient Scottish royalty, so
attractive to the modern tourist, had no charms for Franklin and Marchant, and they merely lunched there ("breakfasted" Marchant says, but they had probably broken their
fast at Edinburgh) and then went on to Falkirk where they
became involved in the crowds gathered for the autumn
cattle fair. Now instead of pursuing the direct route to Glasgow, they turned sharply northward and passed the same
Carron Iron Works whose beginnings Franklin had noted
when he and William rode through these parts in 1759.
The infant forge which had timidly advertised "Dr. Franklyn's Pennsylvania stoves" had developed into a flourishing
industry shortly to be connected with the outside world by
the Forth and Clyde Canal. The Agent, knowing that he
was to visit Carron a few days later, gave the establishment
only a passing glance, his interest being focused upon the
new canal which was the work of his friend and correspondent Smeaton of Leeds.[1] When our voyager first passed
by Carron, Smeaton was on the wave-beaten islet of Eddystone in Plymouth Harbor, putting the last courses on the
famous lighthouse which was illuminated in October 1759.
Franklin had never seen Eddystone, but he was now to view
Smeaton's second important engineering achievement, the
Forth Canal.

Marchant, in whom the Agent seems to have instilled

some of his own enthusiasm, describes the journey up to Falkirk and the appearance of the great ditch as the two colonials saw it on that November day in 1771.

Novr. 6—At half after 6 o'clock set out in a Post Chaise with Dr. Franklin—made our first Stage 16 miles to Lin Lithgo, a considerable Village where we breakfasted and then proceeded to Falkirk a very considerable Town at which there was a Fair —Just beyond Falkirk we crossed the famous Canal now cutting from the Forth which leads from the open Sea at the East of Scotland by Forth & Edinburgh to Stirling &c— This Canal begins near the most noted Iron Works in Brittain called the Caron Works and leads to the River Clyde which from the open Sea the West Side of Scotland up to Grenoch the Seaport for & near to Glasgow. So that a Communication will be formed from Sea to Sea by this Canal when finished. It was at first calculated to cost abt 70,000 Sterl. but it is not now expected to be finished under 200,000 Sterling. Crossing at the Head of the Works we got out of the Chaise & examined it for some Distance then went six or seven Locks or gates for letting in & shutting out the Water the Ground being here uneven. And at this place the Road is to run under the Canal.

The inspection of the canal must have been brief, for in the middle of the same afternoon the travelers were so far advanced that they could descry the great gray rock topped by the battlements of Stirling Castle. The place has changed little since Franklin's day but, of the thousands of American tourists who annually scramble over these same walls and admire the prospect of the Highland hills above the winding links of Forth, very few ever pause to think of Poor Richard puffing and panting along Stirling's ramparts in 1771.

We arrived at Stirling abt. 3 o'clock. We just spared Time to take a View of the Country round & the Forth which runs from Edinburgh. We went up to the Castle and had from thence a most extensive Prospect of the Country below—The Everlasting Hills covered with Snow Adjacent:—And the River Forth on the Side directly under you yield a most delightful Prospect, giving you the true Serpentine:—As in the Distance of 4 miles it makes in its Turnings 24 miles English & from this Eminence you see every Turning.

Marchant's narrative now takes a practical turn suggesting a thrifty appreciation of a good bargain in its reference to the product of the local looms.

At Stirling and the Villages around, the best Tartans, or what we in America call the Plaids, is manufactured. The Scotch call that which the Men or rather Women wear made up into what serves for a Cloak & covering for the Head.

Along the highway which leads northward from Stirling to Doune still stretch the walls of the great estate of Blair Drummond. In our day graceful beeches line the barrier and give a suggestion of the arboreal glories of the domain within. There is no fairer manor in all Scotland, and Sir Walter who visited here extolled the charms of the little river Beith which glides gently on its shaly bed disclosing new beauties at every turn. The present hall, now occupied by Sir Kay Muir, is near the site of the old lodge (destroyed by fire) where Franklin stayed. The trees which the American visitor planted are still shown, and every memory of his stay is sedulously preserved.

The Kames family, whom Franklin had last seen at their Berwickshire estate in 1759, were now installed at Blair Drummond. Lady Kames had inherited this property in 1766 and the family removed there almost immediately. It was a more comfortable residence than their former home on the Border, and more convenient for My Lord's duties in Edinburgh. Here too the justice found ampler scope for the agricultural experiments which were his particular hobby. Our ingenious Benjamin must have been interested in the method which his host had evolved for clearing the estate of a layer of peat which encumbered it. The contrivance was the wonder of the countryside at the time, but is now only imperfectly understood. Sir Kay Muir has made some investigations and thinks that Lord Kames built gigantic sluices by which the peat was washed into the neighboring river Forth. Why the stream was not choked up in the process is not clear. Franklin must certainly have inspected this project and it is to be regretted that his notations, if he made any, have not survived.

Marchant, who had never seen so fine a patrimony in Rhode Island, was frankly delighted.

Novr. 7th. The Ground is all covered with Snow; it began to Snow before we arrived at his Lordships last Evening. However, the Sun for a rarity shining very pleasant his Lordship took Us out with Him to see his Farm And we had a fine Walk of several Miles by the side of a most beautiful River. Our Walk was greatly diversified with here a Nursery of Trees then a considerable Wood of Planted Trees—bold lofty Hills, Plains & Valleys— Stirling Castle from its Highth appearing to Us— The River gliding by the Mills in it, Salmon sporting in it— Upon the opposite Bank a handsome Seat of a Neighboring Gentleman and a little forward still the grand Remains of an Ancient Castle.[2] No longer necessary, since laws are become the Security of Men's Lives and Fortunes.

My Lord's Seat is truly Noble his House & Gardens elegant and His entertainment to Us Sumptuous & Lordly and hospitable. His lady very good very sensible— His Lordship I take to be about 60 years old & yet very alert. He has a Son very sensible & affable and greatly improved by a two years absence at Italy & Rome.

Novr. 8th The Morning is most delightful. We took a Walk of 9 or 10 Miles round & returned with a good appetite to an elegant Dinner. In Short—The Days are now so short that scarce anything can be done but eating, drinking & sleeping. The sun rising 32 minutes after 7 and setting 52 Minutes after 3 o'clock. But in the Morning as well as in the Evening I enjoy much sensible Conversation from his Lordship & Dr. Franklin.

The walk which Marchant describes so enthusiastically, with its views upon the winding river and the ruined battlements of Doune Castle, remains practically unchanged, and

[ 185 ]

the present-day visitor may follow the same path over which Lord Kames guided Franklin and Marchant in 1771.

It may be that Benjamin was not wholly unprepared for the charms of the promenade. At Lord Bath's house in London in 1767 he had met Mrs. Elizabeth Montagu, a cousin to Primate Robinson of Armagh and the writer of Shakespearian essays, who had just visited the Kames family. If they talked of their mutual friends at Blair Drummond her ladyship could give Franklin some premonition of the scenic delights which awaited him. Her own description, contained in a letter to Lord Kames, reflects Marchant's ardor.

I remember perfectly the walk your Lordship mentions and all the beauties of that sweet place. It is happy for a person of your taste to find in his morning's walk the pastoral, the epic and the tragic beauties. The gently murmuring river, the shady banks, the beautiful pastures, the noble castle of Stirling rising in the pride of an impregnable stronghold, defying force and time, and the ruined castle of the Regent.[3]

On Friday the Americans had determined to bring their stay at Blair Drummond to a close, and sent a messenger to Stirling to arrange for a post-chaise. However, their courteous hosts prevailed upon them to remain until the following Monday, inviting them at the same time to share their own family coach as far as Stirling.

Novr. 9 Saturday rose early having determined last Night to set off for Glasgow—His Lordship having offered to & pressed upon Us His Coach & four Horses, as we could not get any Post Chaise. But upon reflecting upon the Matter we concluded rather to give up going to Glasgow than accept His Lordship's too kind offer. And We at present conclude to stay till Monday when His Lordship & Lady set out for Edinburgh for the Court there— We made but a small Walk today as the Weather was rather damp & windy.

Novr. 10 Lords Day. Spent this day chiefly in Reading & Conversation. The Day being very pleasant for Scotland we took a small walk.

The pleasant stay at Blair Drummond had been so long protracted that the Americans decided to abandon their original plan of going to Glasgow and proposed instead to return to Edinburgh. An unlooked-for accident of the road caused them to revert to their first intention. Marchant's diary continues:

Novr. 11th Monday Morning rose before Light & got ready to push for Edinburgh but it was raining and the rising of the Wind increasing to very great Storm which lasted all Day we were put by— But our Entertainment here made the Disappointment agreeable.

Novr. 12th A pleasant Morning the Dr. & I set out with His Lordship & Lady in their Coach & four for Edinburgh— But at Stirling six Miles from His Lordships Seat we obtained a Post Chaise which we took & leaving His Lordship proceeded to Glasgow upon our intended Plan. We had a bad dirty heavy Road & finding no Post Chaise upon the Road we were obliged to go the whole Distance with our First Horses which is 35 Miles from Stirling. We got into Glasgow however by half after six o'clock & here again met with Mr. Church, my Companion from London, who had got in but half an Hour before Us. His Friend Mr. Flemming & one Mr. Stewart of Maryland were with Him & we all supped together.

The "Mr. Stewart of Maryland," while not absolutely identified by the diarist, is almost certain to have been George Home Steuart, eldest son of Dr. George and Ann Digges Steuart of Annapolis. Dr. Steuart had come to Maryland from Perthshire in 1720. He retained an interest in a property at Argaty in Scotland so that when his son, George, Jr., came to Edinburgh in 1758 for his education, he elected to stay and supervise his father's estate. He never went back to Annapolis, married a niece of Lord Rolls through whom he acquired the site of the battlefield of Bannockburn, with valuable coal mines, and died in Scotland in 1800.[4]

The reunion at Glasgow must have been a joyous one.

Dr. Franklin could receive the latest Edinburgh news and relate of his entertainment at Blair Drummond and the fine folk he met there; his young friends could felicitate themselves upon the opportunity to spend an evening with the famous scientist from overseas. It was as well, however, for some of the blithe participants that they were afforded no premonition of their own future. From time to time in the recital of Franklin's second trip to Scotland there comes a sinister suggestion of an impending fraternal conflict. We seem to snuff powder, and our theme unfolds to a vague but ominous accompaniment of Revolutionary drumfire. The destinies of the four youths, one Scotchman and three Colonials, who sat at meat with Franklin on that November evening in Glasgow were to be materially affected by the prospective breach.

During the War for Independence Steuart and Flemming remained in Scotland, temporarily cut off from communication with their friends and relatives in America. Edward Church stayed in Boston, well affected to the patriot cause but distrusted after his brother's treason. Marchant became a member of the Committee of Correspondence in Rhode Island and a delegate to the Continental Congress.

In September 1780, when the American revolt was in its sixth year and whilst Franklin was envoy at Passy, his attention was recalled to the Scottish tour by the arrival of a missive from Alexander Flemming from Kirkliston, asking for intelligence of Marchant and wondering why his letters were unanswered. Marchant was then delegate for Rhode Island to the Congress at Philadelphia and probably little disposed to correspond with the enemy. If Franklin replied, his epistle has not survived.

Four years later, and one year after the conclusion of the war, Franklin was again reminded of the pleasant meeting at Glasgow by a letter from Edward Church written, somewhat unexpectedly, from Dunkirk in France. The stigma cast upon the family name by the defection of Dr.

Benjamin had not helped his affairs and he had essayed to transfer his business from Massachusetts to St. Eustatia in the West Indies. This venture was unsuccessful and in the autumn of 1783 Church left his wife and four children in Boston and came over to Dunkirk. From here he wrote to Franklin asking for an appointment as American consul at Dunkirk.[5] Franklin could nor or did not interest himself in the matter and Church seems to have remained in France for some years vainly seeking an occupation. When Washington became President the exile wrote to him a plaintive missive reciting his woes and his attainments and reiterating his application for a consular post.[6] This appeal was more effective and Church was appointed American consul at Bilbao, Spain (the actual duties of which post he seems never to have assumed) and at Lisbon in Portugal.[7]

One inexplicable circumstance connected with Edward Church's visit to Glasgow in 1771 is that he should have been elevated as a Guild Brother of the town and received the Freedom, an honor not accorded to Franklin, who was in Glasgow at the same time.[8] The embarrassed compiler of the Church genealogy, struck with the discrimination against an illustrious fellow countryman, ventures the apologetic suggestion: "Letters in the possession of Edward Church's descendants indicate that Franklin also received the Freedom of the City of Glasgow." [9]

There is, however, no notation on the minutes of the Glasgow corporation to show that Franklin was so distinguished.

When Benjamin took his stick on the following morning to stroll through the well-remembered streets of Glasgow and look in at the university, he met many friends whose acquaintance he had made on the occasion of his first visit in 1759. The Foulis brothers were there to greet him cordially and display proudly their new issues, Xenophon in twelve volumes, their Milton and their Pope. The brothers had enlarged their collection of dubious old masters, and the gallery was one of the sights of the town. The opinion of an American scientist concerning the authenticity of these works of art was probably of little value; the final disillusionment came five years later when Robert Foulis took the collection to London and saw it sold for a song in Christie's auction room.

Professor Alexander Wilson awaited Franklin in his dwelling on the College Green and exhibited a new type matrix, his own production, which he hoped the great Master Printer would prefer to the specimens recently inspected in Kettilby's shop at Dublin.

Eccentric old John Anderson, Franklin's companion on the journey to St. Andrews twelve years before, was still in college, writing voluminous essays which were never to be read, and still quarreling with his fellow members of the faculty.

Probably Benjamin looked forward to meeting James Watt, whom he had last seen in 1767 in Craven Street and whose experiments with the embryo steam engine he had followed through his correspondence with Matthew Boulton. However, Watt no longer maintained his shop in the University Quad and seems to have been absent from Glasgow during Franklin's visit. Marchant does not mention his presence, and Watt himself tells us that he was engaged in the survey of the Forth and Clyde Canal and "leading a life of much vexation and bodily fatigue, of hunger, cold and wet feet." [10] In all his tribulation Watt found time to act as engineering adviser of the Carron Works and to develop his steam engine in collaboration with Dr. Roebuck of Kinneil. Some of the parts for this engine were then being cast at Carron, and perhaps Franklin's curiosity to see them may partially account for his visit to the Works a few days later.

Other absentees whose presence had afforded so interesting a feature of Franklin's visit in 1759 were John Witherspoon, formerly of Paisley, and James Wilson, formerly of St. Andrews, later of Glasgow University. Both men were far overseas, Witherspoon busied with his academic duties at Princeton and Wilson trying to eke out a living by practising law at Carlisle in Pennsylvania. If the visitor inquired for them the worthy Lord Rector of the University might shake his head, for the rumors from America were to the effect that both of these renegades had become politically disaffected, had allied themselves with the rebel cause and were spreading sedition against the government which had nurtured them. Perhaps the circumstance injected a certain coolness into the Rector's greetings to Franklin.[11]

Marchant, who accompanied his fellow traveler everywhere during the stay, has given us a detailed description.

Novr. 13th Wednesday. We rose, breakfasted & dressed and then I accompanied Dr. Franklin to the College to see some of the Professors his old acquaintances.

We were well entertained in the Morning by viewing the Colleges. A grand Collection of Paintings there antient & Modern tho' chiefly Antient. Not less than several Hundred, many of them done by the best Hands. Here is an Academy of Painting detached however from the University in which youth exercise themselves in that Noble Art. And also in Engraving. Here is also one of the grandest Foundry of Types in Europe carried on by Dr. Willson & his Sons. The Printing Business is also carried on by Messrs. Fowlis and all these within the College Walls. Mr. Anderson, Professor of Natural Phylosophy, carried Us into the different Rooms where the University operates:—Phylosophical &c.

We dined with Mr. Anderson: drank Tea at Dr. Leeds, Professor of Moral Phylosophy, & supped at Dr. Willsons before mentioned. And in all our dining etc had the company of six or eight of the Professors of ye University— [12]

Wrote a letter to my wife from Glasgow for New York and enclosed it in one to my Friend John Murry.

Novr. 14th This was a great First Day in Glasgow— I walked through the town viewed the Cathedral, a most noble Building about Six hundred years old—& which narrowly escaped with one more in the North of Scotland the heated zeal at the beginning of the Reformation. There are three Churches or Places of Worship in it.

The Churches of which there are seven or eight exclusive of what they call meeting Houses (that is to say the Churches of England) are neat & elegant especially a New Church which for situation, elegance, neatness & Convenience is equal to almost anything you meet with in England of the Modern Churches— I attended Worship in this Church in the Forenoon.

In the College they have also a Neat elegant Library Room and a good Collection of Books. Dr. Willson & his Son carried me to their Observatory which is a good Building for the Purpose and will be furnished with the necessary Instruments. I dined in Company with Dr. Franklin, Mr. Church & his friend Mr. Flemming &c at Mr. Cunningham's. An ingenious young man. He has a Grand Brewery, the largest in all Scotland. The Works, Vaults &c of this are very curious and we were well entertained with Them. They brew Porter & What they call Bristol. Both extremely good—

We drank tea at Dr. Wilsons & supped at Mr. Millar's Professor of Civil Law. He has lately published a small Quarto Volume.

The City of Glasgow most agreeably disappointed me.

It is a very well built & regular Town in a very thriving State as to its Commerce and Increase of its Inhabitants.

They have plenty of very fine Stone— The Canal now cutting from Sea to Sea must be of great Commercial Consequence to Glasgow especially.

The Exchange is a large good Building at the Head of ye Cross, in front of it stands a fine Equestrian Statue.

After a stay of three days, Church, Flemming, and perhaps Steuart went directly back to Kirkliston and Edinburgh. Franklin and Marchant left Glasgow early on the morning of Friday, the fifteenth of November, for a sojourn at the Carron Iron Works near Falkirk. Marchant says that the invitation to Carron came from Samuel Garbett, one of the partners, whom Franklin had met at Birmingham in 1759, and from his son-in-law Gascoigne. Smeaton, too, had an interest in the firm and it is possible that he may have suggested a visit. And there is always the interesting hypothesis that Franklin went to Carron to inspect the steam engine which Watt and Roebuck were developing there.

The travelers arrived at Carron on the afternoon of the same day of their departure from Glasgow, and now there stalks into this recital of Ben Franklin's Caledonian wanderings the glamorous figure of debonair Charles Gascoigne, general manager of the works. He was the son of an English army officer, Captain Woodrove Gascoigne, and his wife, the Honorable Grizel Elphinstone, daughter of a Scottish nobleman, Charles, ninth Lord Elphinstone. In his youth he had studied chemistry and then acquired an interest in the Carron Works by the time-honored method of marrying his employer's daughter. At the period of Franklin's visit the manager was enjoying a salary of £4,500 a year, and lived in great state at his mansion Carronpark, situated on the wooded knoll just to the west of the foundry. He received the Americans in his wonted style of lavish hospitality, but there were rumors even then, that the plant was extending its operations at too rapid a pace, that its borrowings were enormous and the creditors much concerned for the safety of their loans. Perhaps the shrewd traveler from overseas marked the extravagance of the establishment and muttered something about "Who Dainties love shall Beggars prove." Financial failure on a large scale was rare in Scotland during the eighteenth century since industry was little advanced and no one was reared high enough to achieve a fall. Gascoigne, however, by his reckless administration did manage to encompass a bankruptcy a few months after Franklin's departure. His innocent father-in-law, Garbett, was forced to flee from Scotland to escape the outraged lenders, and Gascoigne soon followed him.[13]

Once out of Scotland the discredited manager took his revenge in a highly unbecoming manner. The best customer for the cannon made at Carron had been Catherine the Great, Empress of Russia, who was then assembling a fleet of war vessels on the Black Sea. Gascoigne offered his services to his former buyer and was accepted. He not only took over into his new employment the secrets of his former firm, but actually induced many of the skilled artisans to leave Carron and go with him to Russia. Gascoigne never returned permanently to Scotland. Once he stole back under an incognito, but was recognized by exasperated creditors and escaped by night in a fishing smack. Franklin had been in his grave sixteen years when, in September 1806, the Philadelphia newspapers announced the death, at the Ordnance Factory of Petrozavodsky, of General Charles Gascoigne, Knight of the Order of St. Vladimir, the same adventurer who had welcomed the American visitors in 1771 and who was now dying in exile.

Marchant's account of the reception at Carron is as follows:

Novr. 15th. Set out early in the Morning, for Carron Iron Works 27 rough miles from Glasgow. Mr. Garbett and his Son in Law Mr. Gascoigne are the present Proprietors of it.

Dr. Franklin had an Invitation by those Gentlemen to call and see them.

We got at Carron Works about Three o'clock just time enough to dine and found at Mr. Gascoigne's Lord Elphinstone, his Lady, and two Daughters, & it being too late to visit the Works today, they being a mile off we contented ourselves with an elegant entertainment & good Company.

The Lord Elphinstone with whom Franklin supped at Carronpark was Charles, tenth Lord Elphinstone, whose sister Grizel was Gascoigne's mother.[14] Lady Elphinstone was the former Clementina Fleming, and the two Elphinstone daughters were Mary, who died unmarried in 1825, and Clementina, who fifteen years later married James Drummond, the Jacobite Earl of Perth. Lord Charles Elphinstone's younger brother George was the admiral who commanded the blockading squadron off New York Harbor during the American Revolution and who arranged for the transportation of Napoleon to St. Helena in 1815. It is interesting to record that the Lord Elphinstone, Knight of the Thistle, of our own day, the great-great-grandson of the nobleman whom Franklin met at Carron, is brother-in-law to the present Queen of England.

The entertainment at the Gascoigne residence took place on Friday evening and the next day was devoted to a tour of the plant. So few and small were the Scottish industrial establishments of the period that most visitors were taken to see the Carron Works as the almost unique example of the country's economic development. A few weeks before Franklin's arrival, Boswell had brought General Paoli ("that land-louping scoundrel of a Corsican," as the elder Boswell termed him) and the Polish Ambassador at London to inspect the foundry, duly noting in Marchant's exact phrase that his party was "elegantly entertained by Mr. Gascoigne." Some time afterwards there appeared at Carron one Sunday morning a wandering poet named Robert Burns, none the better for his potations at a neighboring public house, who sought admission under an assumed name. The scandalized watchman refused him entrance both because of his condition and because of the breach of the Sabbath, whereat the indignant bard went back to his tavern to compose a rhyming protest.

> We came na here to view your warks
> In hopes to be mair wise,
> But only lest we gang tae hell.
> It may be nae surprise
> But when we tirled at your door
> Your porter dought na hear us,
> Sae may, should we to hell yett come
> Your billy Satan sair us.[15]

To which the assistant manager of Carron, a certain Mr. Benson, replied in kind:

If you came here to see our works
You should have been more civil
Than to give a fictitious name
In hopes to cheat the Devil.
Six days a week to you and all
We think it very well;
The other, if you go to Kirk
May keep you out of Hell.

Curiously enough, the ordnance which the Americans saw being cast during their walk through the Carron Works was to be employed by their own countrymen against the land which molded it. For when the primitive patriot navy came into being four years later, the privateers which went out from Boston and New Bedford and Philadelphia, under stout Nick Biddle and Jack Barry and Paul Jones, were equipped with *carronades,* as they came to be termed, cast at the Carron foundry.[16] Marchant, much impressed but not always assured in his use of technical expressions, describes the operation:

Novr. 16th Saturday—After Breakfast we went to the Works accompanied by Mr. Garbett, a most ingenious Gentleman and indeed we were highly entertained with the Grandest Works I ever saw. Here we saw several Canon one of 32 ton's Casting. Large Pans for Sugar Works containing—Gallons—Pots—Kettles, Iron Money Chests—Stoves and Grates &c &c. Their Bellows is made of Iron, a large Iron Piston being raised up and down by Wheels turned with Water to make them Water Tight, the Pistons are covered with Leather. It is said that all Iron Stone is equally capable of making the best of Iron, the Difference is in the Process which is not yet sufficiently investigated. The Iron Stone is first Roasted in large Fires made in open Air—Then thrown into the Furnace mixed with Cole & a sufficient Quantity of Lime Stone which is absolutely necessary.

They pay a weekly £1500 to their Laborers exceptive of all other charges—

They make a Canon & other wrought Iron 80 Tons one week with another. They shared last Year £12000 Ster.—neat Profits, and they have as yet been Yearly at heavy Extra Charges.

After the visit at Carron the two colonials brought their tour to a close. Sojourns in Highland estates, reunions with old friends on the Glasgow campus, and the inspection of an interesting industrial establishment had made a journey replete with profit. Marchant's zeal for travel, if we may judge from his daybook, was unabated, but Mr. Franklin had been a long time upon the road and was beginning to have uneasy recollections of a neglected office in Craven Street. It was the Sabbath, but our wayfarers having already driven on that day would have no compunctions about further outrage of Presbyterian sanctimony. On Sunday morning, the seventeenth of November, they breakfasted with Gascoigne and Garbett, said their adieus, and took the highway for Falkirk and Edinburgh.

# Chapter XIII

# FAREWELL TO SCOTLAND

D
R. FRANKLIN left me a few days ago for the west but I expect him again in a few days," wrote David Hume to Strahan a few days before his American guest returned to the house in St. David Street. Franklin and Marchant negotiated the twenty-seven miles between Carron and Edinburgh with such expedition that they arrived at Mr. Hume's door at three in the afternoon. There is no intimation of any entertainment on this day of return, and it is possible that Franklin spent the evening in resting and discussing the trip to Glasgow with his host. He found time, however, to write to Strahan and to give a short account of his movements.

*Edinburgh, November 17, 1771*

Dear Sir:—

I have been at Blair Drummond on a visit to my friend Lord Kames, thence I went to Glasgow, thence to Carron Works, viewing the Canal by the way. Extreme bad weather detained me in several places, some days longer than I intended. But on Tuesday I purpose setting out on my return, and hope for the pleasure of seeing you by the Tuesday following.[1]

The Doctor did not depart on the following Tuesday (the nineteenth of November) as he had expected. Indeed he might have remained for a week longer if he had not received news from the South. The London stage arrived bringing a letter from his son-in-law, Richard Bache, whom he had never seen although four years had elapsed since young Bache married Sally Franklin. Richard had gone on a business trip from Philadelphia to Jamaica early in 1771. He returned thence to Philadelphia but was now in England, visiting his mother at the town of Preston in Lancashire. This circumstance explains both Franklin's sudden departure on Thursday, the twenty-first of November, and his choice of the western route in journeying back to London.

For the routine of Franklin's last four days in Edinburgh we are again relegated to Marchant's invaluable diary. One unaccountable omission in our Philosopher's second sojourn in the Scottish capital is his failure to call upon Sir Alexander Dick, then in residence at Prestonfield. Before David Hume became so stout, he set up as a pedestrian and used to make the circuit of Salisbury Crags every morning.[2] This path would take him by Prestonfield and, if his American friend went along, would afford the walkers an opportunity to visit Sir Alexander. It is unlikely, however, from what we know of Hume's condition in 1771, either that he had the physical stamina for such a promenade or that his guest would have been able to keep up with him. Franklin wrote to Sir Alexander in apologetic vein after his return to London:

*London, January 11, 1772*

Dear Sir,

My last Expedition convinc'd me that I grow too old for Rambling, and that 'twas probable I should never make such another Journey.—'Tis an uncomfortable Thing, the Parting with Friends one hardly expects ever again to see. This, with some occasional Hindrances, prevented my calling at Preston Field after my Return from Glasgow; But my Heart was with you and your dear Family, and my best Wishes attended you all.

It is rather surprising that no hint of discord between Franklin and Hume intrudes itself into Marchant's recital of Franklin's stay in St. David Street. Both host and guest were men of strong convictions, and it is not to be supposed that their discussions were always harmonious. Later, when the American debate began to wax in acrimony, Hume spoke of Franklin with considerable sharpness, and perhaps a premonition of future political differences intruded itself into the Edinburgh visit.

This period of Franklin's second stay in Edinburgh is the one usually ascribed for his alleged criticism and review of the manuscript of Adam Smith's *Wealth of Nations,* a supposition based upon the statement of Deborah Logan of Philadelphia.

Dr. Franklin once told my husband that the celebrated Adam Smith, when writing his Wealth of Nations, was in a habit of bringing chapter after chapter, as he composed it, to him, Dr. Price and others of the literati of the day.[3]

This vague reminiscence of Miss Logan's is the only authority for the claim that Franklin corrected or even saw the original draft of the *Wealth of Nations.* To have seen Adam Smith at all in November of 1771 he would have had to cross the Forth to Kirkcaldy, for the economist was in poor health and unlikely to come often to Edinburgh.

On the morning after Benjamin's arrival, Lord Elphinstone and his family, who had followed him up from Carron to the capital, called to invite the two Americans to dine at their house on the High Street below the Castle on the next (Tuesday) evening. The Doctor was already engaged to take dinner on that evening with Lord Kames but Marchant accepted. However, Franklin later called at the Elphinstone mansion and became greatly interested in John, the eleventh Lord Elphinstone, who had served under Wolfe, climbed the heights of Quebec with the regiment of Lascelle, and carried a musket ball in his neck as a souvenir of the campaign.[4]

On the same Monday of Lord Elphinstone's invitation, David Hume gave a large dinner party in honor of his distinguished guest from America. Here the visitor met Lord Kames, back from Blair Drummond, and some old friends from the University—Dr. Black, professor of chemistry, Russell, professor of physics, and Dr. Ferguson. Marchant, who was of the party, was much impressed by the sparkling post-prandial dialogue, observing rather patronizingly, "In such good company I could not fail of being entertained."

On Tuesday Hume and Franklin dined with Lord Kames at his house in New Street, and on Wednesday, the last day of the stay in Edinburgh, with Dr. Ferguson.[5]

By this time the Agent's bag was packed and his arrangements for departure made. He had anticipated the expense of the journey to London by cashing a check for £50 upon the Edinburgh bankers, Chaloner, Leslie, & Seaton.[6] This seems a large sum for a week's journey, but he would wish to repay Marchant, from whom he had borrowed three guineas, and he perhaps had other obligations. Then, too, although he was to travel alone he was allowing himself the extravagance of a post-chaise, an apparent prodigality to be explained by the circumstance that he wished to travel rapidly and that none of the regular coach lines advertised an immediate departure for Preston, which was his first destination.

So now on his last night in Edinburgh, Dr. Franklin might sit contentedly and know that his preparations were finished and that he was to take his farewell repast in most harmonious association. Marchant was there (he had spent the day in the Law Courts under the guidance of Henry McKenzie, the Man of Feeling) and Lord Kames and Dr. Robertson and Professor Russell and Dr. Black. Only Adam Smith, indisposed in Kirkcaldy, and Sir Alexander Dick, still rusticating at Prestonfield, were wanting to complete the circle of Franklin's Edinburgh friends. Dr. Ferguson, who kept up all the customs of his forefathers, prided himself upon the excellence of his claret, the traditional wine of the Scottish gentry from the time when it was drunk as a pledge to the alliance between France and Scotland. One can imagine the toasts and reminiscences and the sentiments of good will as the company bade adieu to their esteemed colleague from overseas whom they were never to see again.

Marchant tells us nothing of the depths of the potations at the farewell dinner. In any event he was given no opportunity to sleep off the fumes, for at daybreak Franklin's post-chaise was at the door and the Doctor entered his room to say good-bye. It had been understood that the Rhode Islander, still accompanied by Edward Church, was to ride down to London a few days later, and that their baggage and some of Franklin's was to be shipped by sea from Leith to Mrs. Stevenson's house in Craven Street. Marchant and Church proposed to catch up with the Agent at Preston, but as a matter of fact the party did not reunite until their respective arrivals in London.

Franklin took three days in which to make the trip from Edinburgh to Preston. The first two days were spent in negotiating the incredibly bad stretch by Hawick and Langholm to Carlisle, where he arrived on Friday night. Carlisle is seventy-two miles from Preston, and the traveler boasts that he made the entire distance in one day and "was not at all tired." We know the Doctor as a hardy tourist, but he must have been inured to the discomfort of a springless chaise and have had the services of an experienced driver to have made such good time. Marchant, who followed in his trail, describes the road as almost impassable after the same inundations through which Franklin had made his toilsome way to Edinburgh on the return from Ireland. "The greatest flood in the memory of Man," says the diarist, "scarcely a bridge in this part of England (all of which were of stone and seemed to bid defiance to time) but were in part or whole destroyed."

When the Agent arrived at Preston late on that memorable autumn evening in 1771, he was received by Mrs. Mary Bache, the mother of his son-in-law, a stately old lady of sixty-eight. Her husband, to whom she had borne twenty children, had died twenty-five years before. Of these children seven survived, and three of them, her two daughters Miss Nancy and Miss Martha, and her son Richard, Franklin's son-in-law, were with her at Preston. Reading between the lines of the missives which were later exchanged, we may glean some of the mutual satisfaction which this for tuitous meeting engendered. The Baches scarcely realized that the benevolent gentleman in mud-splashed traveling costume was the distinguished Dr. Franklin, and were delighted by his affability and simplicity. Franklin in his turn was at once impressed by the worth and solidity of his daughter's husband, and expressed his approbation both to Deborah and to Polly Hewson.[7]

Franklin remained in Preston two days, and none of the towns which he visited in England, Scotland, or Ireland has preserved a better recollection of his stay. Three trustworthy local historians relate the episodes of his sojourn in convincing detail.[8] Obviously all of the actions ascribed to the distinguished American in Preston could not have taken place during the short call in 1771. He returned in July 1772 for a longer stay, and it is probable that it is the occurrences of this time which are described by the Preston writers.

We are told that Benjamin resided, not at the home of Mrs. Bache, but in a house which stood until lately in the Triangle opposite the King's Head Tavern, that he grew extremely attached to the Mayor of Preston, Mr. James Cowburn, and that the two exchanged presents, that he visited Richard Arkwright, the inventor, who had a barber business in the town. As late as the year 1857 there was cherished in the residence of W. Taylor of the Moss cottage in Preston a musical instrument which Franklin made with his own hands; this instrument was shown at an exhibition given by the Lancaster and Chester Historical Society in 1856.

But of all the reminiscences of Franklin's stay in Preston, the most appealing is his association with Colonel John Burgoyne. The dashing hussar officer, who twenty-five years before had eloped with the heiress of the house of Stanley, had lost little of his original *élan*. He was a member of Parliament now, and had gone through several contested and tumultuous elections, on one occasion standing at the polls, pistol in hand, to defend his rights.[9] He had campaigned in France and Portugal, but the calls of war and politics had not tempered his enthusiasm for the arts; he still wrote plays and sometimes acted in them. The local tradition has it that he took part in a play of his own composition, *The Maid of the Oaks,* produced at the theatre in Woodcock Court during Franklin's visit. William Dobson, the Preston historian, writing in 1856 says:

It has been stated that the original house at Cooper Hill, Walton le Dale, Preston, was designed by General Burgoyne and that a lightning conductor was put to it by Dr. Franklin.[10]

It is to be deplored that this account of the intimacy of Franklin and Burgoyne in Preston must be pieced together from such diverse and scattered sources, for the episode is one of compelling interest. General Burgoyne was still the official representative for Preston in the British Parliament when he surrendered at Saratoga, but Franklin had departed upon his French mission and could render no amenities to an old acquaintance in distress. The opportunity came five years later, after Burgoyne had returned to Europe upon parole. Some martinets in the Continental Congress sought to have him brought back to America, pointing out that he was still technically a prisoner of war. The General, sick and discredited, naturally showed little inclination to recross the Atlantic and resume his captivity. He enlisted Edward Burke as his advocate, and Burke in turn appealed to Franklin in Passy. The Envoy, thinking perhaps of the old Preston days, lent his influence to a charitable construction of the parole. Mr. Burke, writing in the winter of 1789, expressed the appreciation of his distinguished and unlucky client: "General Burgoyne presents his best compliments to you with his thanks for your obliging attentions towards him." [11]

We can only surmise as to Franklin's occupations in Preston over the week-end. Whether he went dutifully to take the Lady's Walk [12] as Marchant did two days later, or affected an interest in the old walls and admired the river "meandering between Gentlemen's Seats down to the sea" is not disclosed. The walk still survives for the edification of transatlantic tourists, who are shown a row of trees under which Franklin is alleged to have sauntered, but probably the visitor of 1771 was too preoccupied with conversation inside the house to admit of many promenades abroad. He could relate his adventures by sea and land with interesting details of his stay in Ireland and Edinburgh for the diversion of Mrs. Bache and her daughters. Also he could get to know his son-in-law and hear at first hand the latest news of his family in Philadelphia, which he had left seven years before, and of his grandson, Benjamin Franklin Bache, whom he had never seen. Old Mrs. Bache must have been a congenial and cultured companion. Her spelling is a thought sophomoric, but that was a common failing with the ladies of the period. Marchant relates that he sat up until midnight under the thrall of her sprightly chatter. The cordiality of the connection established between Franklin and his newly found relatives-in-law is attested by their subsequent correspondence. Mrs. Bache, writing to the Envoy shortly after his return to London, says:

*Preston, December 3rd, 1771*
What extreme pleasure did my dear Brother give me and mine to hear you had so agreeable a journey and that our dear Son's leg was so little the worse for his confinement in the chaise. We shall all rejoice to hear it is quite recovered. We are much pleased at the hopes you give us of injoying your good and agreeable company again at my home. You likewise make us happy by naming a longer stay.[13]

And two months later, after Franklin had sent his portrait to Preston,

*Preston, February 5th, 1772*
I received your kind and agreeable present which gave us all great pleasure. It is so like the original. You cannot imagine with what pleasure we look at it. My daughter Marther told Mr. Atherton that Doctor Franklin was come. The next morning he came down and asked whether the Doctor was up and when you was produced it made us all very merry. You are

sometimes in the dining room and other times in the Parlor ware we vew it with pleasure. I think it is now time to return my hearty thanks for it and the oysters.[14]

The "Mr. Atherton" referred to in Mrs. Bache's letter was Richard Atherton, a neighbor and friend of the family, to whom Franklin was introduced in Preston. As early as April 1759 Sarah Bache writes to her brother Richard to say that "Dick" Atherton is rebuilding the front of his dwelling and that she intends to set her cap for him.[15] Atherton became an alderman, entered politics and opposed the election of General Burgoyne to Parliament, after the latter's return from the disastrous American expedition.[16] The alderman is alleged to have taken a part in the circulation of the uncharitable political broadside wherein Burgoyne is termed an "alien Bastard," "alien" because of his French name, and "Bastard" because of the prevalent but erroneous supposition that he was an illegitimate son of Lord Bingley.

Franklin's visit in Preston was shortened by the fact that Richard Bache had hurt his leg in the journey from America to Liverpool and was anxious to have the wound properly dressed in the metropolis. On Monday morning the Agent and his son-in-law, whose bruised limb was carefully supported, mounted to their carriage and took the road for London.

Meanwhile Marchant and Edward Church had left Edinburgh three days after Franklin's departure and followed him across the moors to Carlisle. They, too, made the long jump from Carlisle to Preston in one day, arriving at Mrs. Bache's dwelling at seven o'clock in the evening of Wednesday, November twenty-seventh. Marchant describes the reception:

As Dr. Franklin was to stop here to meet his Son-in-Law, Mr. Bache, whose Mother & Sisters lived in this town, we went to Mr. Bache's to hear of the Dr. and his Son, hoping that possibly they might not yet have set off. The Youngest Sister

Miss Nanny was at Home and very dull at the Loss of Her Brother & the Doctor, as they had gone two Days before. But finding we were somehow connected in Acquaintance with the Doctor & that I knew her Brother, She rec'd us with much politeness & Goodness, insisted upon our Staying the Evening, & her sending for her Mother & Sister who were only at a Neighbors.

They presently came & we had a most pleasant Evening. I was never more pleased with the Company of four such good and agreeable Women. The Mother is now 68 years old, a most stately well looking serious Lady. She sat with us at the Table till 12 o'clock at Night. She had twenty children by one Husband whom she buried 25 years ago & has 7 now living.

She would not let us depart till we promised to come and breakfast with them the next Morning & take a Walk to see the Town &c.

Novr. 28th—We did and after breakfast they took Us to a most delightful Walk at the Edge of ye Town called the Lady's Walk. From Thence we had a good View at once of the Town and several Villages—Gentlemen's Seats & an extra fine Country round with the beautiful meandering of the River from the Town toward the Sea.

Returning now to Craven Street, where Benjamin and Richard Bache had arrived after the journey down from Preston, the pleased father-in-law is disclosed busied with preparations for Bache's embarkation and abounding in sage advice and practical assistance.

I have advis'd Mr. Bache to deal only in the Ready Money Way, tho' he should sell less. It is the safest and the most easy Manner of carrying on Business. He may keep his Store in your little North Room, for the present. And as he will be at no Expence while the Family continues with you, I think he may, with industry and Frugality, get so forward, as at the end of his Term, to pay his Debts and be Clear of the World, which I much wish to see. I have given him £200 Sterl'g to add something to his Cargo.[17]

Yuletide was approaching; winter had enfolded London in its chilly grasp; and already the candles gleamed in the windows of the Stevenson mansion to illuminate the garlands which encircled them. On Christmas Day Commodore James Gambier wrote from his house in Orchard Street, Westminster, to his friend James Bowdoin in Boston: "Dr. Franklin was here in health and talks next year of visiting America."

And on New Year's Day, Thomas Life sat down in his chambers in Basinghall Street to record a conversation which he had with Franklin about the Irish journey, for apparently the Agent expressed himself orally with a far greater frankness than he permitted in his correspondence.

Mr. Jackson and Dr. Franklin have been to Ireland this vacation. I have had no conversation with the former gentleman about his journey but I found from what the Doctor said, that he is impressed with horrid ideas of the poverty and beggary of the poor inhabitants on that side of the water.[18]

Three weeks later came the anniversary of Franklin's sixty-sixth birthday. It was his humorous wont to claim two commemorations, since the adoption by Great Britain of the Gregorian Calendar in 1752 had added eleven days to his original natal date of the sixth of January. However, he usually celebrated on the seventeenth of January, and this particular occasion of 1772 signalized not only his birth but also his safe return from the perilous journey in North Britain.

On that evening Marchant left his lodgings back of the New England Coffee House and walked up the Strand toward Craven Street. It had snowed during the day, "snowed as in America," writes the homesick diarist with recollections of the holiday time in his own country and the ice-bound streets of his native Newport. As he passed St. Bride's he could hear the chime of joy bells and mark how the windows of the tavern glowed in ruddy squares of light. It was evening of another birthday, that of the well-beloved Queen Charlotte, consort of George the Third, and all truehearted Britons were celebrating.

In the house on Craven Street was gathered a goodly fellowship. Richard Bache was there, still nursing his wounded leg, and Mrs. Stevenson, the paragon of landladies, and her daughter Polly Hewson, "my dear girl," solicitous for the comfort of her distinguished patron. Dr. Hewson was absent, but his sister was present with Dorothy Blunt, Franklin's kind hostess from Streatham, and Jonathan Williams, his grandnephew and secretary. To the Agent's right sat a gentleman of the cloth, the Reverend Thomas Coombes, late assistant rector of Christ Church in Philadelphia and now chaplain to the Marquis of Rockingham. He was returning presently to America and was to preach his farewell sermon on the morrow at St. Botolph's in Aldersgate. By the punch bowl, and supposedly not neglectful of its contents, were two Atlantic mariners, Captain Chambers of the New York packet and Captain Falconer of the *Lovely Lass,* who had been entrusted with so many letters and remembrances for Deborah Franklin in Philadelphia.[19]

As the returned wanderer sat happy and contented in the companionship of his good friends and warmed by the birthday cheer, there came the crowding memories of his northern tours, of the bells of St. Paul's pealing for the victory at Minden as he and William drove out over Finchley Heath, of the evening shadows on the castle rock of Edinburgh as they first saw them from the Borough Muir, of the distant prospect of the Grampian highlands on the journey down to St. Andrews, of the generous Commons of Ireland rising in Hibernian cordiality to greet the emissary of liberty from overseas.

The mellowed glow of this pleasing retrospect was not to endure for long; soon the clouds would gather anew. The Agent of Pennsylvania might strive with all his tact and good sense to avoid a schism between the colonies which he represented and their mother country, but his efforts were in vain when a headstrong King and a heedless Parliament drove hard for a fall. Benjamin Franklin was to travel far in the eventful years which followed, to America, to Canada, and to France, but his carefree divertive rambles ended with his trip to Ireland and Scotland in 1771. "I shall probably never make such another journey," he wrote to Sir Alexander Dick. The utterance was all too prophetic.

# NOTES

## CHAPTER I

1 Franklin to Deborah, January 14, 1758. All of Franklin's letters hereinafter quoted are to be found in A. H. Smyth's collection of Franklin's writings, unless otherwise noted.

2 Reports of the Committee on Benjamin Franklin's Accounts. Pennsylvania Assembly, February 19, 1763. The total amount appropriated for Franklin during his six years' stay was £5,000. On March 4, 1763, he was paid £2,214.

3 Franklin to Deborah, February 19, 1758.

4 Franklin to Deborah, September 6, 1758.

5 Minutes of the Incorporated Colleges of St. Salvator and St. Leonard (St. Andrews), Vol. 7, p. 96.

6 See Address of Sir James C. Irvine, *Benjamin Franklin in St. Andrews,* hereinafter quoted.

7 Strahan to Franklin, February 13, 1778, American Philosophical Society, hereinafter referred to as A. P. S. Vol. 44, p. 21.

8 Boswell to William Temple, May 8, 1779. Rush Manuscripts, Ridgway Library of Philadelphia.

9 The British Coffee House is described in many contemporary memoirs, but perhaps best in *Scottish Men of Letters in the Eighteenth Century,* by Henry Gray Graham. London, 1908.

10 The celebrated Dr. John Douglass.

11 The catholicity of Franklin's activities in London and the identity of his associations there are best to be studied at the Connecticut Historical Society, Hartford, in the correspondence and diary of William Samuel Johnson, Agent of Connecticut at London.

12 *Autobiography of Rev. Dr. Alexander Carlyle, Minister of Inveresk,* better known as "Jupiter" Carlyle. London and Edinburgh, 1860.

13 Arthur Murphy, writing to Garrick a few days before Franklin's departure for Scotland, refers to some prank in which he, Franklin, and Garrick had been engaged.

14 Jackson's *History of the Scottish Stage.*

15 Franklin's *Autobiography.*

16 Franklin to Deborah, August 29, 1759. A. P. S. Vol. 46 (2), p. 16.

17 Mrs. Calderwood's *Journey in Scotland.*

18 A highwayman stopped and robbed a chaise on Finchley Common two days before Franklin's departure. *London Daily Advertiser,* August 6, 1759.

19 Aitken's *Life of Steele.*

20 Walpole's letters to Sir Horace Mann.

21 This phrase was found in the notes which Franklin prepared in anticipation of his *Autobiography.* Smyth, Vol. 1, p. 224.

22 Thurot, like John Paul Jones, is said to have been a renegade Scotsman, born of Kirkcaldy, and having served in the British Navy.

23 Walpole is not impressed with the efficacy of the hastily raised and very youthful levies. "If the French load their flat-bottomed boats with rods instead of muskets, I fear all will run away." Letter to H. S. Conway.

24 Franklin first saw George the Third at the Coronation. Franklin to Deborah, September 14, 1761.

25 Governor Denny seems to have saved little during his official career in Pennsylvania. Upon his return he invited Franklin to dine with him at the Star and Garter in Pall Mall at a crown a head, the guest to pay for his meal.

26 The date is fixed by the termination of the entries in the Account Book and is checked by Franklin's subsequent letter of August 29, hereinafter quoted.

27 The firm was later Andrew Regnier & Son. At one time their shop was at Charing Cross.

28 Henry Flower, whom Franklin had known in Philadelphia and whom he disliked, was a pharmacist of a sort who came over to London where in 1766 he published a pamphlet entitled *Observations on Gout and Rheumatism* by "Henry Flower, An American."

29 Elias Bland was a prominent merchant of the period residing sometimes in Philadelphia and sometimes in London. On February 13, 1751, Strahan wrote to David Hall from London: "You will no doubt hear by this ship that Elias Bland has broke some time ago for an immense sum, no less than fifty-five thousand pounds!"

## CHAPTER II

1 *Journal of Thomas Gray*, Clarendon Press, 1935.

2 Walpole to Mann, August 8, 1759.

3 *London Chronicle* of August 11, 1759.

4 Walpole's expression in July 1759. Letters to Mann.

5 The date of William Franklin's registration in the records of the Middle Temple is February 11, 1750. See *American Members of the Inns of Court.* E. Alfred Jones. London, 1924.

6 Charles Hart, *Pennsylvania Magazine of History*, Vol. 35, p. 308.

7 Letter in *London Morning Post*, June 1, 1779.

8 The date given for William Temple Franklin's birth in the records of Père la Chaise Cemetery at Paris and the almost undecipherable inscription on the tombstone are February 28, 1762, but as his grandfather, writing to William Franklin, August 1, 1774, says that Temple is "now in his fourteenth year," the date of 1760, accepted by most historians, is probably the correct one. See Benjamin Franklin to William Franklin, August 1, 1774, British Museum, Manuscript Collections, Folio 9828.

9 Baskerville Correspondence in Birmingham Public Libraries, Reference Library. Boulton Correspondence in Tew Park Collection, Assay Office, 3, Newhall Street, Birmingham. See also *John Baskerville, A Memoir* by Ralph Strauss and Robert K. Dent, London, 1907. See also contemporary numbers of Aris's *Birmingham Gazette* for data as to Baskerville and his establishment. Baskerville's letter to Franklin of August 24, 1773, A. P. S., Vol. 3, p. 164, recalls the former visits. "As the pleasantest time of year is now approaching pray give us yr company for a month and take a bed at Easy Hill. You know all your friends here will rejoice to see you."

10 Franklin to Baskerville, 1760. Day and month not given.

11 Franklin to Thomas Hubbard, April 28, 1758.

12 Memoirs of Miss Catharine Hutton, Timmins Collection, Birmingham Library.

13 Franklin to Baskerville, 1760. Day and month not given.

14 Franklin's Account Book, quoted above.

15 The correspondence as to the steam engine model sent to Franklin is contained in the Tew Collection, already referred to. Boulton, impatient at Franklin's delay in sending back the engine, directs him to give it to a porter to take to the Birmingham Carrier at the Bell Inn, Smithfield. Franklin replies, rather testily, under date of March 19, 1766, "I sent the model last week."

16 Franklin to Deborah, August 29, 1759. A. P. S. Vol. 46 (2), p. 16.

17 Receipt in archives of A. P. S.

18 Manuscript Collections of the British Museum, Folio 6681.

19 Darwin and Tissington to Franklin, March 19, 1763. A. P. S. Vol. 1, p. 72 (Whitehurst).

20 Franklin to Deborah, London, February 21, 1760. A. P. S. Vol. 46 (2), p. 17.

21 F. A. Bruton. *History of Manchester and Salford,* 1924.

22 Franklin makes a casual reference to the Jacobite invasion in the *Autobiography.* Smyth, Vol. I, p. 31.

23 Franklin to Peter Franklin, May 7, 1760.

24 *The Interest of Great Britain Considered.* Franklin was fearful that the acquisition of Guadeloupe might involve the restitution of Canada to the French.

25 Franklin to Lafayette, March 27, 1779. A. P. S. Vol. 45, p. 145.

26 Franklin to Deborah, August 29, 1759. A. P. S. Vol. 46 (2), p. 16.

27 *Autobiography of Dr. Alexander Carlyle. Op. cit.,* Wight was later professor of Ecclesiastical History at Glasgow University.

28 The diary has never been printed and is in the possession of Jonathan Potts's descendants in Philadelphia.

29 See letter from S. (Sarah) Bache to Richard Bache, Preston, April 10, 1759. A. P. S. Vol. 48, p. 12.

30 *Life and Letters of Right Honorable John Burgoyne.* E. B. DeFonblanque, London, 1876. Some lines in which Burgoyne seeks to console his wife, shortly to be deserted when he sailed with the flotilla to France, have survived:

> "The power that formed my Charlotte's heart
> Thus tender, thus sincere
> Shall bless each wish that love can start
> Or absence foster there.
> Safe in the shadow of that Power
> I'll tread the hostile ground
> Though fiery deaths in tempest shower
> And thousands fall around."

31 Franklin to Cadwallader Colden, April 8, 1760. A. P. S. Vol. 45, p. 20b.

32 Franklin's old friend, the evangelist George Whitefield, had been preaching in Edinburgh and was proceeding southward by the western road at the same time that Franklin was journeying northward. They appear to have been in Carlisle upon the same day and it is an interesting speculation whether they might have met.

33 The sentiments are those of John Buchan, now the distinguished governor-general of Canada. See his *Life of Walter Scott,* London, 1931.

34 Smollett's *Humphrey Clinker.*

35 Lockhart describes the incident in his *Life of Scott.*

36 *Letters of Thomas Gray,* Clarendon Press, 1935.

37 See Henry Graham's *Social Life of Scotland in the Eighteenth Century,* with the wealth of source material therein quoted.

38 Gray's letters, already quoted.

39 Franklin may have entered Edinburgh on September first, but after a careful study of the distances and posting stations between Liverpool and Edinburgh, it seems more probable that he arrived there September second.

40 It is hard to avoid using the language of the much-missed "R. L. S." who loved the place and prospect.


CHAPTER III

1 Letter sold at C. F. Heartman's sale of February 22, 1927, quoted in full in Heartman's Catalogue of that date.

2 Alexander Kincaid's correspondence survived until destroyed by fire some years before the writer's first visit to Edinburgh. One of his descendants states that the letters contained frequent references to Franklin's visit.

3 Chambers' *Reekiana,* Edinburgh, 1833. Boswell records that he went to call on Bruce, the African traveler, at Mrs. Reynolds' boarding house in Milne Square. Isham edition of Boswelliana, Vol. 9, p. 162.

4 This is Bishop Popocke's calculation.

5 The English housemaid in Smollett's novel translates this warning as "God have mercy on your soul."

6 Fergusson's poem "Auld Reekie." *Poetical Works,* Glasgow, 1800.

7 Franklin to Lord Kames, January 3, 1760.

8 The transaction of the purchase of the books and the subsequent dunning is to be traced in the Parker-Franklin correspondence printed in the *Proceedings* of the Massachusetts Historical Society, Series 2, Vol. 16, and in various receipts and bills of lading scattered in the archives at the A. P. S.

9 John Balfour and Gavin Hamilton associated themselves together for the printing of the *Edinburgh Chronicle.*

10 Parker to Balfour, November 2, 1761. Mass. Hist. Soc.

11 Balfour to Franklin, November 5, 1771. A. P. S. Vol. 3, p. 78.

12 Franklin to Strahan, December 19, 1763.

13 Franklin to Strahan, September 6, 1759, previously quoted.

14 Hume to Millar, December 18, 1759. *Letters of David Hume,* London, 1932.

15 Franklin to Jonathan Potts, in the possession of the Potts family.

16 The details of the Council Meeting at which the Franklins were honored are to be found in the Municipal Archives of Edinburgh.

17 See *The Lord Provosts of Edinburgh,* Edinburgh, 1932. Provost Drummond served the following terms, 1725–27, 1746–48, 1750–52, 1754–56, 1758–60, 1762–64.

18 The names of the Bailies were George Lind, Andrew Simpson, Joseph Learmouth, and James Mansfield.

19 The minutes of the Council meeting at which Franklin was made a Guild Brother are contained in the Edinburgh Council Record and not in the Burgess Book.

20 The Certificate given to Franklin and now among the archives of the American Philosophical Society is more effusive and speaks of "the affectionate respect which the Magistrates and Council have to a gentleman whose amiable character greatly distinguished for usefulness to the Society

to which he belongs and service to all mankind long ago reached them across the Atlantic Ocean."

21 They were the guides of the community. Marchant, when he came to Edinburgh in 1771, employed one as a constant companion, and it is probable that the Franklins had a special caddy assigned to them.

22 *London Chronicle*, October 3, 1759.

23 A fire occurred in the prison stockade of Edinburgh Castle during the Franklins' visit and a subscription was taken up among the citizens for the relief of the prisoners. *Caledonian Mercury.*


## CHAPTER IV

1 Isham Collection of Boswelliana. New York, 1936, Vol. 12, p. 77.

2 Sir Alexander's son, who later succeeded as Baron William Dick, was not born until 1762.

3 Boswell's letter of April 16, 1768, to William Temple (quoted in the Isham Collection) concerning his courtship of Janet is so brutally frank as to transgress the rules of hospitality and good breeding.

4 Dick Family Archives. See *Curiosities of a Scots Charta Chest*, Edinburgh, 1897.

5 The book which Sally Franklin received was printed by Bremner in the Luckenbooths and is advertised as "A Collection of Scots Reels or Country Dances with a Bass for the Violincello or Harpischord. Sixpence." *Scots Magazine*, November 1759.

6 Lady Dick to Franklin, October 19 (no year given). A. P. S. Presumably 1762.

7 In a curious volume printed by John Balfour of Edinburgh in 1771 and entitled *Essays Physical and Literary*, page 140, Professor Russell describes and commends Franklin's method of protecting buildings from lightning.

8 The diary of Henry Marchant's journey through England and Scotland in 1771, hereinafter so often quoted, and so valuable in the compilation of this record, is in the possession of Marchant's descendants, Miss Alice Clarke and Miss Mary Harris, through whose courtesy it is used. Parts of it were imperfectly printed in the *Literary Diary of Ezra Stiles*, Scribner's, 1901.

9 See letter written by Hume to Millar, December 18, 1759. *Letters of David Hume*, edited by J. Y. T. Grieg, London, 1932.

10 The entire verbose title consists of seven lines beginning *French and Indian Cruelty as Exemplified in the Life and Various Vicissitudes of Fortune of Peter Williamson. . . .*

11 See *General Benjamin Franklin*, by the author. The gift to Peter of the Mohawk headdress "from General Franklyn" is described in a note to Peter's *Indian Cruelty*.

12 This figure turned up at an American Indian exposition in London in the following year.

13 See note to *Indian Cruelty* heretofore referred to. For a plan of the Parliament House at the time of Franklin's visit, showing the location of Peter's "Coffee House," see Chambers' *Minor Antiquities of Edinburgh*, 1833.

14 Fergusson's "Rising of the Session." The lines might be liberally translated as a lament over the fact that Peter's mugs are empty and that the toasts no longer float in his hospitable punchbowl.

### CHAPTER V

1 Correspondence of David Garrick, London, 1825. A suggestion of the difficulties of the dialect practised by the citizens of Edinburgh is contained in Gentleman's description of his vocation while in Scotland. He says that he "played Othello and taught English."

2 This prospectus was found by the author while searching the old files of the Carron Company.

3 Denholm's *History of Glasgow*.

4 *Dictionary of English, Scotch and Irish Book-sellers and Printers*, Plomer, Bushnell, and Dix. Oxford, 1932.

5 See Franklin's Account Book, 1760, quoted above.

6 Already in 1759 Watt was making studies in steam power in connection with James Robison, a student in Glasgow University. At the time of Franklin's first visit to Glasgow he and his father had just completed and were offering for sale at a price of 2s 6d "A Large Sheet Map of the River Clyde from Glasgow to Portincross" (*Glasgow Courant*, October 22, 1759). He journeyed down to London in 1767 and there conferred with Franklin, (Boulton MSS. hereinafter quoted).

7 Marchant's Diary.

8 Rae's *Life of Adam Smith*, Vol. 1, p. 150. A year after the visit of the Franklins to Glasgow, Smith wrote to Strahan, "Remember me to Mrs. Strahan and likewise to Dr. Franklin & son." Smith to Strahan, December 30, 1760, Smith MSS., Glasgow University.

9 The proceedings are to be found in the synodal minutes. Witherspoon's sermon was printed in Glasgow "For James Wilken, Book-seller in Paisley."

10 Franklin's answer is in the files of the American Presbyterian Library in Philadelphia. He discourages the attempt and states that a similar effort in the preceding year to raise money for Dartmouth College had been unsuccessful.

11 The scene at Burlington in 1775, when Governor William Franklin was brought in under armed guard to face Witherspoon, is a little-known incident of rare dramatic quality. The Governor seems to have comported himself with a dignity worthy of his father's son, while Witherspoon's jibes as to his captive's dubious maternity were both ill-timed and ungenerous. Holograph statement of William Franklin in the archives of the Historical Society of New Jersey.

12 Marchant's Diary.

13 Life of John Anderson by John Parsell in *Glasgow Mechanic's Magazine*, Vol. III. See also David Murray, *Memories of the Old College of Glasgow*, Glasgow, 1927.

14 Smyth, *op. cit.*, Vol. X, p. 203 n.

15 See letter, Franklin to Deborah, London, 1760.

16 St. Andrews is more appreciative of Franklin's gift than are some of her sister colleges. Glasgow University has lost the books which Franklin gave. The volume given to the University of Göttingen is in the private library of a professor. Franklin gave, in all, four volumes to St. Andrews.

17 *Scotland Described*, Edinburgh, 1799.

18 Professor Watson, one of the signers of Benjamin Franklin's diploma, bought the college of St. Leonards for £40.

19 The records of the town of St. Andrews lack the fullness and exactitude of those of Edinburgh, so that the details of the Franklin ceremony cannot be set out with more particularity.

20 *Journey to the Hebrides.*

21 This imaginative description is taken from the scholarly essay *Benjamin Franklin in St. Andrews* delivered by Sir James C. Irvine, Principal and Vice Chancellor of the University of St. Andrews, at the Franklin Memorial Dedication, Franklin Institute, Philadelphia, May 20, 1938.

22 "Ode on the Death of Professor David Gregory."

23 Baird's encomium of Franklin's industry as related by him to the Every Night Club of Philadelphia is set out in the *Autobiography*. Baird received his early education at Leyden and was graduated M.D. at Rheims, in France, in 1733. Four years later he took his Doctorate in Medicine at St. Andrews. See Address of Sir James C. Irvine before quoted.

24 Published in Sparks' *Works of Benjamin Franklin*. The change of treatment which Franklin advised was the cessation of the blistering of the patient.

25 Buchan claimed relationship through the Fairfax family.

26 Creech in his *Edinburgh Antiquities* says that the box was made by Robert Hay, a goldsmith, and presented by the Guild of Goldsmithers to the Earl of Buchan.

27 Will of George Washington.

28 John Rush to Benjamin Rush, March 29, 1810. Ridgway Library, Philadelphia.

29 Lockhart's *Life of Walter Scott.*

30 Kay's *Edinburgh Portraits.*


CHAPTER VI

1 *Tour of the Hebrides.*

2 The College Librarian was James Robertson, known as "Little Robertson."

3 *Letters of James Boswell,* edited by Chauncey Brewster Tinker, Oxford, 1924. See also Isham Collection of Boswelliana, *op. cit.*

4 Franklin to Sir Alexander Dick, January 3, 1760.

5 The description is that of Henry Grey Graham, previously quoted.

6 Lord Kames's predilection for a certain word more remarkable for its vigor than its elegance is well known, and Boswell, who occasionally wrote poetry in his youthful days, has commemorated this foible:
"Alemoor the judgment as legal claims,
'Tis equity, you bitch, replies my Lord Kames."

7 Franklin to Mrs. Mary Hewson, Passy, January 27, 1783.

8 *London Chronicle.*

9 *Caledonian Mercury;* the first unofficial bulletin announcing the fall of Quebec arrived in Edinburgh shortly after Franklin's return from Glasgow.

10 "The Harvest Jaunt of 1762." *Boswell's Journal.* Isham Collection.

11 Colonel Charles Thompson Menzies of the Berwickshire Militia is the present owner of Kames House, although no descendant of Justice Kames.

12 "The Harvest Jaunt of 1762."

13 "The Harvest Jaunt of 1762."

14 Isham Collection, Vol. 14, p. 110.

15 Franklin to Lord Kames, January 3, 1760.

16 Franklin to Lord Kames, January 3, 1760.

17 *Ibid.*

[18] Franklin to Sir Alexander Dick, January 3, 1760.
[19] Franklin to Thomas Cushing.
[20] Walpole to Lady Hervey, November 3, 1759.

## THE INTERLUDE

[1] Franklin to Lord Kames, September 17, 1760.
[2] Franklin to Lord Kames, November 1761.
[3] David Hume to Franklin, May 10, 1762.
[4] Shippen Correspondence, H. S. P.
[5] See printed thesis of William Bousch of Virginia, graduate of Edinburgh Medical School in 1778, dedicated to Dr. Benjamin Franklin. Library of Congress. See also manuscript list of American medical students at Edinburgh University. Library of Congress.
[6] Johnson's advice to Lee was, "If you would choose to enter immediately upon physic, go by all means to Edinburgh or Leyden." Letters of Arthur Lee, Harvard University. Boswell tells us in the *Life of Samuel Johnson* that he knew Lee in Edinburgh.
[7] H. S. P. Miscellaneous Papers. A. M. 3841, Vol. 2, pages unnumbered. This letter has never been published.
[8] Franklin to Caleb Whitefoord, December 7, 1762.
[9] Franklin to Sir Alexander Dick, December 11, 1763.
[10] The location of the Elphinstone School is proved by Henry Marchant's Diary.
[11] Mary Hewson to Benjamin Franklin, October 25, 1784. Bache Collection, A. P. S.
[12] William Franklin to Benjamin Franklin. A. P. S., 1768. Vol. 58, p. 46.
[13] The New England Coffee House, conducted from 1759 to about 1765 by Thomas Lever, was on Threadneedle Street back of the Royal Exchange. *Liverpool Advertizer*, August 31, 1759.
[14] Isham Collection of Boswelliana, Vol. 8, p. 122.
[15] Alexander Dick to Franklin, July 5, 1765. A. P. S. Vol. 1, p. 150.
[16] Salary receipt of Governor William Franklin for the year 1778. Archives of Huntingdon Library. See also *Penna. Magazine of History*, Vol. 35, p. 427.
[17] Franklin to Lord Kames, April 11, 1767. A. P. S.
[18] Diary of Jonathan Potts quoted above.
[19] Rush Family Correspondence.
[20] Franklin to Deborah, June 22, 1767.
[21] Franklin to Deborah, March 1, 1769. A. P. S. Vol. 46 (2), p. 64.
[22] The details of the negotiations which led up to Witherspoon's selection as President of Princeton and Franklin's connection therewith are to be found in the letters of Witherspoon, Charles Beatty, and Richard Stockton at the Presbyterian Historical Society, Philadelphia, archives of Princeton University, and archives of New Jersey Historical Society at Newark. Beatty's diary, never published, is in the possession of his descendants at Westfield, New Jersey.
[23] When Stockton went to London he carried letters to Benjamin Franklin from William. *Pennsylvania Magazine of History*, Vol. 35, p. 440.
[24] Witherspoon performed the marriage ceremony at Princeton, January 11, 1776.
[25] Ashbel Green Manuscript, Historical Society of New Jersey.

26 *General Benjamin Franklin,* heretofore quoted.

27 Franklin to Deborah, June 27, 1760.

28 Mills, *Glimpses of Colonial Society,* p. 48.

29 Joseph H. Jones, *Life of Ashbel Green of Princeton,* Philadelphia, 1849.

30 R. Hingston Fox, *Dr. John Fothergill and His Friends,* London, 1919.

31 Strahan to Hall, January 28, 1769. Copy in the establishment of Spottiswoode & Co., Printers, London, successors to William Strahan. See R. A. Austin-Leigh, *The Story of a Printing House,* London, 1912.

32 Whitefield Letters in collection of Frankliniana at University of Pennsylvania.

33 Robert Alexander to Benjamin Franklin, September 3, 1770. A. P. S. Vol. 3, p. 25.

### CHAPTER VII

1 Franklin to John Canton, May 12, 1771. Mason Collection, Yale University. Canton was fifty-two years old when he accompanied Franklin on the Midlands tour. He must have been a delightful fellow traveler since Dr. Kippis describes him as "A man of very amiable character and manners, in conversation calm, mild, rather sparing than redundant."

2 A. P. S. Franklin Accounts, 1771.

3 A. P. S. Vol. 14, p. 22.

4 The correspondence between Franklin and Bowdoin is among the Bowdoin Manuscripts at the Massachusetts Historical Society, Boston. "Jemmy" later made a tour of the Continent and returned to America after the advent of the news of the battle of Lexington. He is alleged to have been in the boat with Washington when the General crossed the Delaware for the capture of Trenton.

5 Additional light might be thrown upon the social relations of Franklin with Priestley and the Manchester circle by the discovery of the lost minutes of the Lunar Society of Manchester, founded in 1766, and numbering among its members Erasmus Darwin, Watt, Boulton, Smeaton, Wedgwood, Day (author of *Sandford and Merton*), and Priestley. These were Franklin's closest friends in the Midlands, and the Manchester scribes assert that he sometimes attended the meetings of the club. The Society got its name from the circumstance that the members dined at two o'clock on the day of full moon "in order to have the benefit of moonlight in returning to their homes at night," an intimation that a measure of conviviality was injected into their serious discussions. See Lord Kelvin's admirable brochure on James Watt, Glasgow, 1901.

6 The correspondence and accounts of Franklin and Whitehurst are at the A. P. S.

7 Craven Street Household Accounts for 1771. A. P. S.

8 Franklin to Jonathan Shipley, September 13, 1775. Printed in Lyell's *Random Reminiscences.*

9 Franklin to Catharine Louise Shipley, April 27, 1787.

10 The journey up from Twyford to Marlborough Street is described in Franklin's letter to Shipley from London, August 12, 1771. It is printed in Lyell's *Reminiscences,* quoted above.

11 Franklin to Samuel Cooper, April 27, 1769.

12 Franklin to Edward Pennington, May 9, 1761.

13 See letters of Miss Martin to Franklin (not yet catalogued) in Bache Collection. A. P. S.

14 J. Kettilby to Franklin, April 27, 1771. A. P. S. Vol. 3, p. 53. The name of the Dublin printer is erroneously given as "Lottilby" in the Hays Catalogue of the A. P. S.

15 Diary of William Samuel Johnson (unprinted), Connecticut Historical Society, Hartford, Connecticut. *The Case of Great Britain and America* alluded to by Johnson was published by James Williams of Dublin in 1769. It has been wrongfully ascribed to George B. Butler. See Sabin, Vol. 3, p. 167.

16 *Alumni Cantabrigiensis*. Cambridge, 1922.

17 See *Book of Baronets' Pedigrees*, Arms Office, Dublin Castle.

18 Franklin to Jackson, May 5, 1753.

19 William to Benjamin, September 3, 1758. A. P. S. Vol. 1, p. 51½.

20 Barrister Blackham's *Crown Office Row*.

21 The will of Richard Jackson is on file in the records of Somerset House, London.

22 Amid the crude notations found among Franklin's papers, of subjects for treatment in the *Autobiography*, was "Jackson." It must always be regretted that he never found time to elaborate the theme.

23 Committee of Correspondence of Pennsylvania to B. Franklin and R. Jackson, Agents in London, September 20, 1766, Library of Congress, Franklin Correspondence, Vol. 1, p. 58.

24 Franklin's Craven Street Accounts, Vol. 67. A. P. S.

25 Franklin Manuscripts, University of Pennsylvania. Jackson to Franklin, May 20, 1771.

26 Lyell's *Random Reminiscences*.

27 Marchant to Ezra Stiles, September 5, 1771. Archives of Yale University.

28 Massachusetts Historical Society.

29 W. Small to Franklin, August 10, 1771. Library of Congress, Franklin Correspondence, Vol. 1, p. 77.

30 Franklin's Accounts for 1771. A. P. S.

31 Issue of September 7, 1771. National Library of Ireland.

32 The discomforts of the crossing from Holyhead to Dublin in the eighteenth century are described by the character in Shadwell's fine old Irish play *The Intriguing Squire:* "All that I know of the vessel was that she stunk confoundedly of pitch and tar. We were a representation of Noah's Ark. The Captain himself was a brute beast and we poor passengers wallowed in the mire we made."

### CHAPTER VIII

1 George Faulkner's *Dublin Journal*, September 7, 1771.

2 Watson's *Directory of Dublin* for 1771.

3 See also *Hibernia Curiosa*, Dublin, 1780.

4 Young's *Tour in Ireland* in 1779.

5 Library of Congress. Printed in Hale's *Franklin in France*.

6 While the volume which Franklin bought is not absolutely identified, it is considered by the officials of the National Library of Dublin to have been *Philosophical Essays* by Henry Ecles of Lismore, published in Dublin in 1771. The author refers to Franklin's theories on electricity as "fallible and insufficient."

7 It is understood that the late Professor Henry Stewart Macran of Trinity proposed to write a brochure concerning Franklin's visit to Trinity, but he died before the completion of his task.

8 Benjamin Franklin to William Franklin, January 30, 1772.

9 Walpole's *George the Third.* Vol. 4, p. 348.

10 Franklin to Samuel Cooper, January 13, 1772.

11 Franklin to James Bowdoin, January 13, 1772. A. P. S. Vol. 45, p. 50.

12 *Memoirs of Right Honorable Henry Grattan,* by Henry Grattan, London, 1839.

13 Charlemont Letters. Charlemont to Malone, Dublin, May 15, 1779.

14 *Dublin Chronicle.*

15 Barrington in his *Personal Sketches,* London, 1831, gives a whimsical description of Sir Edward's affectations: "By repeatedly writing letters of congratulation he had at length extorted a reply from George Washington which he exhibited upon every occasion, giving it to be understood by significant nods that he knew vastly more than he thought proper to communicate to anybody."

16 Franklin to William Deane, April 11, 1773. A. P. S. Vol. 45, p. 63. When Franklin was almost on his deathbed, December 31, 1789, he regretted to Newenham that he had not sent a fishing apparatus which he had promised to Deane.

17 Franklin to Cadwalader Evans, London, July 18, 1771.

18 William Philips, Esq., Director of the Dublin Society for Improving Husbandry.

19 Franklin to Bishop Shipley, London, December 14, 1771. Mason Collection, Yale University. Some doubt is cast upon the identification of "Mr. Jackson" with Dean Jackson of Christ Church by the circumstance that Franklin, usually punctilious, does not use the title "Dean." In other respects, however, the description seems to accord. There was in Dublin at this time a printer named Isaac Jackson at the sign of the Globe in Meath Street, but he does not seem to have possessed a country house.

20 *Hibernian Journal.* October 4, 1771.

21 Francis O'Kelly. See pages 3–14 of Vol. I of the *History of the Times.* "The Thunderer in the Making," 1785–1841. London, 1935.

22 *Personal Reminiscences* of John O'Keefe, New York, 1876.

23 Smyth, Vol. 10, p. 80.

## CHAPTER IX

1 No less than five contemporary Dublin newspapers are available for the details of the opening of the Irish Parliament in 1771.

2 An examination of the regimental lists of the British armies in America during the War for Independence discloses the fact that they were officered largely by Scotchmen and recruited largely from Celtic Ireland.

3 Henry Marchant's Diary, already quoted.

## CHAPTER X

1 In recent years some doubt has been thrown upon Franklin's authorship of this document.

2 Debates of the House of Lords for 1781.

3 Franklin to Samuel Cooper, London, February 5, 1773.

4 Franklin to William Franklin, London, January 30, 1772. A. P. S. Vol. 45, p. 45.

5 East Hampstead Park, Berkshire.

6 Lord Hillsborough's letters to his agents concerning the improvements at the village are preserved among the Governmental Records of the Public Record Office at Belfast.

7 Young's *Tour in Ireland, 1776*, Dublin, 1780.

8 Franklin to Thomas Cushing, January 13, 1772.

9 A revengeful administration removed Downshire from his command of the Ulster militia and erased his name from the Privy Council.

10 The muck-raking research of our own day has suggested a closer relation between Lord Kilwardin and Charlotte Charpentier Scott, hinting that she was the nobleman's illegitimate daughter, but no proof worthy of consideration has been advanced for so scandalous an assertion. Sir Walter Scott appears never to have known of the friendship between Franklin and his wife's guardian. When the writer and Sir Walter Maxwell-Scott searched the library at Abbotsford for Franklinian items, they found only a Gaelic edition of *The Way to Wealth*.

11 Franklin to William Franklin, January 30, 1772, already quoted.

12 Richard Cumberland's *Memoirs*.

13 Boswell's *Jaunt to Ireland*, 1769. Isham edition.

14 The details of this linen transaction are to be found in Franklin's accounts for 1771 at the A. P. S.

15 Boswell's *Jaunt in Ireland*, already quoted.

16 The contemporary Chester newspaper, *Adam's Weekly Courant*, reports that all the Irish packets had rough passages and that the *Nancy* lost some of her passengers overboard.


### CHAPTER XI

1 William Franklin to Thomas Wharton, October 28, 1771. Historical Society of Pennsylvania, Wharton Correspondence.

2 Sir Alexander Dick was twice married.

3 Creech's *Fugitive Pieces*, Edinburgh, 1815.

4 Williamson was also occupied with plans for a penny post which he inaugurated shortly afterwards. The roguish Fergusson, who wrote his will in rhyme, left Peter a humorous bequest:

"To Williamson and his resetters
Dispersing of the burial letters
That they may pass with little cost
Fleet on the wings of penny post."

5 Hume's house is now occupied by the London and Lancashire Insurance Co., Ltd. The gable and upper story are unchanged since Franklin's time. The inscription "Here lived David Hume, 1772-1776," is erroneous since Hume moved into the house in 1771.

6 *Letters of David Hume*, Oxford, 1932. Letter #462.

7 The information as to Edward Church is mainly derived from the genealogy *Descendants of Richard Church*, by John A. Church, Rutland, Vt., 1913. See also *General Gage's Informers*, by Allen French, University of Michigan Press, 1932.

8 Dr. Benjamin Church's defection is best to be studied in Mr. French's book, quoted above, and in the *Diary of Ezra Stiles*, before quoted.

9 *Literary Diary of Ezra Stiles*, before quoted. Stiles terms the go-between

who carried the clandestine letters between Benjamin Church and Fleming a "daughter of pleasure."

10 Samuel Fayerweather to Franklin, December 5, 1768. M. H. S.

11 Franklin to John Winthrop, January 13, 1772. Vol. 45, p. 52. A. P. S. In addition to the sum sent for the diploma fee, Winthrop sent Franklin by Marchant fifty-two shillings to pay for a copy of the proceedings of the Royal Society. Winthrop to Franklin, October 20, 1770, *Proceedings* of Massachusetts Historical Society, Second Series, Vol. 15, p. 12.

12 Marchant refused the degree.

13 Balfour to Franklin, A. P. S. Vol. III, Part 1, p. 78.


CHAPTER XII

1 Franklin and Sir John Pringle visited Smeaton at Austhorpe, near Leeds, and were received in the curious tower built on the lines of a lighthouse which the engineer had constructed as a study. Smyth, Vol. 1, p. 167.

2 The "Ancient Castle" which Marchant describes is Doune Castle.

3 This letter is quoted in the *Life of Lord Kames* by Tytler of Woodhouselee, Edinburgh, 1807. Mrs. Montagu first met Lord Kames at a party given in London by Dr. Gregory of Edinburgh.

4 *Letters of a Maryland Medical Student.* Maryland Hist. Mag., Vol. 31. *Steuart Genealogy*, Historical Society of Maryland. See also *Old Kent of Maryland*, by George Hansom, Baltimore, 1876.

While the above-described George Home Steuart is in all probability the one who met Franklin in Glasgow, there is a suggestion that the diarists may refer to Charles Stewart, a Scotchman who came over to America and lived for a time in the southern colonies. Later he held the position of Cashier and Paymaster of Customs for his Majesty's Forces in New England, went out much in Boston society and was a favorite of the belles of Beacon Street. While in the South Stewart had acquired a negro slave called James Sommerset whose name became as conspicuous in the jurisprudence of the period as did that of Dred Scot a century later. In an evil hour the Paymaster decided to visit England and to bring Sommerset along as a bodyservant. Once landed on the free soil of Britain, the darkey ran away and defied his master to reclaim him. When Franklin was at Glasgow in November 1771, the slave was still at large, but a few weeks later he was caught and put upon a ship at Tilbury for deportation to America. Proceedings in Habeas Corpus were instituted by Sommerset's sympathizers and a *cause célèbre* ensued in the spring of 1772. The great Mansfield presided, and Franklin was so interested that he induced Marchant to attend the sittings and to make for him a written syllabus of the case. The Sommerset case is reported in King's Bench, 12 George III, 1771–72, and is referred to in the *Archives* of the Massachusetts Historical Society, Second Series, Vol. 10, pp. 11–60. When John Quincy Adams visited the home of Henry Marchant at Newport in September 1789, he met Charles Stewart and embarked with him upon the Long Island Sound packet which bore them to New York. At that time the erstwhile cashier was practising law in Halifax.

5 Edward Church to Franklin, November 19, 1784. Vol. 32, p. 179. A. P. S.

6 Edward Church to George Washington, May 11, 1789, quoted in the Church genealogy already referred to.

7 Edward Church had a fluent knowledge of Spanish and Portuguese

through the circumstance of his having been born and having spent some years at Fayal in the Azores Islands, where his father was in business.

8 Church genealogy already referred to.

9 Church genealogy already referred to. There can be no doubt as to Edward Church's elevation as Guild Brother. His certificate is quoted in the Church genealogy and is still in the possession of his descendants. Church refers to the honor conferred upon him in his letter to Franklin from Dunkirk. The Lord Provost of Glasgow at the time was Colin Dunlop.

10 Watt to Dr. Small, December 24, 1771.

11 When Witherspoon returned to Edinburgh after the Revolution, in July 1784, and sought to deliver an address at a banquet of the American residents, the Edinburgh newspapers refused to publish an account of the gathering.

12 Boswell and Paoli, who visited the college a few weeks earlier, were "regaled with sweet meats and wine in the College Hall," but while Franklin dined with individual professors, he was not accorded an official reception.

13 The descriptions of Franklin's visit to Carron and of Gascoigne's career are drawn from a personal examination of the documents at Carron and from a series of excellent pamphlets issued by the Carron establishment. See also *The Story of the Forth,* by H. M. Cadell, Edinburgh, 1895. One of the papers in the Carron collection gives the interesting suggestion that Gascoigne was associated with John Paul Jones during the latter's Russian sojourn. This statement could be verified only by a search of the archives of the Russian Imperial Marine.

14 William Fraser, *The Elphinstone Family,* Edinburgh, 1897.

15 Burns's couplet is printed in most editions of his works. The incident of his visit is given in the series of brochures issued by the Carron establishment and entitled *Famous Visitors to Carron.* See also *The Story of the Forth,* by H. M. Cadell, Edinburgh, 1895, already quoted.

16 Nelson's flagship, the *Victory,* carried these same carronades, as did Rodney's fleet which engaged De Grasse off Martinique in 1781. One of the partners of Carron was Samuel Shrapnel, who gave his name to the explosive shell still in use.

## CHAPTER XIII

1 Franklin to Strahan, November 17, 1771.

2 When Aaron Burr visited Edinburgh in 1809 he took the same walk in company with Captain M'Dowell, the grandson of one of Franklin's hosts.

3 *Pennsylvania Magazine of History,* December, 1868.

4 Lord John Elphinstone was later Governor of Edinburgh Castle.

5 The events described in this paragraph are taken from Marchant's diary.

6 Franklin's Account Book for 1771. A. P. S.

7 Franklin to Mary Hewson, November 29, 1771. Franklin to Deborah, January 28, 1772.

8 P. Whittle, *History of the Borough of Preston,* Preston, 1837. Charles Hardwick, *History of the Borough of Preston,* Preston, 1857. Archives of the Preston Library, Preston, Lancashire.

9 The details of Burgoyne's parliamentary career and of his relations with Franklin in Preston are given in William Dobson's erudite *History of the Parliamentary Representation of Preston,* Preston, 1856.

[10] Dobson's *History*, quoted above.

[11] Burke to Benjamin Franklin, August 15, 1781. Archives of University of Pennsylvania.

[12] Now called the Avenham Walk, with charming views over the river Ribble.

[13] Mary Bache to Franklin, Bache Collection, A. P. S. (uncatalogued).

[14] *Ibid.*

[15] A. P. S. Vol. 47, p. 12.

[16] William Dobson, *History of Parliamentary Representation in Preston*, previously quoted.

[17] Franklin to Deborah, London, January 28, 1772.

[18] Thomas Life to William Samuel Johnson, January 1, 1772, Correspondence of William Samuel Johnson, New York City Public Library, Vol. 3, p. 357.

[19] The description of the birthday festival is taken from Marchant's diary.

# INDEX